Community Political Systems

Community

Political

Systems

EDITED BY *MORRIS JANOWITZ*, UNIVERSITY OF MICHIGAN

GREENWOOD PRESS, PUBLISHERS
WESTPORT, CONNECTICUT

CONTRIBUTORS

Victor Ayoub, ANTIOCH COLLEGE

Phillips Cutright, UNIVERSITY OF CHICAGO

Scott Greer, NORTHWESTERN UNIVERSITY

Amos H. Hawley, UNIVERSITY OF MICHIGAN

Daniel Katz, UNIVERSITY OF MICHIGAN

Melvin Reichler, UNIVERSITY OF MICHIGAN

Peter H. Rossi, UNIVERSITY OF CHICAGO

Robert O. Schultze, BROWN UNIVERSITY

Harry Scoble, UNIVERSITY OF WISCONSIN

Henry Valen, INSTITUTE FOR SOCIAL RESEARCH, OHIO

Basil G. Zimmer, UNIVERSITY OF MICHIGAN

Library of Congress Cataloging in Publication Data

Janowitz, Morris, ed.
   Community political systems.

   Reprint of the ed. published by the Free Press,
Glencoe, Ill., which was issued as v. 1 of International
yearbook of political behavior research.
   Bibliography: p.
   Includes index.
   1. Political psychology. 2. Community power.
I. Title. II. ·Series: International yearbook of
political behavior research ; v. 1.
[JA74.5.J36 1978]   301.5'92'091732   78-6602
ISBN 0-313-20501-9

Preface

THE PUBLICATION of this first volume of the *International Yearbook of Political Behavior Research* represents another step in the development of the behavioral approach to the study of political phenomena. This is not the place to review in detail a line of development which is associated with the work of Arthur F. Bentley, Graham Wallas and Max Weber in the first two decades of the century, which was fertilized by the writings and teaching of Charles E. Merriam and Harold D. Lasswell in the twenties and thirties, but which entered its active phase only after World War II.

There are a number of indices of accelerated development of political behavior research in recent years. This research was greatly stimulated by the establishment and the subsequent activities of the Committee on Political Behavior of the Social Science Research Council. If one compares the pages of the *American Political Science Review* in the decades before 1950 with the material found in this official journal of the American Political Science Association in the few years since 1950, the changes in research orientation appear dramatic indeed. In 1956, The Free Press published *Political Behavior: A Reader in Theory and Research,* which included representative, then available, theoretical, methodological, critical and empirical studies focused on the political behavior approach. In that year, too, a series of panels devoted to the political behavior approach were initiated at the annual meeting of the Association, and research in political behavior has been reported since in panels on various substantive concerns of political science. More and more, books in the fields of politics, public administration, and international relations, as well as theoretical works, reflect the behavioral orientation. Special professorships in political behavior have come to be set up at almost all major universities, and political sociology has become an important subject of inquiry in university departments of sociology.

Yet, the rapidity of this development in recent years calls for a word of caution. Political behavior studies represent an *approach* to the investigation of political phenomena. They do not constitute a new "field" of political science or sociology. They constitute an approach because they seek to bring to inquiry in *all* fields of political science greater theoretical sophistication than earlier empirical work exhibited, particularly by insisting on the necessary unity of theory and research; because they demand more methodological rigor and careful specification and control of the relevant empirical variables; and because they attempt to enlighten political inquiry by drawing on the

7

tools and findings of the other social sciences. For this reason, the setting up of independent panels on political behavior research at professional meetings or the establishment of separate professorships in political behavior may be less wholesome than one might suppose. It may well lead to a kind of scientific segregation — long forced on, and indulged in by, the practitioners of political theory — which is the very purpose of the political behavior approach to avoid. Desirable cross-fertilization of political theory, methodology, and empirical research can meaningfully take place only within the substantive fields of the entire discipline of political science or political sociology. Ideally, all students of politics, whether they concentrate on public or private governmental processes, electoral phenomena, parties or political movements, public administration, or international relations, should be at once theorists, methodologists, and empirical researchers.

In order to avoid scientific segregation, each annual volume of the *International Yearbook of Political Behavior Research* will be centered in a single, major research area and will accommodate both theoretical and empirical studies longer than the normal professional journal article but shorter than the conventional monograph. Each volume will be edited by a special issue editor, in co-operation with the general editor and with the advice of an international editorial advisory board. Beyond the present volume on *Community Political Systems,* the following annuals have been projected: a volume on the socialization, recruitment, and mobility of political leaders in different societies; on civil-military relations; on comparative political systems on three continents; and on political movements and ideologies. Political scientists and political sociologists interested in contributing to these volumes are invited to write to the general editor.

STANFORD UNIVERSITY   *Heinz Eulau*

Contents

Community Political Systems

Converging Perspectives
in Community Political Analysis

BY *MORRIS JANOWITZ*

MEMBERSHIP in a human community can be considered a universal phenomenon. The growth of industrialism weakens, or more accurately, transforms traditional community affiliations, but does not eliminate them. The dominant trend toward "urbanism as a way of life" increases the importance of occupations and associations in linking a person to politics and to the nation state. Yet, the community must be understood as a social reality, a political context, and as an ideological symbol if contemporary political behavior is to be analyzed.

Community organization is taken as an indispensable mediating unit in various parts of the world in the search for economic development, social stability, and political order. In India, the political planners have assumed that economic development without undue coercion rests on stimulating initiative and self-help in village communities. In West Africa, the new population centers are the locus of political struggles for national identity and the training ground for developing political leadership. Centralized economic, governmental, and social services in most of Western Europe have limited localized decision-making. Yet all European mass parties — democratic and totalitarian — are forced to develop a community basis in order to wield political power. In the United States, regional differences and social heterogeneity have meant that national political organizations are less national and more expressions of regionalism and the structure of metropolitan communities. In all parts of the world, regardless of the level of urbanization, nationalism as a political ideology is built on, or at least must accommodate itself to, appeals to localism and to symbols which stress the importance of community — rural, urban, or metropolitan.

In the development of the interdisciplinary analysis of political behavior, the study of community political systems lends itself to a comparative treatment, perhaps more so than the nation state. Human communities are complex social systems, yet the political arrangements they develop are manageable objects of research. Yet, despite the number of community studies in the literature of social anthropology and sociology, few make explicit reference to political institutions, and few relate community organization to the larger political systems in which they operate. In part, this is due to the paradox that politics at the community level is diffuse — diffuse in its goals and in its penetration into the social fabric.

In the absence of a body of comparative research about community political systems, as a first step, five case studies from the United States are presented in this volume which deal with different but related aspects and approaches to community political systems. They supply a basis for a more systematic approach in that they make possible comparisons within, rather than between, nation states. The inclusion of a single cross-national comparison, from Norway, a nation with many comparable economic and social traditions, gives substance to the assumption that community political systems are understandable only in terms of differences in national political arrangements.

These studies represent independent efforts at research and their relevance for comparative interpretation emerges from convergence in the perspectives of the investigation rather than from any explicit research design. The discovery, or perhaps rediscovery, of political community systems by research workers in the United States is in itself an expression of convergence. Social problems, that is, intellectual and ethical concerns with social instabilities, have a natural history. The decade 1950–1960 produced an explosive population growth and a strain on community organization, with the result that the "metropolitan problem" has become a renewed focus for controlling social and political change. Social scientists responding to these trends have become concerned with the cumbersome and unadaptive character of decision-making at the community level. The studies presented in this volume are samples of the first efforts. Work under way includes literally dozens of efforts, some of lasting scholarly import and others mainly of immediate administrative consequence.

If an intellectual history of social science is ever to be written, the question will have to be answered why so little effort has been expended to co-ordinate what, in effect, are "grass roots" movements in the social sciences. In part, progress in any intellectual sphere starts with unco-ordinated efforts. In part, the mechanisms for co-ordinating social science efforts lag behind its tasks. The fact that the revived interest in the analysis of community political systems has been unmanaged is not necessarily a disadvantage. The work that has been done, as represented by the reports in this volume, reflects the diversity and complexity of the subject matter and prepares the ground for truly systematic comparative analysis. It reflects a keen interest in relating empirical realities to theoretical generalizations rather than arbitrarily applying formal models.

Nevertheless, common intellectual concerns have produced considerable convergence in posing problems about political power in a community setting.

One, in each study, the urban community is the arena in which political power is exercised. The range encompasses the small aggregate (trading center as well as satellite town), the middle-sized industrial complex, and the giant metropolis, as represented by St. Louis. In each case, the intent has been not to use the community as a research site but rather as an object of analysis.

Definitions of the human community are far from satisfactory since the community has imprecise and incomplete boundaries. In these research studies, the community is thought to be a social system, rooted in geography, which directly supplies its members with the major portion of their daily sustenance needs. Modern economic trade relations are world-wide, but the scope of daily transactions, more or less, delimit ecological boundaries of the urban community. In addition, each study is concerned in varying degree with administrative and political parameters, as supplementary definitions of the community. Under modern conditions, no community is sovereign, for the community is not the source of legal authority or the political structure which monopolizes the means of violence. This does not deny that the community produces an independent decision-making process, or that the community can be conceptualized as an independent political decision-making system.

Two, each study focuses on leadership. The concept of leadership is both a conceptual tool and a basis for making value judgments. Leadership becomes a social science concept as soon as power exercised by leaders is assumed to be reciprocal. Reciprocal relations are not equal relations but rather patterns of influence in which one group clearly has more power and more influence than the other. Analysis of community power structures is the analysis of how power is exercised and under what conditions power is compatible with particular political and moral goals.

Three, in varying degrees, common theoretical elements in these research papers exist because their frame of reference is compatible, although not necessarily by design, with the orientation outlined by Max Weber in his classic essay on "Class, Status, and Party." The central problematic issue is an analysis of the limitations which confront economic leadership in the exercise of political power. Economic processes are seen as creating a leadership — national, regional and on the community level. In the United States, in particular, there is no feudal tradition; the civil service is weak; and society is organized so as to be comparable with business values. The classic community study of Middletown in the 1920's and 1930's, by Robert and Helen Lynd, is grounded in this assumption. But the current renewed interest in community political systems is in part a questioning of the observations of Floyd Hunter who rediscovered the dominance of business interests in social welfare activities. But the facts of these studies do not obscure the other facts, namely, that in the United States there has been a withdrawal, a default, or an inability of business to exercise political power in community affairs.

Community struggles are not merely economic. Leadership in these research studies is seen as deriving from the status or symbolic organization of the community. Leaders compete on the basis of ethnic, religious, and traditional affiliations which reflect the complexity of community stratification systems. The web of government operates because men are concerned with maintaining an environment appropriate for their familial, friendship, and religious association.

Four, thus, politics is seen as a specialized form of behavior, requiring skill and long-term commitment with characteristics distinct from the rest of the group life of the community. In fact, there is much to be gained by thinking of politics as a profession, even though politics at the community level requires many part-time professionals. By the use of such a perspective, it is possible to focus on the inherent limitations imposed on political behavior and on economic and status groups in their efforts to achieve political dominance. None of these researchers is forced to over-simplify the relationships of "politicians" to the economic and social stratification systems of the community.

As long as the scale of economic organization was no greater than the trading city, businessmen could combine the direction of their private enterprise with the guidance of political decisions in their immediate environment. Part-time activities such as doing good works in the locality, handling the ceremonial aspects of public life, and maintaining personal ties were readily possible. But when a city grew into a large metropolis and developed elaborate relations with the hinterland, the task became more complicated at the very time that the scope of top community decisions was enlarged. Paradoxically, the growth of the national economic system and the centralization of economic decision has been accompanied by a persistence and proliferation of the areas of community decision-making, for example, public education, physical planning, and social welfare. While the goals and processes of decision-making which are community wide are diffuse, the issues are real and of crucial importance. Moreover, decision-making at the community level involves the crucial function of the recruitment and training of emerging national political elites.

Robert Schulze in his analysis of an industrial satellite community, approaches the problem in historical depth. He is able to trace out historically the gradual withdrawal of the dominant economic leaders from the management of local community affairs as their perspectives lead them into participation in the wider society.

His data reveal the gradual turning over of civic leadership to smaller businessmen, and to men professionalized in organization and communication skills. His is a study of an extreme example of withdrawal from the immediate environment. By contrast, Harry Scoble's analysis of a selected number of issues in a small community focuses on community political power at a given point in time. Nevertheless, the patterns that emerge are remarkably similar. There is no single pinnacle of economic domination of the political process. Factionalism among leadership groups enables the electorate to exercise considerable reciprocal power by being able to choose among competing blocs.

Peter Rossi and Phillips Cutright's study of political party organization in Stackton is also a study of a deviant case since in this industrial community the political party organization is dominated by working-class elements and is organized along an old-fashioned patronage formula. Nationality and racial affiliations are crucial in maintaining the effectiveness of the political organization and the influence of business leaders is most indirect and curtailed. The findings of this study are important correctives to national studies of voting behavior since, in the community context, the effectiveness of the local party precinct workers in influencing political behavior can be established. Stackton is a carry-over from earlier times when party workers were stimulated by patronage. A comparable study on new middle class communities in which party workers are stimulated by ideology and desire for social participation remains to be completed.

The analyses of potentials and resistances to governmental change in two metropolitan centers, Flint and St. Louis, by Amos Hawley and Basil G.

Zimmer, and Scott Greer respectively, focus more on public attitudes. Attitudes are but the first step in analyzing the political arrangements of metropolitan communities. Clearly business leadership is confronted not only with an inability to exercise power, but with a lack of priorities as to its self-interest. Most metropolises are confronted with real and imagined problems for which existing political and associational arrangements are inadequate. Perhaps the greatest defect is in raising the demands which the public will consistently make on governmental agencies. The demands of higher and higher levels of consumption and satisfaction are not carried over in the public sphere.

Any effort to synthesize these results seems to focus on models of coalitions that are required if a community decision is to be effected. Community government is a parliamentary-type form of government that must operate without a suitable legislative mechanism. The political party is ineffective in co-ordinating the demands of the variety of associations which seek access to the community-wide decision-making process.

From a comparative point of view, aside from the absence of rigorous equivalence in operational definitions, the greatest weakness in the present efforts to study community political systems is an underemphasis on the process of legitimization of authority. All other things being equal, the community is a political context in which consensus tends to emerge. The analysis of party images in a Norwegian community by Henry Valen and Daniel Katz underlies this function of local politics. If consensus is overemphasized it is because of the questions asked by the researcher. While the community is not sovereign, community political systems are involved in adjudicating labor conflicts, controlling racial and religious tensions, and suppressing crime and deviant behavior. While this group of research reports is aware of these problems, they do not focus on them.

The efforts thus far make it possible to design more rigorously comparative research. The efforts to date have been the result of individual scholars, and the prospects of extensive comparative analysis clearly require the development of new, more simplified methodologies. However, to the imaginative researcher another alternative is open which is still in the case study model, namely a more experimental approach. Because of the diffuse nature of politics in the community setting, adequate images of the parts involved are not available to those who participate in community decision-making. How do community leaders react to efforts to identify the component parts of community political systems? The moral issues are not as complex as intellectuals would make them seem. Let it be assumed that effective decision-making at the community level is the prerequisite for democratic procedures in larger political systems. Everywhere community leadership faces a common problem, highlighted by these essays; namely, the issue is not the manipulation of the citizenry by a small elite, but rather the inability of elites to create the conditions required for making decisions. The experimental situation is to discover what would be the political consequences if the major actors had a clearer understanding of the structure of community power in which they are involved. The prediction is that such knowledge would enhance the processes of group representation and the formulation of community consensus.

The Bifurcation of Power
in a Satellite City

BY *ROBERT O. SCHULZE*

I: The Problem

As A SOCIAL FACT, power has long been recognized as one of the crucial components in human interaction. As a sociological concept, however, it has been difficult to delineate and harder yet to operationalize with much precision. "There is an elusiveness about power that endows it with an almost ghostly quality. . . . We 'know' what it is, yet we encounter endless difficulties in trying to define it. We can 'tell' whether one person or group is more powerful than another, yet we cannot measure power. It is as abstract as time yet as real as a firing squad."[1]

Of course, for Marx and his followers, power and power relations have been enshrouded in no great mystery. Persons who control the means of production are the key wielders of power, and ever have been. Interestingly, even non-Marxists — American sociologists among them — have agreed that in a democratic-capitalistic system, the control of property and production has constituted a major source of power. But what is often not adequately recognized is that, given a business-oriented system of values, economic power has long served as a *legitimate* basis of wider social and political power.[2] If this has not been acknowledged formally in our legal-constitutional system, it has nonetheless been a commonly accepted tenet of informal custom in our society. "He who pays the piper calls the tune" has thus been considerably more than an empty, well-worn saw in American culture.

Yet some social scientists have for some time suggested that this "sophisticated" view of power may not be so sophisticated after all. If the structure and dynamics of power fail to follow a nice democratic model, it need not mean that they neatly fit the raw rubric of economic determinism. Economic power often has to be translated somehow into political power before it can become broadly effective, and this process appears to be becoming increasingly complicated. Hence, growing attention has been paid to alternative centers of power. Lasswell has charted the rising power of governmental leaders, and Mills, however begrudgingly, has admitted the military and political elite to the top power triumvirate of American society.[3] Taking even more pluralistic views, Galbraith and Riesman have emphasized the "counter-

19

vailing power" of a diversity of national voluntary associations and other "veto groups."[4]

On the other hand, at the level of the *local community,* the "piper payer" thesis has proved remarkably resilient in both theoretical thinking and empirical research. Yet despite this persistent emphasis on the influence of economic dominants in community control structures, there have been at least two notable gaps in research:

(a) No attempt has been made to study a community's economic dominants as *a category* — that is, to specify all persons in positions of economic dominance, and then determine the patterns of their local involvements.[5]

(b) With one exception, students have been pretty much satisfied with charting the "merely contemporary." The systematic study of the roles of economic dominants in community control structures *in historical depth* has been largely ignored.[6]

A major objective of the research reported here was to begin to fill these two gaps in the study of community power.[7]

A Conceptualization of Community Power. Power is an abstract concept. In specifying its meaning, most sociologists have followed Max Weber's classic formulation:[8]

In general, we understand by "power" the chance of a man or of a number of men to realize their own will in a communal act even against the resistance of others who are participating in the action.

Subsequent definitions have not differed significantly from that of Weber.[9] On the other hand, a few have emphasized the *act as such* rather than the *potential to act* as the crucial aspect of power.[10]

It seems far more sociologically sound to accept a Weberian definition which stresses the potential to act. Power may thus be conceived as an inherently group-linked property, an attribute of social statuses rather than of individual persons. Whether or not the specific individuals in these statuses cash in on their control potential in their concrete role behavior is obviously an important matter, but it is not important to the conceptual clarification of the key term, power. In the present research, accordingly, power will denote the *capacity* or *potential* of persons *in certain statuses* to set conditions, make decisions, and/or take actions which are determinative for the existence of others within a given social system.

The social system with which this study will be concerned is the American urban community. Admittedly, sociologists have little agreed how to conceptualize the power structure of such a group. In part, this lack of consensus derives, of course, from the very complexity of the urban community with its vast network of sub-groups and statuses, all having some potential for determinative action. To no less an extent, it stems from the fact that power statuses and power relations are considerably more difficult to define in loosely-structured groups with diffuse goals than in those more formally organized groups characterized by fairly specific objectives.[11]

It is suggested that this conceptual quandary can perhaps best be resolved by *postulating certain broad values as most crucial in a community's viability as a social system, and then by conceptualizing its power structure in terms of those statuses presumed to have greatest potential for the maintenance of these values.* In this study, accordingly, two such values are considered pre-eminent in American community life: first, the goal of maintaining the community as an economic system which provides for the sustenance and physical well-being of its members; and secondly, the goal of maintaining the community as a socio-political system within which its members may organize their lives and toward which they may experience some meaningful sense of identification and belonging.

Persons presumed to have greatest potential for control over the maintenance of the local economic system are here designated as the *economic dominants.* Those presumed to have the capacity to exercise greatest control over the maintenance of the local socio-political system are designated as the *public leaders.* While the definitions of these two power types will later be spelled out more carefully, for the present they may be operationally identified roughly as follows:

the *economic dominants* are those persons who occupy the top formal statuses in the major economic units within the community area; the *public leaders* are those persons who, in the opinions of the heads of the local voluntary associations, exercise major influence and leadership in community affairs.[12]

In thus attempting to view community control structure in terms of both *economic* and *reputational* criteria within an overall framework of *community values,* this study endeavors to utilize and perhaps to relate three familiar approaches to the conceptualization of power:

(a) that which views power in terms of certain functional statuses (and requisite skills) which give their occupants decisive control over the key values in a social system — an approach associated with Harold Lasswell;[13]

(b) that which views power primarily in terms of preponderant control over the crucial sustenance or economic activities in a social system — an approach derived mainly from Marx, but perhaps best represented in American sociology by the work of Robert Lynd;[14]

(c) that which views power primarily as a function of the subjective evaluations of more or less representative or significant elements in the population of a social system — an approach most closely identified with W. Lloyd Warner.[15]

A Rudimentary Theory of Community Power Structure. Two assumptions underlie this study. First, a theoretically fruitful and empirically tenable distinction can be made between the most powerful persons and units in the urban community, and those having less power. That power cannot be realistically conceived in the form of either a single or simple pyramid does not mean that crucial community power relations are, therefore, so nebulous, ill-defined, mercurial or diffuse that they cannot be charted at all. Second, as power structures, like other social structures, have not been immune to specialization as a result of the complexity of modern urban society, crucial power statuses change — in both kind and number — as the social system of which they are part changes. Specifically, as the functional relationship of the community to the larger society alters, so too do the nature and form of the community control structure.

On the basis of these assumptions, it is hypothesized that the power structure of the relatively isolated and self-contained community tends to be monolithic, that is, that the persons who have greatest power in its economic system tend to be the same persons who have greatest power in its socio-political system. As the community becomes increasingly involved and interrelated in the large societal complex, however, its power structure bifurcates, resulting in two crucial and relatively discrete power sets, the economic dominants and the public leaders.[16]

This bifurcation can best be explained in terms of the changing relationship of the community to the larger society. The period of "local capitalism" passes. It has been a time during which, in Warner's words, "there was no extension of the factory social system outside the local community. The factories were then entirely under the control of city ordinances and laws, but also the more pervasive, informal control of community traditions and attitudes."[17] In such a period, rationality and sentiment combined to encourage the wedding of economic dominance and public leadership.

With increasing urbanization, the local community loses control over its economic system. In particular, its industrial base, in earlier periods owned and directed by local persons and groups, becomes divorced from local domination as an increasing number of plants are linked — whether through ownership, contractual, or buyer-seller relationships — with large economic organizations beyond the community.[18] With this growing interdependence, the activities of those units which are economically dominant in the community thus become ever more directed toward, and by, populations other than the local one. By thus effectively widening their resource base, these units come to occupy an even more powerful position in the community.

At the same time, however, these units become increasingly subject to influences which militate against the effective exercise, the actual cashing-in, of their enlarged potential for determinative action at the local level. Foremost among these is the fact that the local community has grown ever less important to the survival and prosperity of its dominant economic units. The relevance of local community organizations and activities, and the impact of local policy determinations on these units diminish. The development and maintenance of extra-community relationships become increasingly crucial.

As this occurs, the occupational and public relations imperatives of the persons in key statuses within these dominant economic units stimulate non-local, beyond-this-community, orientations. Insofar as their social and career objectives are concerned, the economic dominants find that decisive and sustained involvement in community affairs, in either the interpersonal or organizational sense, no longer has central relevance. At the same time, increased mobility and the absorption of units into national industrial organizations make it less and less likely that the occupants of key economic statuses will be persons indigenously recruited. Their social and family ties, like their occupational orientations, are ever less likely to have local roots. And thus, rationality and sentiment again join forces, but this time they induce withdrawal rather than involvement in the decision-making processes of the local community.[19]

Regardless of increased functional linkages with other groups in society, however, it is suggested that the local community endeavors to maintain its integrity as a meaningful social-political area in which its members live their lives. To be sure, it may be argued that heightened involvement in the larger society enhances rather than diminishes local efforts to preserve the identity of the community. Thus, the community experiences not a decline in localism, but a "new localism" as increased interdependence forces local leadership to define the "outer world" and to attempt to so organize the community that its integrity is maintained. The functional necessity for leaders whose orientations, commitments, and efforts are directed primarily toward *this community*, rather than toward *other* communities or groups, is therefore maintained and perhaps even intensified.[20]

If this argument is tenable, it would logically follow that the local leader, in order to act and be perceived as such, must be a person who refers most of his behavior to local community groups, who has developed a wide core of local interpersonal and organizational relationships, and who maintains a sustained and active interest in local community affairs. What is here hypothesized, then, is not merely that the community power structure tends toward bifurcation, in the sense that it consists of two different sets of individuals in the economic dominant and public leaders statuses, but that the persons comprising these two sets will be notably distinguishable from one another in terms of their involvements, commitments, and relationships in the community. Furthermore, it is suggested that the public leaders, by reason of their mutual participation in the community's political and civic life, would tend to constitute a closely-knit, informal elite group. Lacking this diversity of local ties which might orient them toward the community and relate them to the public leaders and to each other, the economic dominants, on the other hand, would be unlikely to comprise an integrated power group.

Finally, there is the question of the relationship between these two community elites. I made no attempt to develop detailed hypotheses about this relationship. It was suggested, however, that the likelihood that the two elites would be related in a predictable (and stereotyped) pattern of dominance-subdominance, with the economic dominants calling the tunes for the men "out front," the public leaders, was slim. If the developments already hypothesized, in fact, occur, the public leaders and economic dominants would be separated by ever-widening social, psychological and physical distances. Viewed casually, both segments might still appear to represent "business interests," but such a perspective would overlook the growing split within the business class itself.[21] Their diverse orientations and commitments would make it ever more difficult for the economic dominants and public leaders to think and act in concert. The economic dominants' relative indifference to local affairs, together with their lack of group cohesion, would seem to suggest that a considerable measure of autonomy would accrue to the public leaders in the initiation and direction of community action.

Research Design. The operational difficulties encountered in attempting a community power structure study, although obviously different from, are hardly less perplexing than, the theoretical problems of conceptualization.

The first methodological problem was the selection of the specific "field" in which to carry out a test of theory outlined in the preceding pages. In his recent and provocative discussion of community power structure research, Rossi concluded that we have had sufficient "depth" studies of single communities, and that "research on decision-making should (now) be extensive rather than intensive and comparative rather than the case-study technique."[22] With that desideratum few would disagree, but, because of limited resources, I fell back on an intensive case study of a single community. I can but voice the usual hope that the methods and findings reported here will somehow be useful and suggestive to the study of other communities.[23]

The community selected — I have called it "Cibola" — is a Midwestern city of some 20,000 inhabitants, located just beyond the Standard Metropolitan Area of one of the largest urban centers in the United States. It was chosen as the subject for this study for several rather unscientific and thoroughly practical reasons: it was convenient to my home base of operations; its modest size made it appear reasonably manageable for an essentially one-man research effort; and most important, I had already done field work there, conducting interviews in connection with other studies by two of my colleagues.[24]

It cannot be claimed, of course, that Cibola is America, nor America, Cibola. Criteria of typicalness did not figure in its selection for study. Yet, in retrospect, it may be argued that what Cibola has experienced is probably somewhat illustrative — though in the extreme — of what has happened to many communities over the past half century. Cibola has felt the full impact of the metropolitan and bureaucratic drift of American life.

Throughout the 19th century, it remained a slowly-growing and relatively self-contained community, surrounded by a rural hinterland, and not too much influenced by the presence of a larger community some thirty miles distant. Since 1900, however, it has become increasingly involved in the urban complex of its rapidly growing neighbor, Metro City. Like so many other American communities, it has become a metropolitan satellite.[25] Likewise, its industrial plant has undergone considerable transformation, much of it having been formally or informally absorbed by large corporations. By 1955, over 80 per cent of the industrial workers living in Cibola were employed by absentee-owned firms, and one plant, the branch of a huge national concern, had almost 10,000 persons on its payroll.

It might be claimed, therefore, that Cibola is perhaps ideal-typical, representing not the present mode, but rather approximating the polar extreme of the American community endeavoring to exist in the twin shadows of two social giants: the metropolis and the corporation. In this sense, the Cibola experience, while not representative of the present condition of other small and middle-sized American cities, may nevertheless be suggestive for the future fate of such communities.

The research operations fell into two major tasks: first, the historical reconstruction of the economic dominants of Cibola's past, including a determination of the nature and extent of their formal involvements in the political and civic life of the community — an extensive digging operation largely involving what is loosely called "library research"; and second, field work in the contemporary scene in an effort to define the roles and relationships of the community's current economic dominants and public leaders — a task primarily entailing intensive interviews with the occupants of these statuses and with selected informants, but also including a review of relevant documentary data. This work was accomplished over a two-year period, extending roughly from mid–1953 until mid–1955.

There was available in Cibola and environs a vast and informative (if scattered) variety of historical documents relevant to the community's industrial, financial, and political past. These data — city directories, newspapers, city council minutes, company and Chamber of Commerce files, tax records, commemorative city and county histories, and the like — were reviewed as carefully and systematically as seemed practicable. For example, the Pottawatomie County tax assessors' records were examined for every tenth year from 1844 to 1954 in an effort to determine the major property holders throughout most of Cibola's history; city and county directories, published periodically in Cibola and Pottawatomie County for over 70 years, were reviewed and relevant information — such as the dates of incorporation, capital assets, number of employees, and officers of the local banks and industries, plus the names and titles of city, school, and county public officials — was collected.[26] Drawing on these sources and, for the more recent periods, on such standard references as Poor's Register, Polk's Bank Directory, and the Reference Book of Dun and Bradstreet, a considerable body of pertinent historical data was accumulated. Because of the variety of documents consulted, it was possible to cross-check the accuracy of much of this information. On the basis of these sources, criteria for the selection of the economic dominants for the several periods of Cibola's history were developed. These criteria are indicated in Appendix A.

Investigation of the contemporary structure and dynamics of community power was a somewhat more straightforward task, involving for the most part intensive interviews with the current (1954) economic dominants and public leaders. These interviews, consisting mainly of open-end questions, were intended to elicit four general types of information: (a) the usual sort of vital data covering such variables as age, education, length of residence, membership in voluntary associations, occupancy of political and civic offices; (b) degree of familiarity and acquaintance with others in public leader and economic dominant statuses; (c) perception of the community power structure(s), in terms of both individuals and organizations; (d) perception of community power processes by means of a discussion of (i) hypothetical community action situations, and (ii) a series of two recent episodes of community-wide import. The latter included:

1. The local efforts in 1945–1946, successfully culminated in 1947, to change the form of city government from a mayor-aldermen, to a city manager system.

2. The post-war efforts to cope with the problem of community growth, specifically, the unsuccessful local attempts to annex large sections of land in the surrounding township (1947–1954).

The major shortcomings of the interviews seemed to derive not so much from occasional blocking and reticence as from the fact that I sometimes did not know the "right" questions to ask. While generally aware of what I was trying to "get at," most of those interviewed did not think of particular community power situations as wholes which could be recounted from beginning to end in a nice orderly manner. In truth, power does not appear to operate in any such rounded and closed terms. It rather manifests itself in contacts and decisions mixed in with, not set apart from, a lot of other everyday contacts and decisions, and a man cannot simply say that in one instance he was acting as a community power figure and in another, as a businessman, a member of a golf foursome, or a friend having lunch with other friends. Power-oriented activities and relationships are not discrete, distinct segments in men's lives; they are imbedded in a larger social context of day-to-day living. If the student knows enough about the situations to ask relevant and meaningful questions, he is likely to elicit quite direct and candid answers. For I found, as did Hunter, that most men do not regard actions and decisions pertinent to community power processes as either secret or nefarious. They may be private in the sense that one does not broadcast them, but they are not things about which men are reluctant to talk simply because they fail to jibe with the ways high-school civics texts tell us American communities are run.

II: The Past

A Brief Economic History of Cibola. Cibola's economic history may be conceived in two broad divisions: the era of local capitalism, 1823-1900; and the era of non-local capitalism, 1900–1954. Each of these, in turn, may be sub-divided:

Era of   ⎫ Period of pre-industry, 1823–1860
Local   ⎬
Capitalism ⎭ Period of local industry, 1860–1900

Era of   ⎫ Period of metropolitan involvement, 1900–1940
Non-local   ⎬
Capitalism ⎭ Period of absentee control, 1940–1954

1823–1860 were the years of the town's beginnings. Throughout most of this period, Cibola remained a small, struggling frontier village. This was a time of speculation in land and banks, but it witnessed as well the founding of a number of flour and saw mills, precursors of later industrial development. It was a period of intense rivalries between men seeking economic pre-eminence, but by its closing decade a small handful had gained ascendence, bringing a new and previously unknown stability to the economic and political life of the community.

The Civil War marked the end of one period and the beginning of another in Cibola, no less than throughout the entire nation. The pioneer days were over, the foundations laid. But the social and economic structure which rose from these foundations was not the small village, agrarian society envisioned by some of the founders. It was, instead, a society growing ever more urban and industrial and, in such a setting, the farmer, the landowner, and the miller gave way to the manufacturer and the financier.

These new developments were reflected in Cibola by its incorporation as a city in 1858, and by the founding of the community's first stable bank (The Cibola National) a few years later, in 1863. Thereafter, a diversity of local industries developed, manufacturing carriages, paper, dress stays, baseball bats, grass-seed sowers, agricultural implements and other products. In 1867, the Pottawatomie Carton Company was founded, the only local industrial firm which has survived from that time to the present. Throughout this 40-year period of steady economic growth, all of Cibola's industries were locally-owned, and each was managed by its owner(s).

The period 1900–1940 witnessed the beginnings of Cibola's ever-deepening involvement in the industrial complex of Metro City. On March 6, 1896, the first gasoline-driven car assembled in Metro City was driven through the streets of that community, and three years later Metro City's first automobile manufacturing factory began operation. By 1904 Midwest State was leading all others in the production of motor cars.

The development of automotive transportation made Cibola increasingly accessible to Metro City, and gave impetus to the steady spatial expansion of both communities. But, more important, the location of major segments of the auto industry in Metro City led to marked change in the character of economic activity in all communities in its hinterland. And despite the almost unanimous opposition of the directors of Cibola's older established industries, no less than fifteen new industrial plants began operation in that community between 1901 and 1910. Most of these industries soon established contract relationships with manufacturing units in Metro City, and Cibola more and more became a supply link in the automotive production chain. The new plants, however, remained relatively modest operations, and with but one minor exception, until 1932, the "outsiders" who established these industries themselves moved to Cibola and took up residence there. In several instances, in fact, local, long-established economic dominants "bought their way in," and thus gained control of "invading" industries. Throughout this entire period, therefore, manifest control of its industrial plant remained almost wholly in local hands.

By the last decade of the 1900–1940 period, however, the steady encroachment of Metro City and its motor-car empires was joined by the impact of the Great depression. It is doubtful that the local economic dominants could have long held out against either of these forces; confronted by both of them, their ranks were soon broken and their control of local economic life almost completely shattered. In 1932, Luther Wade, founder of one of America's great automobile manufacturing companies, built in Cibola a branch plant which shortly became the community's largest industry. And by 1933, all three of Cibola's banks — including the old National, for so long the cornerstone of local financial and industrial hegemony — had collapsed.

The dismemberment of the long-existing pattern of economic control by local dominants, signaled by the depression and the coming of Wade Motors, was culminated in the period during and following World War II. Until the late 1920's, all of Cibola's industries had been locally-owned; by the late '30's, three of its five largest manufacturing plants remained under local control; by the late '40's, this number had been reduced to one; and in 1952 that one lone survivor passed under absentee control. In 1954, there remained in Cibola but three locally-owned industries employing more than 75 workers — the largest with 115 employees, being the veteran Pottawatomie Carton Company[27] — and altogether, the number of persons on their payrolls amounted to only about three percent of the total number on the payroll of the largest plant in the Cibola area. In the 1940–1954 period, then, the economic structure of Cibola became almost entirely divorced from local control. It was now thoroughly dominated by large, absentee-owned corporations — all of them locally represented by managers brought in from "the outside."

The Local Involvements and Political Participation of Economic Dominants During the Era of Local Capitalism, 1823–1900. The original settlement, founded in the spring of 1823 and called Woodward's Grove, was located on a stretch of prairie just west of a bend in the Pottawatomie River, roughly a mile south of the present central business district of Cibola. By flatboat, Woodward's Grove was a good day's trip from the small community which was to become Metro City; overland, by ox-wagon, the journey took three days. Indians were camped nearby, food was always a problem, and there was the constant threat of sickness which the settlers called "ague," believed to have been caused by exhalations of decaying vegetation, but later discovered to have been malaria. By 1824 there were but thirty-eight families in the entire county.

In a rough, frontier environment such as this, it is difficult to designate certain individuals as economic dominants. The men who broke the wilderness and settled these early villages came perhaps seeking wealth and privileged position, but hardly any of them had these things when they arrived. Of the original pioneers, the settlement's founder, Benjamin Woodward, alone may be said to have been in a more advantaged economic position than his neighbors. It was he who staked out the county's first claim. He built the first home in the area and also the first grist mill, opened in 1825 and operated by him until 1830. Likewise, Woodward erected the village's first tavern, and a short time later, built a second. It thus appears that he not only processed the produce of the local farmers by day, but provided two places where they might dispose of their proceeds by night.

In addition, Woodward seems to have been intimately involved in what we may loosely call the public life of that early settlement. He was its first postmaster, its first justice of the peace, and the first sheriff of the county. It was at his home that the earliest communal festivity was held on Independence Day in 1824. It is reported that among the special provisions supplied by Woodward for this happy occasion was "a half-barrel whiskey," and that before the meal he read the Declaration of Independence, delivered a patriotic address, and led the settlers in singing "Hail Columbia." In the person and leadership of Benjamin Woodward, then, Cibola's economic, political, and civic life had its humble origins.

Despite hopeful beginnings, fortune did not deal kindly with these earliest settlers, nor with Woodward's Grove. Within a few years, the village was resettled a mile to the north — at the juncture of the river and a road recently laid out by the federal government — and was renamed Cibola. Woodward himself sold his interests at the Grove and in 1830 moved the mile north to the new village.

This settlement was to thrive, and by the time of Woodward's death in 1837 its inhabitants numbered over 1,000. By 1838 a local economic base had been laid, a county historian reporting that in that year the village contained "a bank, a banking establishment, two churches, a flouring mill, two saw mills, a woolen factory, a carding mill, an iron foundry, a druggist, eight or ten stores, five lawyers, and four physicians." Within a decade of its resettlement, some men had thus begun to achieve positions of economic dominance in Cibola — but not many, for most of the business units listed and most of those soon to be established were owned by but a handful of its citizens.

Throughout the entire 1823–1860 period, a total of only twelve persons met the requirements for categorization as economic dominants.[28] Of these, seven are known to have been associated with at least one other dominant in banking, milling or related business ventures, and six had two or more such connections.[29] Furthermore, the business ties which obtained served to link the majority in a potential power bloc as shown graphically in Figure 1.

At least one of these webs of economic relationship was short-lived. With the dissolution of the Bank of Cibola in 1839, Mark Norton and Arden Ball became rivals in the local struggle for economic ascendence. By the mid–1840's, however, it was clear that Norton, in alliance with Follmar and Johnson, had gained the position of greatest economic affluence in Cibola. The activities of these three men, may, in fact, be said to have brought into co-ordination the major control spheres of community life: the financial industrial (milling), and political. While each of them was among the major landowners in the township, and while the involvements of each were diverse, each yet appears to have concentrated his efforts — Norton in mills and other (pre-)industrial holdings, Follmar in banking, and Johnson in politics — as suggested by the following listing of the economic and political statuses which each occupied.

The combination of economic and political involvements reflected in the careers of Norton, Follmar, and Johnson was by no means atypical of Cibola's economic dominants throughout this period. Ten of the twelve, in fact, occupied public office (the average number of offices held by each dominant having been 2.4).

Especially noteworthy was the fact that the economic dominants of the 1823–1860 period, like those of the next, evidently made a concerted effort to be "in on the ground floor" when new governmental activities were initiated. Thus, for example, economic dominants of the pre-industrial period were the *initial* occupants of the following local offices: village president, village trustee, village recorder, village assessor, postmaster, foreman of fire company, county sheriff, county highway commissioner, and mayor.[30]

Furthermore, the economic dominants of this early period seem to have involved themselves in a few rather less official organizations and activities aimed at controlling the body politic. The most interesting of these was the Cibola Vigilance Committee, formed in 1837 for the ostensible purpose of advancing the Whig cause in the gubernatorial election of 1838. This was, in fact, a vigilante group, the aim of which apparently was to "assist" the village officials in ridding Cibola of certain "undesirables." A Cibola historian writes:

The proceedings of this organization were of guarded secrecy and the methods employed in dealing with shady characters of the town was doubtless drastic and certainly effective. There is, however, no record that these meetings were violent or illegal. The result of the activities of the Vigilance Committee, combined doubtless with those of the local authorities, was that before the end of the year 1839, one hundred and twelve men had been convicted of crime, $10,000 worth of stolen goods recovered, and numbers of undesirable citizens driven from the community. Considering the small population of the times, this record is no less than astounding.

Almost half of the period's economic dominants — Norton, Johnson, Edwards, Ball, and Prewitt — are known to have served on the "Central Committee" of this vigilance organization, and its meetings were held at the home of Abiel Hawks, the manager of the Norton-owned "Western Hotel."

Figure 1

BUSINESS LINKS AMONG ASSOCIATED ECONOMIC DOMINANTS, 1823–1860

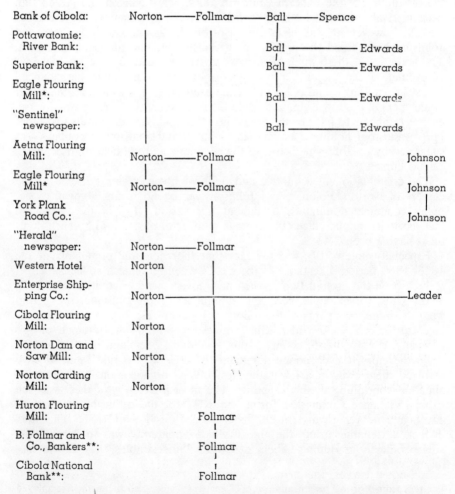

Bank of Cibola:	Norton——Follmar——Ball——Spence	
Pottawatomie: River Bank:		Ball ———————— Edwards
Superior Bank:		Ball ———————— Edwards
Eagle Flouring Mill*:		Ball ———————— Edwards
"Sentinel" newspaper:		Ball ———————— Edwards
Aetna Flouring Mill:	Norton——Follmar	Johnson
Eagle Flouring Mill*	Norton——Follmar	Johnson
York Plank Road Co.:		Johnson
"Herald" newspaper:	Norton——Follmar	
Western Hotel	Norton	
Enterprise Shipping Co.:	Norton————————————————Leader	
Cibola Flouring Mill:	Norton	
Norton Dam and Saw Mill:	Norton	
Norton Carding Mill:	Norton	
Huron Flouring Mill:	Follmar	
B. Follmar and Co., Bankers**:	Follmar	
Cibola National Bank**:	Follmar	

*The Eagle Flouring Mill is listed twice; originally, it was owned by Ball and Edwards, and later it passed into the hands of Norton, Follmar, and Johnson.
**Follmar established these two connections in the 1860's, after the death of Norton, and after the terminal point of Cibola's first economic period, thus, a dashed line is used to indicate these late-established Follmar links.

	ECONOMIC STATUSES	POLITICAL STATUSES
MARK NORTON:	Co-owner, Norris dam and saw mill	Postmaster
	Owner, Norris carding mill	Village trustee
	Owner, "Western Hotel"	Village assessor
	Partner, Enterprise Shipping Company	
	Co-founder and director, Bank of Cibola	
	Owner, Cibola Flouring Mill	
	Co-owner, Aetna Flouring Mill	
	Co-owner, Eagle Flouring Mill	
	Co-owner, "Herald" newspaper	
	Major property-owner	
BENJAMIN FOLLMAR:	Director and cashier, Bank of Cibola	Foreman, Village Fire Company
	Co-owner, Aetna Flouring Mill	Alderman
	Co-owner, Eagle Flouring Mill	Mayor
	Partner, Follmar and Conlin, Bankers	
	Founder, B. Follmar and Co., Bankers	
	Co-founder and director, Cibola National Bank	
	Co-founder, "Herald" newspaper	
	Owner, Huron Flouring Mill	
	Major property-owner	
CHAUNCEY JOHNSON:	Lawyer	Village recorder
	Co-owner, Aetna Flouring Mill	Township supervisor
	Co-owner, Eagle Flouring Mill	Justice of peace
	Director, York Plank Road Co.	Probate judge
	Major property-owner	Mayor
		State representative
		Member, school board
		Member, state board of education
		Member, board of control, state college
		Member, state canal commission

By the waning decades of the 1823–1860 period, however, the rough edges of community life had been considerably smoothed down. Even the long-time rivals, Norton and Ball, now joined forces and, together with Johnson and Follmar, led the drive to incorporate Cibola as a city. This was accomplished in 1858, and Chauncey Johnson was elected the first mayor. Four years later Mark Norton, the dominant figure throughout most of the early times, was dead. The pre-industrial period in community life was at end. Now a city, its population numbering almost 4,000, Cibola was about to enter a forty-year span in which the development of industrial and financial enterprises by *local* entrepreneurs went unrivaled.

As noted earlier, the first decade of the 1860-1900 period was marked by the founding of two major economic units, the Cibola National Bank in 1863, and the Pottawatomie Carton Company in 1867. Both had their roots in the earlier period, for Benjamin Follmar and his banking associate, Isaac Conlin, respectively, were prime movers in their organization. For the next seventy years, the National was Cibola's largest and most powerful bank, and for approximately the same period, Pottawatomie Carton remained the community's major industry.

Within a few years of their founding, control of these two dominant units was consolidated through the interlocking directorships and officerships of three men, Isaac Conlin, Lambert Barth, and Grant Moseley I. The economic supremacy of the National Bank and Pottawatomie Carton did not go unchallenged, however, and by the 1880's, rival interests had centered themselves around a new financial group, the Cibola Savings Bank. This cleavage was reflected in the local networks of economic linkages which reached their peak during this period. Fully *76 per cent* of Cibola's dominants were welded into two formidable economic blocks, shown graphically in Figure 2.

Figure 2

BUSINESS LINKS AMONG ASSOCIATED ECONOMIC
DOMINANTS, 1860–1900

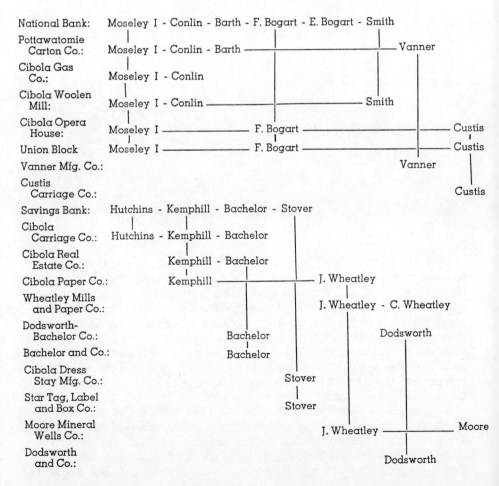

In the area of overt political participation, both segments in the hierarchy of economic control were well represented.[31] Twenty-one persons have been categorized as economic dominants in the 1860–1900 period, and fully *83 per cent* of them held public office. All but one of the eight dominants in the National Bank bloc were officeholders, as were five of the eight in the Savings Bank grouping. And if the National segment appears to have been slightly more politically active as a category, this was perhaps offset by the tenacity with which some dominants in the Savings bloc held office: Kemphill, for example, served sixteen years as city treasurer; Dodsworth, with but two brief lapses, was elected city alderman over a twenty-year period; and Bachelor served as a member of the school board for twenty-one years.

During this heyday period of local industry, the average number of public offices occupied by each dominant was 1.3, and once again, they were officially much in evidence at the inception of new civic ventures. The most noteworthy of these was that directed by the initial Water Commission of Cibola, a municipal group charged with the planning, development, and installation of the community's first central water system — the single most ambitious and costly project ever taken by the city government. Every one of the five members of this commission — Grant Moseley I, its chairman, Henry Custis, Oliver Thomas, Clark Wheatley, and Henry Stover — was an economic dominant.

As Mark Norton had eventually emerged as the dominant figure during the early period in Cibola's history, Grant Moseley I was to dominate the local power structure in its second half-century. In 1885, Moseley I assumed the presidency of the National Bank, and two years later, of Pottawatomie Carton. To these were added other economic officerships (Figure 2). Although he served as chairman of the important Cibola Water Commission, and was mentioned in the local press of the period as a "strong Democrat," Moseley was not widely active as a public office-holder. On the other hand, he had *direct* business and financial ties (via co-officer- and directorships) with a sizeable number of local officials — specifically, four mayors, four school board members, three city commissioners, two aldermen, one city treasurer, one county supervisor, and a postmaster — and he, no doubt, maintained many more indirect connections through the credit functions of the bank and the employment and business activities of his other holdings. Furthermore, several of Moseley's kinfolk, including his son and a brother-in-law, were overtly active in local government.

Moseley I was rather grandly described in a Midwest State publication of his time as "one of those rare men who build cities and lay foundations of the Commonwealth." From the perspective of Cibola, this characterization represented but little exaggeration — as suggested by the manner in which the community celebrated his 91st birthday in 1909. On that day the public schools were closed, and 91 "representative" citizens sent Moseley 91 American Beauty roses, each with the personal card of the sender attached. Each bloom was carried by a child from the Cibola Central School, the children visiting Moseley's home at two-minute intervals, beginning at eight-thirty in the morning, and continuing until all of the 91 roses had been presented. Several of the older respondents in this study remembered that day well, reporting that Moseley had a kind word for each child, many of whom he knew by name.

Grant Moseley I died in 1912 at the age of 94. After his death, his children gave to the community their father's large old residence as a memorial. It was not inappropriate that in 1914 it officially became (and yet remains) what it had perhaps unofficially been for many years, the Cibola City Hall.

The Local Involvements and Political Participation of Economic Dominants During the Era of Non-Local Capitalism, 1900–1954. As the twentieth century opened, Cibola's growing financial and industrial complex seemed solidly in the hands of home-towners. The Moseleys had expanded their local "empire," and indisputedly were the community's most powerful family. Shortly, to be sure, the direct and indirect business ties of Grant Moseley II linked him with 17 economic dominants, as illustrated in Figure 3.

In one way or another, however, the "outside" world, and particularly the soon booming industrial activity in Metro City, were stimulating a reorientation of Cibola's economic life. In the 1890's, one local dominant, Samuel Pruitt, who had been state representative and chairman of the Republican County Committee, extended his business interests in Metro City where he established and assumed the presidency of the huge Queen Marie Soap Company. Yet his roots remained in Cibola, and he continued for many years to commute and to serve as treasurer and vestryman of St. Mark's Episcopal, the town's "elite" church.

New companies were formed by Metro City industrialists, but throughout the first two decades of the period, all of the latter became residents of Cibola, and in addition, long-established local dominants soon acquired stock and officerships in several of these firms. Two of the largest concerns in which Grant Moseley II gained positions of dominance — the American Manufacturing Company and the Midwest Stove Company — had been founded by recent in-migrants.

Yet there was little doubt that the economic dominants of Cibola were becoming more cosmopolitan. Grant Moseley II founded the Pottawatomie Country Club and the Cibola Theater Group — organizations which smacked hardly at all of sober, small town provincialism. And shortly thereafter, he became a member of two exclusive associations outside the community — the Tappan Hills Country Club and the Metro City Club — in which the elite from the larger metropolitan area gathered. Nevertheless, the bulk of Moseley's ties appear to have remained local: he was elected alderman in the first decade of the century, and afterwards he served as treasurer of the school board and member of the police commission. In addition, he was president of the Rotary Club, and director of the Chamber of Commerce (both newly formed organizations), and commissioner of the Boy Scouts.

Compared with earlier periods, however, the political participation and leadership of the vast majority of Cibola's economic dominants declined sharply. In the 1860–1900 period, fully 88 per cent of the dominants linked with the National Bank had been office-holders, while between 1900 and 1940, this proportion declined to 28 per cent. Likewise only 11 — *28 per cent* — of the 43 persons categorized as economic dominants in the 1900–1940 period occupied public office.[32]

By the 1920's, the pattern of interlocking economic interest depicted in

Figure 3

BUSINESS LINKS OF GRANT MOSELEY II AND ASSOCIATED ECONOMIC DOMINANTS

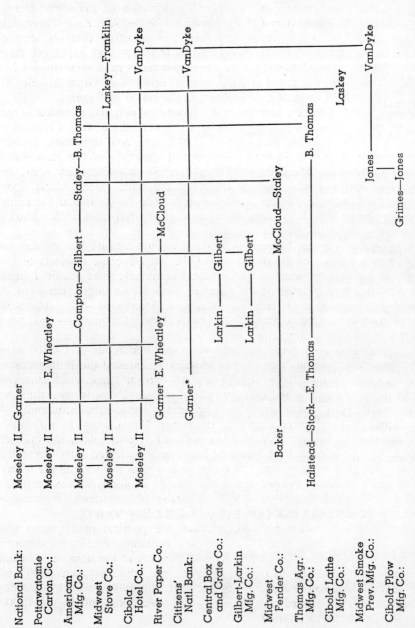

*Garner had resigned his directorship in the National Bank before assuming an officership in the Citizens' Bank. These two banks were linked, nevertheless, through an association of Moseley II and VanDyke.

Figure 4

BUSINESS LINKS OF ECONOMIC DOMINANTS
ASSOCIATED WITH THE CIBOLA SAVINGS BANK, 1900–1940*

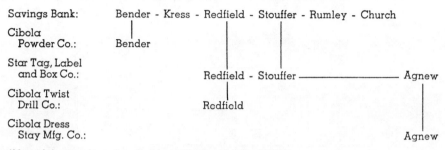

*Most of the ties shown here had been dissolved by the 1920's.

Figure 3 began to disappear, and by 1933 it was completely shattered. Within a two-year period (1932–1933) all three of Cibola's banks collapsed. By the late 1930's there remained in the community but seven major industrial units and *none* of these was interlocked.

The decline in economic dominant participation in the public life of the community closely paralleled the breakdown in the local web of economic interdependence. Of the relatively few dominants who had been elected to public office between 1900 and 1940, most were active during the first two decades of the period. Prior to 1920, for example, Moseley II, Wheatley, and Larkin had served on the city council; Church had been mayor and state representative; Moseley II, Kress, and Rumley had been school board members. In the 1920's only one additional dominant entered the elected ranks (VanDyke as mayor), and *in the 1930's Larkin, alone among all economic dominants, held an elective public office.*[33]

The pattern of economic dominant participation in the public life of Cibola during the most recent period, 1940–1954, will be our concern throughout most of the remainder of this chapter, and therefore, it will be but briefly sketched here. During this period of expanding absentee control, the dominants' withdrawal and disaffection from local political involvement continued. Economic linkages within the community, to be sure, persisted, but their scope and nature were now markedly altered. (See Figure 5.)

Figure 5

BUSINESS LINKS OF ECONOMIC DOMINANTS,
1940–1954

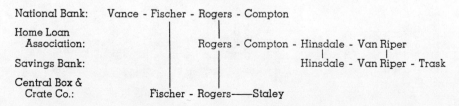

It should be emphasized that the network shown here was *the only one* existing among any of the thirty-one economic dominants of the 1940–1954 period, and that it wholly includes the smaller locally-owned units. In this bloc were eight dominants — *26 per cent* of the total. Conversely, *74 per cent* of the dominants had no secondary economic ties in Cibola, and *42 per cent* were members of chains-of-command extending beyond the community (i.e., they were the managers of absentee-owned corporation plants).

While the major banks of former periods apparently were centers of rival power, each interlocked with its own set of industrial firms in the community, Figure 5 further reveals that the two present banks were now indirectly linked *with each other.*[34] It might thus appear that when control of the economic life of Cibola was centered within the community, its banks could "afford" to be focal points of separate and possibly competing interest segments. With major economic control wrested from local hands, however, the banks apparently had greater need to act in concert.

Finally, it should be noted that the name of Moseley was conspicuously absent from the 1940–1954 economic network. Grant Moseley III, since 1948 president of the Pottawatomie Carton Company, was formally linked with no other dominant.

The economic power structure of Cibola was now one increasingly dominated by large, absentee-owned firms, none of which were formally linked, neither with each other nor with locally-owned banks or industries. At the same time, a certain retrenchment, a kind of closing-of-the-ranks was discernable among the still-locally-owned units.

This economic pattern appears to have been reflected in the dominants' record of political participation. Collectively, they have been the least formally active of those of any period; only *23 per cent* of them have held public office. And all of those constituting this 23 per cent have been the heads or directors of locally-owned firms. *None of the thirteen absentee firm dominants of the 1940–1954 period occupied any public office in Cibola.*[35]

Our historical review has documented that, following the turn of the century, there occurred a marked withdrawal of the economic dominants of Cibola from sustained, overt participation in its public life. We find, for example, that the "average" economic dominant of the nineteenth century held over three times as many public offices and remained in them almost three times as long as did his twentieth century counterpart.[36] Tables 1-4 further summarize this general drift.

Table 1

ECONOMIC DOMINANTS IN PUBLIC OFFICE*,
1823–1954

Period	Number of Economic Dominants	Number of Economic Dominants in Public Office	Percentage of Economic Dominants in Public Office
1823–1860	12	10	83%
1860–1890	21	17	81%
1900–1940	43	11	26%
1940–1954	31	7	23%

*Includes all public offices, elective and appointive, in the city, school district, township, and county. Also see footnote (32) above.

Table 2

ECONOMIC DOMINANTS IN *ELECTIVE* PUBLIC OFFICE, 1823–1954

Period	Number of Dominants in Elective Office	Percentage of Dominants in Elective Office	Percentage of Politically-Active* Dominants in Elective Office
1823–1860	10	100%	100%
1860–1900	14	67%	88%
1900–1940	7	16%	64%
1940–1954	4	13%	57%

*In this and the following two tables, "politically active" refers to all those dominants who had ever held any public office.

Table 3

ECONOMIC DOMINANTS ON CITY GOVERNING BODY*, 1823–1954

Period	Number of Dominants on Governing Body	Percentage of Dominants on Governing Body	Percentage of Politically-Active Dominants on Governing Body
1823–1860	9	75%	90%
1860–1900	12	57%	71%
1900–1940	5	12%	45%
1940–1954	3	10%	43%

*This group has been variously designated as the village board of trustees, the board of aldermen, and the city council.

Table 4

ECONOMIC DOMINANTS IN COMMUNITY'S HIGHEST PUBLIC OFFICE*, 1823–1954

Period	Number of Dominants in Highest Office	Percentage of Dominants in Highest Office	Percentage of Politically-Active Dominants in Highest Office
1823–1860	6	50%	60%
1860–1900	7	33%	41%
1900–1940	2	5%	18%
1940–1954	1	3%	14%

*This office was designated as village president until 1858; thereafter, as mayor.

While a variety of complex factors, no doubt, operated, the following three seem most significantly related to the dissociation of the economic dominants from involvement in local government affairs:

1. The establishment of direct supplier relationships with large, non-local manufacturing companies (especially ones in Metro City) by a growing number of Cibola industrial units after 1900.

2. The subsequent location in Cibola of an increasing number of branch plants by large, absentee-owned corporations.

3. The relative dissolution of the extensive network of business ties (interlocking officerships and directorships) which traditionally had served to link major proportions of Cibola's economic dominants in a variety of important banking and industrial enterprises within the community.

It is suggested then, that the trend toward widening, extra-local economic involvement significantly altered not merely the industrial and financial control patterns in the community, but its political power structure as well. This historical outline of this transition having been sketched, the task remaining is to explore the pattern of community power at the contemporary stage of its development.

III: The Present

Both objective and subjective techniques were employed in delineating the top statuses in the current power structures of Cibola.[37]

In keeping with the historical definitions already used, the current economic dominants were defined as those persons who occupied the foremost occupational positions in the community's dominant economic units.[38] At the time of this research there were thirty-three industrial and three banking units in the immediate Cibola area. Most of the industries were small, the median number of employees being only fourteen. A few, however, were of moderate size, ranging from 250 to 2,000 employees, and one, with almost 10,000 workers, would have been regarded as a giant concern in any community.[39] By our definition, the heads and interlocking directors of the eight largest industries and the three largest banks were categorized as economic dominants. These are indicated in Table 5 which also reveals that a few Davids and several Goliaths have been subsumed under one rubric. In the subsequent presentation of data, accordingly, care will be taken to indicate any significant differences between the dominants from the largest, absentee-owned firms, and those from the smaller, locally-owned units.

In devising a reputational approach to community influence and leadership, it was assumed that the local voluntary associations constituted the broad "grass roots" base of organized community power. Accordingly, the judgments of the heads of these associations were utilized in determining Cibola's public leaders.[40]

As in the case of defining the economic dominants, an arbitrary line had to be drawn somewhere, and once again, it is evident that certain persons qualified for inclusion in the subject category more solidly than did others. The public leader "line" was drawn after the eighteen most-frequently nominated (living) persons for several reasons. Very few of the association heads viewed the city as being "run" by a small clique of four or five individuals; however, we often heard comments like this: "I'd say there are about fifteen or twenty people who pretty much run things around here." Furthermore, it was found that after the top eighteen, duplicate nomination scores ("times named") began to occur with increasing frequency, suggesting perhaps the "fanning-out" of leadership and influence into somewhat lower levels of power. And finally — although this was discovered long after the selected operational definition had been used — we found that both the economic dominants and the public leaders, when asked the identical set of "perception of influence" questions originally addressed to the association heads, nominated substantially the set of persons indicated in Table 6 as most influential in the community.[41]

Table 5

ECONOMIC DOMINANTS OF CIBOLA, 1954

Dominant Economic Units	Number of Employees or Total Assets	Economic Dominants*
Metro Gear Division, U. S. Motors Corp.	9,492	Albert Larmee, General Manager Harold Leeds, Asst. Gen. Mgr. Personnel & Community Relations
Cibola Mfg. Division, Wade Motors Co.	1,989	Cal Lamkin, General Manager Nelson Leidy, Plant Manager
Lathe Mfg. Division, Hall Products Corp.	650	Daniel Porter, General Manager
Midwestern Division, Metro Mfg. Corp.	283	Earl Schuck, General Manager
Argent Division, Grove Mfg. Corp.	250	Harry Sherlock, General Manager
Pottawatomie Carton Co.**	115	Grant Moseley III, President
Cibola Machine Products Co.**	90	Edwin Shuster, President & Manager
Central Box & Crate Co.**	77	George Staley, President
Cibola Savings Bank**	$14,043.724.	Robert Trask, Chairman of Board and President
National Bank of Cibola**	$ 9,921,000,	Eugene Vance, Chairman of Board
Cibola Home Loan Assn.**	$ 1,018,000.	Deming Rogers, President

*Economic dominants via interlocking directorships: Deming Rogers (President, Cibola Home Loan Assn.; Director, Central Box & Crate Co.; and Director, National Bank of Cibola); Carl Fischer (President, National Bank of Cibola; Director, Central Box & Crate Co.); Alfred Van Riper (Director, Cibola Savings Bank; Director, Cibola Home Loan Assn.); Elmer Compton, Jr. (Director, National Bank of Cibola; Secretary-Treasurer, Cibola Home Loan Assn.); Ralph Hinsdale (Director, Cibola Savings Bank; Director, Cibola Home Loan Assn.).
**Indicates locally-owned units.

Comparison of the individuals listed in Tables 5 and 6 reveals that *the economic dominants and the public leaders consisted of two almost wholly discrete sets of persons: of Cibola's seventeen economic dominants only two were perceived among the community's eighteen public leaders.* Grant Moseley III, president of the largest locally-owned industry, was unquestionably regarded as one of the top influentials in Cibola; on the other hand, Deming Rogers, merchant and president of the locally-owned home loan association, fell just above the minimum limits for inclusion in each of the control categories.[42]

The historical reconstructions have suggested that the community's power

Table 6
PUBLIC LEADERS OF CIBOLA, 1954

Name (Occupation)	Times Named	Rank Order
William Houston (Chamber of Commerce executive)	153	1
Robert Drew (mayor)*	110	2
John Milan (city manager)	108	3
Grant Moseley III (industrial executive)	105	4
Bernard Rush (educator-attorney)	102	5
James Forme (attorney)	73	6
Oliver Ford (wholesaler)	51	7
Norbert Johns (realtor-insurance broker)	50	8
Cleveland Chapman (educator)	48	9
Arthur Schlaff (judge)	40	10
Charles Bernard (clergyman)	37	11
Bard Stevenson (educator)**	35	
Paul Warne (merchant)	30	12
James Taylor (bank executive)	29	13
Grant Moseley II (retired; ex-banker and industrialist)	27	14
Clarence Peters (industrial executive)	26	15
Naylor Guyer (Chamber of Commerce executive)	24	16
Philip Haas (salesman)	22	17
Deming Rogers (merchant, banker)	20	18

*At the inception of our study, Drew was employed as personnel manager in the plant of an absentee-owned corporation. During the course of the research, however, he resigned from this position, and, in partnership with another Cibolan, established a local insurance agency.
**Stevenson had died a few months prior to the initiation of our research, and therefore—even though still perceived as a public leader—he could not be operationally included in that category.

structure had not always been similarly bifurcated. We know, at any rate, that the economic dominants of earlier periods were, in very large measure, active participants in the public life of Cibola, and we may thus presume that most of them would have been regarded by their contemporaries as public leaders in the community. For the current years, we are certain that this was not the case.

Why were Cibola's economic dominants not regarded as community influentials? Conversely, why were the men perceived as public leaders so regarded? And finally, what was the relationship between these elites? To answer these questions we must begin by comparing the patterns of local involvement of persons in these two power categories.

General Characteristics. When we consider such standard sociological variables as age, education, length of residence, employment status, and occupational mobility, differences between the public leaders and economic dominants do not appear significant. This, however, results from the lumping-together of the dominants representing locally-owned and absentee-owned units. When we distinguish between the latter two, rather consistent and suggestive differences become evident. (See Tables 7 — 11.)

The differences reflected in these tables suggest that we might more realistically approach Cibola's current power structure in terms of three (rather than two) elite types: the local-firm economic dominants, the absentee-firm economic dominants, and the public leaders.

Oldest, least well-educated, least mobile, and with deepest roots in the community, the ten local-firm dominants were the economic descendants

Table 7

AGES OF PUBLIC LEADERS AND ECONOMIC DOMINANTS

	Public Leaders	Total	Economic Dominants Local	Absentee
Median age	53	50	60	48
Range	43-83	34-69	34-69	38-51
N	(18)	(17)	(10)	(7)

Table 8

EDUCATIONAL LEVELS OF PUBLIC LEADERS AND ECONOMIC DOMINANTS

	Public Leaders	Total	Economic Dominants Local	Absentee
High school, trade or business school	27%	41%	50%	29%
Some college	22	12	12	14
College graduate	50	47	40	57
Total	99%	100%	100%	100%

Table 9

LENGTH OF RESIDENCE IN CIBOLA OF PUBLIC LEADERS AND ECONOMIC DOMINANTS

	Public Leaders	Total	Economic Dominants Local	Absentee
Median years	30	22	39	0
Mean years	35	26	43	3
Percent native-born Cibolans	28%	30%	50%	0%

Table 10

EMPLOYMENT STATUS OF PUBLIC LEADERS AND ECONOMIC DOMINANTS

	Public Leaders	Total	Economic Dominants Local	Absentee
Self-employed	44%*	41%	70%	0%
Salaried employee	54	59	30	100
Total	98%	100%	100%	100%

*The retired public leader has been classified as self-employed, his prior status.

Table 11

OCCUPATIONAL MOBILITY OF PUBLIC LEADERS
AND ECONOMIC DOMINANTS

Degree of Intergenerational Mobility	Public Leaders	Total	Economic Dominants Local	Absentee
1 rank lower than father	5%	0%	0%	0%
Same rank as father	28	30	50	0
1 rank higher than father	39	41	40	43
2 ranks higher than father	22	30	10	57
3 ranks higher than father	5	0	0	0
Total	99%	101%	100%	100%

*Ratings were based on the seven-point Lenski-Landecker occupational-prestige scale. See Gerhard E. Lenski, "Status Crystallization: A Non-Vertical Dimension," American Sociological Review, 19 (1954), pp. 405-413.

of the men who had once "run" Cibola. Two of them, in fact, had been perceived as public leaders, indicating that complete bifurcation had not yet occurred. However, the fact that a much larger proportion were not regarded as community influentials suggests that they were possibly so committed to the largely defunct system of local economic control that they were unable to act effectively as community leaders.

The seven absentee-firm dominants, on the other hand, were the youngest, best-educated, most mobile of the three types, and their community roots were the most shallow — if indeed it could be said that they had any community roots at all. The data led us to suspect that perhaps Cibola, either as an integrated economic system or as a meaningful area of social and political activity, was of no great relevance to their lives.

All of them business or professional men, the public leaders appeared to stand between the local-firm and absentee-firm dominants in terms of each of the variables so far considered. May we say that this tentatively indicates that the public leaders served to bridge the old and the new systems of economic control? Their roots were perhaps deep enough to permit strong identification with the community, yet not so deep that they were irrevocably entangled in the old and waning system of local-firm domination. It has already been suggested that the task of maintaining the social and political viability of an increasingly dependent community demands that its leaders be locally-oriented, but also that they be able to transcend merely provincial interests, for they must somehow relate the community to the larger "outer" world.

Political and Voluntary Associational Involvements. That the public leaders had, in fact, established relationships in the larger social system while remaining primarily committed to the local community is evident when the overt political and voluntary associational activities of the three elites are reviewed. We find, for example, that five political offices at the non-local level had been occupied by public leaders, and that their mean number of memberships in non-local associations was considerably greater than those of either the absentee-firm or local-firm dominants.

Unquestionably, however, the most notable findings revealed by the political and associational data are the significant differences in community commitment among the public leaders and economic dominants. Notwithstanding their manifestly deeper community roots, the local-firm dominants' involvements in Cibola's political and civic system had been appreciably less intensive and extensive than those of the public leaders.

While no more than one of them could have been considered a professional politician, fully *94 per cent* of the public leaders (seventeen of the eighteen), had held office in the city, county, and/or state governments[43] Slightly more than half of the local-firm dominants and none of those from absentee-owned firms had held local public office.[44] Furthermore, the public leaders had served a median of eight years in public office as contrasted with

Table 12

PUBLIC OFFICES IN CIBOLA, POTTAWATOMIE TOWNSHIP, AND MIDWEST STATE EVER OCCUPIED BY PUBLIC LEADERS AND ECONOMIC DOMINANTS

PUBLIC OFFICE	Public Leaders	NUMBER IN PUBLIC OFFICE Economic Dominants Local	Absentee
Elective:			
Mayor	3	1	0
Alderman	2	2	0
Councilman	4	1	0
School Board Member	3	4	0
Township Supervisor	3	0	0
Circuit Judge	1	0	0
State official	2	0	0
Total	**18**	**8**	**0**
Appointive:			
City Manager	1	0	0
City Attorney	1	0	0
Board of Review Member	1	1	0
Board of Appeals Member	1	1	0
City Plan Commission Member	5	2	0
Police Commission Member	1	0	0
Fire Commission Member	0	1	0
Park Commission Member	1	0	0
Public Works Commission Member	0	1	0
State official	2	0	0
Total	**13**	**6**	**0**
GRAND TOTAL	**31**	**14**	**0**

the local dominants' median of four years. And finally, the public leaders had maintained a record of sustained interest in important civic offices unmatched by that of the local-firm dominants. Thus, since 1930, the public leaders had been continuously represented on the Cibola city council, five of them having served as councilman and/or mayor, while only one economic dominant (Grant Moseley III—also a public leader) had been on the council during the most recent 25-year period.[45]

Despite the abundance of political activity, it should not be inferred that occupancy of political office, per se, insured perception as a public leader. Although all but one of those currently accorded that status had in fact held such offices, so had a considerable number of other persons not recognized as community influentials.[46] Clearly, community involvements in addition to ones overtly political were requisite to achievement of public leader status. And foremost among these appears to have been active and responsible participation in the voluntary associational life of the community.

While the legal control of Cibola was the function of its municipal government, its extra-legal direction was largely channeled through important voluntary associations, and particularly, through its Chamber of Commerce. In this area of activity, the difference between public leader and economic dominant involvements was even more striking than in the political arena.[47]

The quantitative dimension of voluntary associational memberships is indicated in Table 13. While the elite segments claimed a larger number of organizational memberships than did less powerful elements in the population, the community ties of the public leaders and the local-firm dominants were clearly more extensive than those of the absentee-firm dominants.

Table 13

VOLUNTARY ASSOCIATION MEMBERSHIPS OF PUBLIC LEADERS AND ECONOMIC DOMINANTS

	Public Leaders	Economic Dominants		
		Total	Local	Absentee
Median number of memberships in all voluntary associations	10.5	7.0	8.5	4.0
Median number of memberships in local associations	9.0	3.0	6.0	1.0
Median number of memberships in non-local associations	2.5	3.0	2.0	3.0
Mean number of memberships in all voluntary associations	13.7	6.8	8.6	4.1
Mean number of memberships in local associations	9.6	4.2	6.1	1.6
Mean number of memberships in non-local associations	4.2	2.5	2.5	2.7

Several managers representing non-local firms saw little need to become involved in community associations. During our interview, after I had written down the names of the local organizations to which Daniel Porter, general manager of the Hall Products plant, belonged — and there were hardly any — he remarked:

I don't believe in belonging to an organization just for the sake of belonging. If I don't have enough time or enough interest to be active, I don't join.

Another absentee-firm dominant, Earl Schuck, general manager of a plant which manufactured automobile accessories, said:

I would try to get into things more if I honestly felt it would help the company, but I honestly don't see how it would. What all this amounts to anyway is community relations, and there're two conditions under which you need to mess with it. Either you're a small outfit with your whole operation in town in which case you can't afford not to get involved, or you're really big, like (U. S. Motors), and you *can* afford it and maybe need it for the sake of public relations. Our company is neither. Nobody in (Cibola) decides whether or not to use our product. You don't buy a car because somebody or some outfit you either know or don't know has made some of its parts. That's the advantage of marketing a product that doesn't sell directly to the consumer market. . . . So I've never really tried to get into things here. What we need most—any company does — is business, and this town can't do anything about that.

But even for the "really big" corporations, "Making Friends for (U.S. Motors) in the *Local* Community" (the title of a kit for executives issued by one firm) via extensive organizational activity was a hopeful-sounding policy to which everyday-reality did not necessarily correspond. Here is an excerpt from an interview with the general manager of one of Cibola's largest absentee-owned plants:

Q: "Now you've said that the local organizations you belong to are the Chamber of Commerce and the Advisory Council of the (Cibola) Boys Club. What about some of your subordinates; are they active in any groups in town?"

A: "Our approach is to have the different men on the staff take active roles and perform community tasks required. They're encouraged to the extent of their abilities. We want them not to put their foot forward too fast, not too aggressively, so as to seem to capitalize for self-aggrandizement purposes, but we do encourage them to be active in community affairs."

Q: "Of what sort? Are any of them besides you, for example, members of the Chamber of Commerce?"

A: "Yes, when we first came here we took out — I think it was ten — memberships in the Chamber. The company always tries to support organizations of that sort. Of course, I took one of the memberships, and so did (X — his assistant)."

Q: "What about the others; who did they go to?"

A: "To tell the truth, we had quite a time getting rid of the others. I'm not even sure that by now they're all in particular individuals' names. It's rather inconvenient, you see, for most of us to really participate the way we'd like to and know we should. I was put on the Chamber's board of directors almost right away, and I appreciate being on it, but unfortunately, I've been able to attend only maybe two or three meetings. Now (X), I think, is on the Chamber's Industrial Affairs Committee and I believe he's attended meetings more regularly."

And when I asked (X), the plant's assistant general manager in charge of personnel and community relations, he said:

"Yes, I'm on the Industrial Affairs Committee. Also the National Affairs Committee. I try to make these meetings. I go to functions I don't really care about so they'll feel we're interested in the community and its problems. I'm also connected with the Boys Club. I think I'm a sponsor or something. It's a very worthwhile project."

These interview excerpts rightly remind us that we need to distinguish between the quantitative and qualitative aspects of membership in voluntary associations. In general, and to the extent that they belonged at all, the absentee-firm economic dominants were "card-carrying" members rather than active participants in Cibola's civic life. Their organizational ties tended to be segmental and formal, with the trappings of local attachment dictated mostly by corporation public relations policies emanating from Metro City or other large centers — not from any locally-nurtured sense of belonging or commitment.

On the other hand, the public leaders, despite the large number of their associational ties in the community, were not mere "joiners." As revealed in Table 14, they had consistently assumed roles of responsibility in a considerable number of local organizations.

If the economic dominants were relatively parsimonious in their overall organizational involvements, their parsimony, nevertheless, was not random. As indicated in Table 15, they concentrated in large measure on the strategic associations, the ones that "really counted."*

Table 14

OFFICERSHIPS IN LOCAL ASSOCIATIONS BY PUBLIC LEADERS AND ECONOMIC DOMINANTS

	Public Leaders	Economic Dominants		
		Total	Local	Absentee
Percent having served as president of at least one local association	89%	24%	40%	0%
Number of associations served as president	20	5	5	0
Number of presidencies occupied	36	5	5	0
Percent **currently** serving as president of at least one local association	44%	6%	10%	0%
Percent **currently** serving as officer or board member of at least one local association	94%	35%	40%	30%
Number of local associations **currently** served as officer or board member	21	9	8	1
Number of officer or board memberships **currently** held in local associations	41	13	11	2

Note: **currently** indicates during 1954.

Table 15

PUBLIC LEADER AND ECONOMIC DOMINANT MEMBERSHIPS IN THE MOST INFLUENTIAL ASSOCIATIONS

	Percent Belonging to Association			
Association	Public Leaders	Total	Economic Dominants	
			Local	Absentee
Chamber of Commerce	78%	94%	100%	87%
Rotary	50	47	70	14
Kiwanis	44	18	30	0
Lions	11	0	0	0
Junior Chamber of Commerce*	0	0	0	0

*All of the public leaders and all but two of the economic dominants were beyond the upper age limit for membership in the JCC.

In the most influential organizations, as in Cibola's general voluntary associational life, however, it was the public leaders who occupied the key offices, as indicated in Table 16. Nowhere was this more clearly illustrated than in the Chamber of Commerce. The presidency of that association had been held by ten of the eighteen public leaders, and by but one of the seventeen economic dominants.[49] Although public leaders were pervasively involved in the associational life of Cibola, their participation had not been spread so thin that it precluded almost constant (and official) attention to the community's crucial organizations.

Interestingly, however, Table 16 also reveals that two board memberships in influential associations were currently held by absentee-firm dominants. Both of these were in the Chamber of Commerce, and they were occupied by the general managers of the two largest industrial units in the Cibola area. Even more interesting, and more suggestive for our understanding of the

Table 16

PUBLIC LEADER AND ECONOMIC DOMINANT OFFICERSHIPS IN THE MOST INFLUENTIAL ASSOCIATIONS

	Public Leaders	Economic Dominants Total	Local	Absentee
Percentage having served as president of at least one of the five most influential associations	61%	12%	20%	0%
Number of presidencies occupied in the five most influential associations	14	2	2	0
Percentage **currently** serving as officer or board member in at least one of the five most influential associations	44%	18%	10%	30%
Number of officer or board memberships **currently** held in the five most influential associations	12	3	1	2

Note: **currently** indicates during 1954.

evolving relationship between economic dominance and public leadership, was the manner in which these two executives assumed their positions on the Chamber's board.

Until 1953, all board members were chosen by vote of the Chamber membership-at-large from a slate containing twice as many nominees as there were board openings. In the latter year the Chamber's nominating committee "put up" the name of Cal Lamkin, general manager of the Cibola Manufacturing Division of Wade Motors. It was not customary to place an individual's name in nomination without his consent, and a figure of Lamkin's importance in the community's economic structure would obviously not have been nominated had the committee not anticipated his election.

To the considerable embarrassment of the Chamber's officers, however, Lamkin failed to muster sufficient votes to win election to the board. A crisis of no mean dimension ensued among the directors of the Chamber for not only was Lamkin the top local representative of the second largest employer of local workers, but Wade Motors was also the largest single financial supporter of the Chamber.

"Of course," said a Chamber official, "(Lamkin) had no one to blame but himself. He can't expect to get elected just by saying, 'I'm (Cal Lamkin) of (Wade).' Look — he doesn't even belong to Rotary or Kiwanis. He just hasn't been active enough in town."

But if Lamkin was not "active enough," the Chamber's directors were: they immediately amended the organization's by-laws, increasing the number of board members from fifteen to eighteen, and providing that the three additional members be appointed by the board rather than elected by the total membership. It is hardly necessary to add that Lamkin then became a director of the Cibola Chamber of Commerce via appointment. And shortly thereafter, so too did Albert Larmee, general manager of the most recently arrived dominant economic unit, the huge Metro Gear Division of U.S. Motors.[50]

If the Chamber of Commerce was the last formal stronghold of economic dominant involvement in Cibola's civic life, it was also apparently a pretty tenuous one. At least (as Table 17 indicates), membership on its board had been assumed by dominants with declining frequency since its founding in 1920. But the reason suggested by the Lamkin episode was presumably not the major one for this withdrawal, for I could find no evidence that other dominants had been unsuccessful contestants for board seats.

Table 17

ECONOMIC DOMINANTS AS BOARD MEMBERS OF THE
CIBOLA CHAMBER OF COMMERCE, 1920–1955

Period	Median Number of Memberships Per Year on Board of Directors	Number Serving as President
1920–1927	6	3
1927–1934	3	2
1934–1941	3	0
1941–1948	2	1
1948–1955	1	0

Differences in overt involvement in the civic life of Cibola were also reflected in the extent to which the power elites were "in the public eye." Local articles appearing on the front page of every third issue of the *Cibola Daily Beacon* during a twelve-month period, June 1953–May, 1954 (the months during which most of the association heads had been interviewed), were reviewed.[51] The frequency, prominence, and context of local persons' citations were tabulated. While this content analysis failed to reveal that the public leaders (as a category) had been uniquely treated, it did indicate gross disparaties in the manner in which they and the economic dominants were "covered." As Table 18 shows, the public leaders unquestionably received far greater attention in the local press.[52]

Not indicated in Table 18 are facts such as these: 44 per cent of the public leaders and *none* of the economic dominants had been mentioned in ten or more articles; fully half of the public leaders received more extensive coverage than the most-frequently-mentioned economic dominant.

The *Beacon* analysis also revealed that the public leaders were cited in a

Table 18

COVERAGE OF PUBLIC LEADERS AND ECONOMIC
DOMINANTS IN THE *CIBOLA DAILY BEACON*

	Public Leaders	Total	Economic Dominants Local	Absentee
Median number of front page articles in which mentioned	7.0	1.0	1.0	1.0
Mean number of front page articles in which mentioned	11.6	1.9	2.1	1.7
Median prominence score*	16.0	1.0	1.0	1.0
Mean prominence score*	33.7	4.9	5.2	4.5

*The prominence of the placement of each article and picture was rated on a 5-point scale, ranging from "lead" article or picture on top-half of page (5 points) to one-column article beginning on bottom-half of page (1 point). The median and mean scores for the three control segments were then computed from the total prominence scores of the individuals in each category.

far wider range of subject matter contexts than were the economic dominants. The median number of subject-matter contexts in which the public leaders were mentioned was 4.5 — as contrasted with a median of 1.0 for the economic dominants. The public leaders were cited in a total of twenty-one contexts, while the economic dominants had been mentioned in but eleven. There was but one content category in which the economic dominants were mentioned in more than five articles, that of industrial activity. On the other hand, the public leaders figured in articles at this or greater frequency in thirteen subject-matter areas: municipal business, municipal politics, township politics, state politics, Chamber of Commerce, Junior Chamber of Commerce, industrial, educational, social welfare, recreational, youth-oriented, veterans, and service club activities.

We may conclude, therefore, that the press coverage further supported what had already been suggested by the political and voluntary associational data: the overt involvements of the public leaders in Cibola's civic life were significantly more extensive and intensive than the involvements of the economic dominants.

Interpersonal Contacts. That the formal opportunities for interpersonal contact afforded by political and voluntary organizational activities were not unrelated to the formation of more informal ties is suggested by the data on acquaintanceship patterns among Cibola's elites. Each public leader and economic dominant was asked to indicate on a nine-point scale the extent of his acquaintanceship with each of the others in the power categories.[53] As measured by composite mean selection scores, the perceived closeness of relationships among the various elites are shown in Figure 6.[54]

Considered collectively, the public leaders clearly constituted a closer friendship group than did the economic dominants. The overall public leader relationship fell almost midway between "close personal friend" and "friend," while the economic dominants, in aggregate, could be characterized as no more than "acquaintances." While no public leader indicated a relationship with any other public leaders more distant than "acquaintance," 14 of the 17 economic dominants were *unheard of* by at least 1 other dominant, 12 were

Figure 6
PUBLIC LEADER-ECONOMIC DOMINANT
ACQUAINTANCESHIP SCALE: MEAN SELECTION SCORES

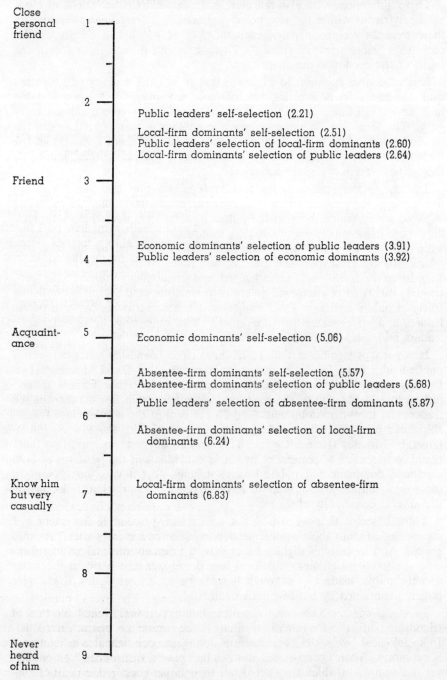

Close
personal   1
friend

            2

                    Public leaders' self-selection (2.21)

                    Local-firm dominants' self-selection (2.51)
                    Public leaders' selection of local-firm dominants (2.60)
                    Local-firm dominants' selection of public leaders (2.64)

Friend   3

            4   Economic dominants' selection of public leaders (3.91)
                    Public leaders' selection of economic dominants (3.92)

Acquaint-   5
ance   Economic dominants' self-selection (5.06)

                    Absentee-firm dominants' self-selection (5.57)
                    Absentee-firm dominants' selection of public leaders (5.68)

                    Public leaders' selection of absentee-firm dominants (5.87)

            6
                    Absentee-firm dominants' selection of local-firm
                        dominants (6.24)

Know him
but very   7   Local-firm dominants' selection of absentee-firm
casually   dominants (6.83)

            8

Never
heard   9
of him

unheard of by at least 2 other dominants, 8 by at least 3 others, and 5 by at least 5 others. There was 1 economic dominant who was *unknown* to almost 70 per cent (11 out of 17) of his fellow dominants!

These differences were also reflected in the mutuality of selections of close personal friends within the two power segments. Among the public leaders there were 24 reciprocal pairs, each member of which had designated the other as a "close personal friend." There were but 6 such pairs within the ranks of the economic dominants.

It is of course apparent in Figure 6 that it was the sparsity of absentee-firm dominants' friendship ties which largely accounted for the considerable interpersonal distance characteristic of the overall economic dominant category. The local-firm dominants knew one another almost as well as did the public leaders. And while it was the locals and the absentees who indicated least familiarity, it is not without interest that the absentee-firm dominants themselves were but slightly acquainted.

Turning to the inter-category relationships, we find that the friendship ties between the public leaders and economic dominants, while not as strong as those which bound together the public leaders, were nevertheless appreciably more numerous and intimate than those linking the economic dominants with each other. These differences were further reflected by the incidence of reciprocal "close personal friend" selections. There were 19 intimate friendships pairs linking public leaders and economic dominants (as contrasted with 6 pairs composed solely of dominants, and 24 pairs consisting solely of public leaders). Only 2 of these 19, however, were between public leaders and an absentee-firm dominant.[55] The remaining 17 linked public leaders and local-firm dominants.

It is perhaps significant that 11 of these close friendship pairs between a public leader and a local-firm dominant involved either Grant Moseley III or Deming Rogers, the two dominants also perceived as public leaders. Stated differently, 65 per cent of the reciprocal close friendship ties between public leaders and local-firm dominants, and 63 per cent of the mutual close friendship links between public leaders and all economic dominants were maintained by Moseley III and Rogers. This strongly suggests an important functional consequence of occupancy by single individuals of the positions of both economic dominant *and* public leader: namely, that it was the persons in these dual statuses who appear to have served as the principal links among the several community elites.

Thus, it seems that we would not be stretching social reality too far if we concluded that Cibola's public leaders constituted a closely-knit friendship group. And to an only slightly lesser extent, intimate informal relationships tended also to exist among the local-firm dominants and between the latter and the public leaders — although it must be remembered that these were largely maintained by but two individuals.

In sharp contrast, the absentee-firm dominants were linked by ties of friendship neither to the other influentials in the community nor to each other. In sociological terms, the absentee-firm dominants constituted a category — not a group. Their occupational statuses had placed them *in* the community, yet the manner in which they acted out their larger social roles did not suggest that they were *of* the community. But it did not follow, of course, that they were therefore unimportant *to* the community.

IV: The Dilemma

What has been described so far mostly concerns the shifting *structure* of power, the changing *potentialities* for control. And whatever I have been tempted to "read into" all this regarding the actual *dynamics* of power has been based in large measure on inference alone. How power *really* worked, how much autonomy the public leaders *really* had, to what extent the economic dominants *really* pulled or failed to pull the crucial strings — these are important questions, but questions far less amenable to systematic treatment and definitive resolution. Nevertheless, it seemed that an attempt at tackling them had to be made. These questions were approached through an effort at "reconstructing" the power alignments and processes in two recent community episodes, both of them stemming from Cibola's widening involvement in the metropolitan complex, and both apparently having signal importance for the viability of the community.

The City Charter Episode. When World War II began, Cibola was still operating under a system of municipal government quite similar to the one established by the first city charter of 1858. As the community had grown, various lay boards had been added, and new wards created, but the essential form of city government had remained unchanged. The central governing body consisted of a mayor and ten aldermen. All of these officials were selected in partisan elections, with each of the five city wards naming two aldermen, and with the mayor elected at large. All department heads were appointed by the mayor and aldermen, as were the members of the twenty-five lay boards and commissions, each charged with the policy direction of a designated area of municipal business, although final say-so in all matters was in the hands of the mayor and aldermen. The charter contained no provision for the central purchasing of supplies, and its loose statement regarding competitive bidding was easily evaded.

In the opinions of some local persons this form of municipal government, which had perhaps worked well enough when Cibola remained a small and relatively self-contained town, was inadequate to the problems which the community faced in the 1940's. During the war, the area's population had shot up over 100 per cent, and with this rapid growth, the demands on city services and utilities had greatly increased. One public leader, Oliver Ford, describes matters forcefully:

By sometime in 1944 there was actually a certain breakdown in the existing city government. The old officials were proud of their low tax rate, but that was nothing to be proud of in view of the facts. What were we getting for our taxes? The streets were in terrible shape. . . . The gas plant had been allowed to get terribly run down. The water works were antiquated and inadequate. The whole thing struck me as inefficient as hell.

By 1943, agitation for bringing the city charter "up to date" had been initiated. In 1944, at the solicitation of the Chamber of Commerce, a series of meetings, attended by Mayor Norbert Johns, the city council's ways and means committee, and top Chamber officials (including James Forme, its president, and William Houston, its executive secretary), were held in the offices of the Chamber. It was agreed that the old charter needed revision. In 1945, a charter commission was elected, and within a year, it proposed that an entirely new charter be adopted. The principal provisions of the proposed charter were: that the city governing body consist of a seven-man council to be named in a *non-partisan, city-wide* election; that the council would hire a *city manager* who, in turn, would appoint all municipal department heads (e.g., chief of police, fire chief, manager of public utilities), excepting the city attorney and city clerk who would be appointed by the council; that the municipal supplies and services be contracted for by competitive bidding and that a centralized purchasing system be instituted.

This proposed charter was defeated by a two-to-three vote in an election held in March, 1946. Referendum petitions were circulated almost immediately, calling for the resubmission of the charter to popular vote at the forthcoming general election. On November 5, 1946, the new charter, identical in every detail to the one rejected eight months earlier, was approved, and again, although conversely, the vote was roughly three-to-two. Five months later a new seven-man council (including Grant Moseley III and Robert Drew) was elected, and on April 14, 1947, the approved charter became effective, with Moseley III having been selected by his fellow councilmen as Cibola's first mayor under the new system.

Who were the initiators and prime movers in the charter campaign, and what were the alignments, pro and con?

When I discussed these questions with Clarence Peters, one of the public leaders, he commented:

It's hard to say just how or when the move for a new charter began. There'd been talk about it off and on for years. But I think the thing that got [Grant Moseley III] and [Oliver Ford] and some of us pretty serious about it was when we were on the Chamber's board during the war. We worked closely with some of the city officials and we really got a good idea of the shape things were in. It was pretty bad by the end of the war.

I think, [said absentee-firm dominant, Earl Schuck] that [Moseley III] got together with [Ford] and [Forme] and that group. Then, of course, they broadened out a bit by working through [Houston] and the Chamber of Commerce.

It was the overwhelming consensus of the public leaders and economic dominants interviewed that the persons just mentioned, Ford, Forme, Houston, and most notably, Moseley III, were the initiators and prime movers of the 1945–1947 charter efforts. As early as 1943, to be sure, Grant Moseley III had begun attending meetings of the city council as an "interested citizen."

For some damn reason [said Moseley] I'm not exactly sure why — just curiosity maybe — I attended almost every city council meeting for a period of almost two years prior to the real move for charter revision. I never saw so much petty bickering and cheap politics. There were two colored members and eight whites, and these two groups were always at loggerheads. And, by God, the colored members were generally the ones who were right! But it wasn't just these personal sorts of things. The main argument for a change was simple business efficiency. You had about twenty departments, each with a lay board of at least three people, and each with an average budget of some $20,000. Obviously, each of them tended to spend up to the hilt. There was no pooling of funds, no central purchasing, nothing. They never really took competitive bids.

Likely as not they'd just send a man down to a local hardware store when they needed a pane of glass or something. One hardware man built up quite a little trade by getting this kind of business from the city.

One of the few public leaders who had opposed the new charter (and the only one who opposed it publicly) asserted.

In the last analysis, you can put it this way: [Grant] wanted to be mayor and this seemed the easiest way. He thought it was a good way to get the [Moseleys] back in power.

Oliver Ford, another public leader, discerned a different (although perhaps not incompatible) motive:

Sure [Grant] and I are good friends, and I supported him in the charter blowup. But it wasn't just out of friendship. The thing was, [Grant], like most of the rest of us, saw a need to clean out a lot of deadwood, and he was willing to stick his neck out. For several years things had gotten too sectional. There was too much short-sighted bickering between different areas and different groups. Maybe you can get away with that when you're a hick town, but [Cibola] wasn't a hick town anymore. We needed people willing to go to bat for the whole city after the war, and there wasn't anybody around who could do that better than [Grant Moseley III]. He has his faults, God knows, but there's no one who will go down the line for [Cibola] like he will.

The interviews with the public leaders and local-firm dominants revealed that for many, the struggle for the new charter symbolized a major effort at community survival. Cibola had been engulfed by social and economic forces threatening its identity and its way of life. It had been "invaded" by exceedingly large numbers of persons whose wartime situations led them to seek a job, a bed, a drink, a good time, but not a community. Its principal industries, one by one, had succumbed to outside ownership and control. Its municipal services were inadequate and in disrepair. Those who strongly identified with Cibola needed to prove to themselves perhaps that there was, after all, a city to govern, a community with which to identify. And who seemed better fitted to spearhead an effort at local revival than a man with roots deep in the town's past, the head of its largest and oldest – though no longer very powerful — home industry, the man whose grandfather had "built cities and laid the foundations of the Commonwealth"?

As the vote at the spring election of 1946 revealed, however, there were obviously many Cibolans who did not view charter revision as a good thing for the community, symbolically or otherwise. A breakdown of the initial vote by wards supported the locally-popular opinion that sizeable numbers of Negroes and blue-collar workers cast ballots against the new charter — their fear presumably having been that abolition of the ward system in favor of city-wide elections would no longer insure them a voice in the council. Considerable opposition also came from certain small businessmen, many of whom were reportedly "used to things the way they were," and more than a few of whom apparently had profited from the non-bid-taking, non-centralized purchasing practices of the old council. One of the leaders in this element was Ralph Hinsdale, an economic dominant who, in addition to being a director of the Savings Bank and Home Loan Association, was one of the largest lumber- and hardware-men in the city. Associated with this "crowd" were numerous city officials and employees, and many ward and party politicians, led by public leader Norbert Johns, the incumbent mayor. Also suggested in the charter fight were vestiges of the old National versus Savings Bank rivalry. In addition to Hinsdale, the Savings Bank contributed two other charter opponents: John Church, the bank's president and for over twenty years the city attorney, and James Taylor, the Savings' vice president.[56] On the other hand, a member of the charter commission and an avowed proponent of the new charter was the National Bank's president, Eugene Vance, he and Moseley III having been the only local-firm dominants who exerted leadership in the campaigns for adoption.

To the best of my knowledge, the four just mentioned: Moseley III, Vance, Church, and Hinsdale were the sum of Cibola's economic dominants who were active in the charter struggle, and all of them represented locally-owned firms. Meanwhile, all sixteen of the public leaders residing in Cibola in 1947 were clearly involved in the charter fight: fourteen as proponents, two as (sometime) opponents.[57] Ten of the fourteen proponents *publicly* advocated passage of the new charter through endorsements in the press and/or addresses before associational and other meetings. And finally, as we have already seen, Grant Moseley III (working closely with public leaders Oliver Ford, James Forme, and William Houston) was the acknowledged leader in the charter effort, while the leader of the opposition was public leader Norbert Johns.

Nor could I uncover any evidence that economic dominants were "behind-the-scenes" instigators of the charter move. None of the absentee-firm dominants suggested that they had played initiatory roles, nor did any of the local-firm dominants, excepting Moseley III. There was strong indication, in fact, that various key dominants favored the new charter only after having been "sold" on the idea by one or more of the public leaders.

The banks lend in the area, of course [said James Taylor, the Savings' vice president] and we knew you had to have certain city improvements before you'd get much building, and therefore much loans for building. It became clear to us during that summer [between the first and second charter elections] that the charter might accomplish this — and that, I think, was probably the main reason the banks favored the change.

It had become evident to me [the Wade Motors' general manager, Cal Lamkin, commented] that the whole business of city services badly needed improving. Things like utilities, fire and police protection, streets and the like. [Grant] and the others made sense to us when they argued that it was just good business to support the change.

Yes [said Bernard Rush] the industries here all *went along* with the switch to city manager. [Wade Motors] especially backed the move, and I think it was the non-partisan elections provision of the new charter that particularly appealed to them. This was about the time that [Wade Motors] was beginning to develop a civic interest in the communities in which its plants were located. The [Wade] people didn't feel they could work in a town on a partisan basis, but they could if things were non-partisan.

These statements, together with other evidence, suggested that the public leaders were not simply "fronting" for the larger economic units in the charter movement. But if theirs was not an initiatory role, the dominants certainly were consulted and their support solicited.

Our procedure [said James Forme] was pretty much the one followed in any issue of general community importance. A group of us got together and hashed over the idea. When it seemed feasible, we checked with [Bill Houston] at the Chamber of Commerce to see what he thought in the line of general support on the part of business and others. [Houston] foresaw some opposition on the part of some of the smaller businessmen, and of course, considerable opposition from the old city hall crowd... but we knew right along we'd run into this. Then we contacted the bigger plants and the banks to see how they'd take to the idea. As I recall, all of the industries were on our side from the time we first brought it up, and even the [Savings] Bank swung along eventually.

Whether the charter proponents would have persisted in their efforts had one of the dominant economic units continued to attempt a veto must remain a moot question. So must the question of whether at some later time the economic dominants themselves might not have played a more initiatory role in changing the form of local government had the 1946 effort not succeeded. The fact is that these things did not occur, while what I have described apparently did.

The fact also remains, however, that among the first city councilmen elected under Cibola's new charter was public leader Robert Drew, the personnel manager of the local Wade Motors plant. And upon the subsequent resignation of Grant Moseley III as mayor, Drew was named by his fellow councilmen to that post. Both Drew and Lamkin, the Wade general manager, denied that Wade Motors was thereby "represented" on the city council. Both strongly asserted that Drew has been a "free agent" while serving in local government:

As a matter of fact [said Lamkin] I can remember only one instance in the whole six or seven years that [Bob Drew] served as councilman and mayor that he ever asked me our position on an issue before the council. . . . And I told him to do whatever he thought best, regardless of the company's interest.

Be that as it may, the interviews with the association heads and public leaders clearly indicated that many Cibolans, however much they regarded Drew as *their* representative and mayor, also thought of him as *"the Wade man"* on the city council.

Drew's days as a "Wade man" were nevertheless numbered; in 1954, while continuing to serve as mayor, he resigned his position with Wade Motors and entered private business in Cibola. What precipitated this action, I cannot be sure. Quite a few persons interviewed expressed surprise that Drew "would give up a really good-paying job with a big outfit like [Wade Motors] to open an insurance office in [Cibola]." A few public leaders added that they were "afraid that [Bob] was having to get into things as mayor that [Wade] wasn't eager to have one of its boys get involved in." Both Drew and Lamkin denied that a conflict of interests had developed, yet both were obviously reluctant to pursue the subject. "[Bob] had his reasons," said Lamkin. And Drew said, "Let's say that I thought I'd be better off making the switch, and let's let it go at that."

Possibly suggestive, however, were several comments made by Lamkin during our interview:

The company has decided that it won't encourage its executives to live in the communities where they work if they don't already or if they don't want to. . . . The company doesn't feel its people — at least its executives — have to live in a town in order to have good community relations. Just about the opposite, as a matter of fact. You're always subject to a hell of a lot of local pressures if you're there. If they know where you are, you're always a target. . .

And later he remarked with characteristic forcefulness:

You've got to remember that what I do doesn't just affect us here. The man who represents [Wade Motors] in this area could affect [Wade's] reputation a hell of a lot of other places as well... Look what happened ten, fifteen years ago when the old man [Luther Wade] let [Harry Bender] get his damned nose into everything. The company's *never* lived that down. But we've learned our lesson... and today we play it conservative.... Why, if I went out and got myself [fouled] up in local politics, you'd see a new boy in these shoes so damned fast it'd make your head swim.

Whatever the "true" facts and motivations underlying the Drew case, it conceivably suggests the limitations presently imposed upon participation by "representatives" of dominant economic units in the public life and councils of the community. Sustained and responsible involvement in local affairs may sooner or later result in conflicts (whether of time, interest or loyalty) with the "representative's" obligations to the organization which employs him. It seems not unlikely that Drew's resignation from Wade Motors may have been the result of such conflicts. That this was no isolated case and that a "hands-off" policy regarding involvement in potentially controversial types of community affairs was perhaps becoming increasingly prevalent among local, as well as absentee-owned firms, was indicated by an interesting episode involving the *only other* subordinate official in a dominant economic unit who had served on the Cibola city council since the adoption of the new charter in 1946.

The affair concerned the superficially trivial matter of the purchase of two police cars by the city. In addition to Drew, another dominant economic unit was "represented" on the council in the person of James Taylor, vice president of the Savings Bank.

The patrol car deal [explained one public leader] wasn't important in dollars and cents terms, but a lot of people took it as important in other ways. It seemed that the city needed two new police cars. The regulations covering purchases of this sort were clearly set down in the new charter — which most of us had recently supported. They called for taking bids and awarding the deal to the lowest bidder; unless his product was obviously inferior. Bids had been placed by both [Wade] and [Kane-Abbel][59]. [Bob Drew], the mayor, stepped down when this was being considered because of his connection with [Wade], and [Jim Taylor], who was then mayor *pro tem,* took over. You might know how it turned out — [Kane-Abbel's] bid was lower than [Wade's]. Had it been a *lot* lower, I doubt that much would have been said, but what made it ticklish was that it was only about $10 per car lower. Nevertheless, it *was* lower and the regulations were quite clear...

It wasn't an easy decision to have to make. Here [Wade] was paying us over $60,000 a year in taxes, and [Kane-Abbel], being located in the township wasn't paying anything. Yet nobody was in much of a position to say that [Kane-Abbel's] product was clearly inferior — that wouldn't have looked good for [Cibola] considering the cars were made here. I don't have to tell you that [Jim Taylor] had a real problem on his hands.

James Taylor described his predicament:

As I told you, I hadn't been much in favor of the new charter at first, but various people had convinced me that it was the best and most businesslike way to run the city. Now here some of these same people were coming to me and saying, "[Jim], let's overlook the regulations this time." Business people and others came and reminded me that [Kane-Abbel] paid their taxes in the township. They didn't have to tell *me* that! And then I was told that nobody in [Cibola] would really object if we gave [Wade] the contract. That may have been so, but I still felt we'd worked out an orderly and fair way of handling this sort of thing, and the more pressure was applied, the more determined I got to stick by the rules...

A member of the board of directors of the Savings Bank, reminiscing about the patrol car episode, said:

For some time we'd felt that [Jim] was getting too much mixed up in things on the council. We'd asked him to go easy — after all, we do business with everybody in this area.

As I recall, it was on this occasion that [Jim] reminded us that he worked for us at the bank during the days, but that what he did with his evenings was his own business. 'When my council work starts to interfere with my job at the bank, then and only then will I agree that the council activities are too much.' He may not have put it quite that strong, but that was the idea. But hell, what he was doing on the council *was* interfering with his job at the bank whether he realized it or not!

Taylor again:

The bids on the police cars were read at three different council meetings as required, and at no time could anyone come out and say that [Kane-Abbel's] was an inferior product. So I ended up by recommending that their bid be accepted — which it was. Of course, there were hard feelings. I'm sure [Cal Lamkin] was pretty displeased, though he never said anything to me about it. But quite a few of my friends did. They said nobody cared about the cars actually; it was the principle of the thing. But that's what *I* was concerned with, too! I'll tell you I wasn't the most popular man in town for awhile there, but I'd done what I thought was right.

One significant consequence of this episode was described by Taylor:

A short time after all this police car business, a strange thing happened. It seems that the board of directors at the bank decided to hold their weekly meetings in the evening, and they set the time so that it fell on the same night of the week as the city council meetings. I couldn't very well go to both, of course, so I ended up leaving the council.

If the new charter had indirectly caused headaches for Jim Taylor, its adoption also created problems (and of a less circuitous sort) for its proponents who eventually included all but one of the public leaders. While the power of the economic dominants no longer involved the development by them of extensive and well oiled local ties, the public leaders' claim to power, on the other hand, rested in large measure on the maintenance of personal and organizational relationships and incentives within the community. Through supporting a charter which presumably would modernize and revitalize the machinery of local government, the public leaders had inevitably disrupted the balance of things within the community's power structure. In so far as they were concerned, therefore, the issue did not end with the adoption of the charter in 1947. Yet, remaining before them was the task of coming to grips with several major concomitants of the recent civic struggle.

First, the charter fight had necessitated broadening the effective base of local decision-making. After the Moseley III - Ford - Forme group had failed in their direction of the initial effort at adoption, younger business and professional men in the community (operating largely through the Junior Chamber of Commerce) had been enlisted to "run" the second campaign. The aggressive manner in which they handled the renewed pro-charter effort manifestly had borne fruit in November. In the meantime, however, men representing these elements which hitherto had had a smaller voice in community affairs had been allowed to make inroads into the upper levels of the local elite structure. And once the fight had been won, they could not be conveniently sloughed off.

Likewise, the public leaders, following the charter's defeat in March, had been obliged to try to "win over" certain key leaders in the Negro and working class sub-communities. The second charter vote indicated that they succeeded in these efforts. But in the process, promises and commitments had been made, as evidenced by the fact that since 1946 one prominent Negro leader and one pivotal labor union official almost invariably have been named to "represent their elements in the community" on important citizen committees appointed by the Chamber of Commerce and the city council. In all of these instances, a somewhat wider sharing in the decision-making processes resulted.

Of equal significance was the fact that the charter struggle had alienated a considerable number of second and third echelon power figures in the community: small businessmen, ward politicians, and officials associated with the old city government. The fact that the public leaders felt an urgent need to resolve this alienation, and the manner in which they endeavored to do so, throw light on the process (and problems) of public leadership in a small city such as Cibola.

When the charter fight was all over [said one public leader] we had to try to cement things together again. In a town this size, and knowing each other as we do, you can't just scuttle the men who lost. They were men who had worked hard for the town before — men like [Norbert Johns] and [Wallace Burns — another former city official], and they got a real slap in the face during the charter campaign. But the Chamber of Commerce didn't forsake them. You must try to forget and start in again, and that's what we've tried to do — though it wasnt easy. . . . The Chamber has tried to remain aware of the feelings of these men who lost.

This comment summarized most public leaders' attitudes following charter enactment, and just as accurately, it suggested the principal channel through which the proposed reconciliation was to take place. Clearly, the perceived need was to close ranks, to present a common and cohesive leadership front in the face of inevitable future challenge to the community. Large economic concerns might have turned their backs on vanquished competitors; professional politicians might have "thrown the rascals out"; but the men intimately involved in the informal leadership structure of a small community could afford neither to flaunt nor to be vindictive for they realized that if the effort to renovate the local government was to result in the lasting alienation of significant segments of community opinion, theirs would have been a Pyrrhic victory indeed.

Acting principally through the "good offices" of William Houston and the Chamber of Commerce, the public leaders therefore embarked upon a concerted effort to re-enlist the civic loyalties and energies of those elements in the community which had been defeated in the charter struggle.

I don't recall [said Houston, the Chamber's executive secretary] that there was ever any debate about the fact that we should demonstrate to men like [Johns] that the community appreciated their devotion and didn't want it to end over the charter issue.

Cleveland Chapman, the local college president, who did not arrive on the scene until two years after the charter campaign had ended, commented:

I gathered that the old council crowd headed by [Norbert Johns] had taken the whole affair very personally. The wounds were just beginning to heal about the time I was elected president of the Chamber in 1950. I recall that I was advised by [Bill Houston] and others to be very careful to include representatives of the [Johns] group on all committees I appointed — which of course, I was. Even today, however, when Chamber appointments and community service awards of one sort or another are given, there are likely to be hard feelings if the [Johns] element feels it's been slighted.

This public leader strategy was reflected by the election of Norbert Johns as president of the Chamber of Commerce in 1949. The following year, the board of directors named Wallace Burns, a close friend and political ally of Johns, to the Chamber's presidency. In 1952, Johns was selected as president of the Community Chest organization, and in 1953, he was presented with the Chamber of Commerce award as "(Cibola's) Citizen of the Year." Thus, the defeated, like the collaborators, had their payoffs.

And how effective, in fact, was the new charter in stimulating a revitalization of the civic and government life in Cibola? Unquestionably the quality of municipal services improved — and with no significant tax increase. Most of the public leaders (and economic dominants) indicated that they had no complaints about the city's current management. Yet there was also discernable in their remarks a certain feeling of detachment, an absence of a sense of meaningful involvement in the affairs of municipal government. One of the rather more sophisticated public leaders remarked significantly:

When you start thinking about it and talking about it like we are now, you sort of realize there was something damn paradoxical about our whole enthusiasm for getting a new charter. I never really saw it this way at the time, but here we were — smacked between the eyes with the realization that things had all of a sudden changed a lot ín [Cibola]. . . . There were a lot of big companies, that hadn't been here a few years before, moving in, and they were run by outsiders. So what did we do? We revamped the city government so that it was set up rather like a big company, and we brought in an outsider to manage things. That's rather interesting, isn't it?

Another public leader — and his comments were atypically harsh — said:

I suppose the city manager form has worked fairly well. . . . But look at the city council. It no longer has any standing committees — not one. They really don't know what's going on anymore. About all the council now does, in effect, is appoint a city manager and then resign! Under the old system you had more prominent people, better citizens, in the city government. Who are the elected officials now? Does anybody know them?

Under the old system, the committees were really relied on by the council. The city manager, however, doesn't want to know too much, and he doesn't want others to know too much. Admittedly, we've got a good manager; he's efficient as hell apparently, but so was Hitler. In a town like this you need something more than efficiency.[60]

The Annexation Episode. Whatever the long-range consequences, the public leaders had resolved the charter issue to their immediate satisfaction. The problem of annexation, however, proved to be quite another matter.

While Cibola's population had increased sharply over the 1940–1950 decade, like most American cities, the community had witnessed an even greater population growth in the area surrounding its legal perimeter. Long predominantly rural in character, the neighboring township had grown ever more urban — a development which was greatly accelerated by the wartime construction of the huge Big Bend plant roughly two miles east of Cibola.[61] In terms of the many economic and social factors, the Cibola-north Pottawatomie Township area had become an interrelated whole. In terms of legal boundaries, however, the area remained devided. And the consequences of this "artificial" division posed large political problems for local leadership.

As population density in the area increased during the 1940's, the inadequacy of the township's sewage, water, fire, and police systems became evident. Largely because of its refusal to levy adequate property taxes, however, the township governing board was unable satisfactorily to meet these pressing needs. Cibola's leaders became increasingly alarmed by the rapid and largely planless growth around the community's borders. Investors and builders, few of them local citizens, had begun to speculate in township land; housing developments, consisting almost entirely of cheaply-constructed units, were mushrooming; health problems resulted from the inadequacy of sewer and water facilities; the "temporary" wartime housing units near the Big Bend plant had become overcrowded and deteriorated; and elsewhere in the township, suburban and rural slums were emerging.

While the township was able to boast of an extremely low property tax rate, Cibola, in order to provide adequate municipal facilities for its own and the area's expanding population, had been forced to impose a sizeable property tax.[62] More significantly, by 1950, almost every square foot of useable land within the city limits was occupied. Cibola's population was expanding; its need for revenue-producing (industrial) property was no less great than its need for home sites, yet its supply of land was near exhaustion. And all the while, the township's population was increasing at a rate five times as great as that of Cibola. In the face of these developments, Cibola's leaders were not hard pressed when asked to indicate the major problem confronting the community, nor did they have to strain their imaginations to foresee the day in which effective control over Cibola's political and social life might be wrested from the local community much as had control over its economic life.

Accordingly, from 1947 until 1954, apparently intense and certainly varied efforts were undertaken to annex to the city sizeable sections of land in the township. The local organizations which fostered and guided these endeavors were the Chamber of Commerce and the city council. With one exception, the top posts in both of these groups were occupied by public leaders throughout the entire period: Moseley III and Drew served successively in the mayor's office, Milan was city manager, and the presidents of the Chamber were Peters, Stevenson, Taylor, Johns, Burns, Chapman, Hass and Warner.[63]

A series of committees, the Greater Cibola Committee, the Cibola Area Development Committee, etc., were jointly appointed by the city council and the Chamber's directors, in an effort to develop annexation proposals acceptable to both the city and the township. Representation on these committees was inclusive of most of the well-organized and potentially influential groups in Cibola (at least one lesson learned in the 1946 charter fight not having been forgotten). At the same time, the public leaders themselves were prominent in the composition of each committee. The most recent one, for example, included Warner as chairman, and Ford, Moseley III, Houston, and Johns were among its members. Although a few public leaders thought that some of the annexation proposals were too ambitious, none opposed any of them. Nevertheless, these efforts failed.

I tried like hell for five years as mayor to work out something with the township [said Grant Moseley III] but we didn't get anyplace. I sat around the conference table with the township officials night after night; I had them over to my home for lunch and for dinner; I took them into [Metro City] to ball games; I even tried priming them with highballs. I think I tried everything to get them around to some common ground on which we could make some annexations. Nothing worked.

I was chairman of one of the Chamber's committees that tried to work the thing out [James Taylor said] but we got nowhere. Then after I was elected to the council, I convinced [Moseley III, then mayor] to let me form another joint committee. The idea that we could sit down with the township people, talk sensibly, and work it out seemed awfully reasonable to me, even though I realized that what we were asking the township officials to do was relinquish some of their power... We've made a little progress — working agreements for the extension of city water lines to some parts of the township — that sort of thing. But in all this time, no *land* had been released by the township.

The reasons for the failure of the city's efforts were perhaps most succinctly suggested by William Houston, executive secretary of the Chamber:

Everybody paid lip service to the idea of orderly development of the area, but our real problem was that we had nothing to offer the people who carried weight in the township. The officials there are an entrenched bunch, and they knew perfectly well that for every acre of land they might let us have, they'd lose money on the state sales tax diversions. . . . Of course, they tried to convince the township voters that there'd be a large increase in their property taxes if they came into the city. I don't know that they have in fact convinced them; there's never been a vote on the thing, so we don't know. . . . [64] Finally, there was the [Big Bend] plant; they had almost a self-sustaining setup out there — with their own water supply and their own police and fire protection. What advantage could they see to coming into the city?

With the (by now) usual exception of Grant Moseley III[65], active economic dominant involvement in the annexation issue was limited to one firm: the Kane-Abbel Corporation, operators of the Big Bend plant during most of the 1947–1954 period.[66]

At no time were relations between Kane-Abbel and Cibola's public leaders cordial. Anticipating that the new auto manufacturer's venture would be short-lived, the community influentials in effect used Kane-Abbel as a handy and vulnerable whipping-boy toward which could be directed blame for a multitude of perceived community ills; the rapid influx of Southern migrants, the growing power of the labor unions, and of the Negro sub-community, the fluctuating employment situation with its erratic impact on local business, etc. That all of these conditions were inevitable in the community's growing involvement in the metropolitan complex, and that they clearly antedated the Kane-Abbel operation — these facts were conveniently ignored or forgotten by most of Cibola's leaders.

Nor were the reported attitudes of hostility nothing more than after-the-fact verbalizations of the local leaders. Kane-Abbel officials had early been cognizant of community sentiments, and had generally reciprocated in kind.

Certainly [said a former Kane-Abbel executive] we were aware of local feelings right along — not that they made much difference. This unfriendliness wasn't a one-sided proposition, however. [Kane-Abbel] was very little concerned with the community or with community relations. About the only [Kane-Abbel] man who took an interest in [Cibola] and got along well there was [Norton Hudson], who was supposed to be in charge of public relations at first. But he got kicked upstairs into advertising. Then when the annexation ruckus started, we worked closely with the township people, and that really ended things as far as the possibility of good relationships with [Cibola] were concerned.

The "annexation ruckus" to which this informant referred was the most ambitious of the several efforts to expand the community's limits. Initiated in 1950, it proposed to increase the city's land area from three to eighteen square miles, and to incorporate, among other things, the Big Bend plant. Suddenly, avoidance of local involvement became a luxury which the Kane-Abbel Corporation felt it could no longer afford; its management feared that the sizeable increase in its property taxes which would result from annexation might well prove one straw too many for Kane-Abbel's shaky financial structure to bear. Accordingly, the corporation surreptitiously supported the officials and others in Pottawatomic Township in their opposition to "the big grab."

In all [said another former Kane-Abbel official] the corporation ploughed over $40,000 into the effort to defeat [Cibola's] annexation plan and to develop a substitute proposal. [Kane-Abbel] paid all the court fees in the litigation hassles that followed — although you could never prove it.[67]

But avoiding annexation did not save Kane-Abbel. By 1953, the sales of its cars were dangerously lagging, and meanwhile, a new and far less friendly national administration had taken over in Washington. (Several of its key officials were ex-U.S. Motors' executives.) Shortly, crucial Air Force contracts held by Kane-Abbel were cancelled. There were large-scale layoffs at Big Bend, and it was rumored that the corporation would soon suspend operations at the huge plant altogether. Nevertheless, in September 1953, the *Beacon* carried a full-page advertisement in the form of an "open letter" in which Clyde Kane, Jr., the corporation's president, gave assurances that Kane-Abbel was not planning to abandon the community. Kane's message was an interesting compound of candor and something less than candor:

We have been your neighbors for nearly eight years. . . . During this period the Management of this company has not always shared and taken responsibility in community events and affairs to the extent that you felt we should do, and certainly not to the extent that we would have liked . . . if it appears we have been self-centered, it is not because of any lack of understanding of the community problems, or any lack of desire to work with you on them. . .

I have been asked many times if [Kane-Abbel] planned to move its entire operation away from this area. I've answered this question the same way each time it has been asked, and I shall repeat that answer now. All our plans are based on continuing operations both here and at [a plant in another state]. Our goal is to increase the work load at [Big Bend]. . . . Let us assure you that in addition to the growth and development of our work at [Big Bend] and elsewhere, we will undertake the responsibility that is ours, to keep you better informed of all operations. We look forward to sharing with you, to a greater extent, civic and community affairs.

Sincerely,
[Clyde Kane, Jr.]

Despite "all our plans," Kane-Abbel rapidly liquidated its holdings in the Cibola area; within a month of the appearance of Kane's supplicating letter, the Big Bend plant had been sold to U.S. Motors Corporation.

But the arrival of this latest — and most stable — industrial giant did nothing to implement the resolution of Cibola's long-standing annexation problems. While the corporation did not underwrite opposition to the community's expansion plans (as had Kane-Abbel), neither did it encourage such plans. Early in 1954, several Chamber of Commerce officials (including leaders Paul Warne, its president, and William Houston, its executive secretary) made an effort to " 'feel out' what (U.S. Motors') attitude would be if we reopened the drive for annexation." In Warne's words:

[Larmee, the general manager] and [Leeds, his assistant] were very cordial and all, but they did most of the talking. I gathered that [U. S. Motors] wasn't particularly concerned about the tax increase that would have come with [Big Bend's] annexation; that would have amounted to a drop in the bucket as far as [U.S. Motors] was concerned. But they were quite aware of the fact that there'd been a lot of opposition to annexation in the township. They told us they didn't want to get involved in local squabbles the way [Kane-Abbel] had. I think they were afraid it would be bad for public relations. In any event, they ended up by saying that they wanted to play fair with everybody, and they thought the only way to do this was to be *neutral*. They told us they wouldn't oppose any new attempt we might make at annexation, but they wouldn't endorse it either. Under the circumstances, though, the situation amounted to this: if we couldn't get [U.S. Motors'] help, and if we couldn't go before the people and say that they were in favor of annexation, it would be like saying they were opposed to it. . . . That's what it all added up to, and in view of that we saw no sense in trying to start the whole business over again.

When I asked a top U.S. Motors official at the Cibola plant what he considered the major problem facing the community, he answered without hesitation:

Annexation. They've got to work out this annexation thing. [Cibola] will be dead as a doornail if it doesn't expand. And privately, we have no objection to [Big Bend's] being taken in even though it would cost us more money. But [U.S. Motors] will never in the world take active sides in an issue like that. We're playing it strictly hands-off. We sell too many cars to everybody to get involved.

The fact that a growing number of dominant economic units were reluctant to "get involved" was perhaps the root of the community's failure to resolve its expansion problems. Several public leaders claimed that had they and the economic dominants acted in concert, they could have exerted sufficient pressures on the township and county officials and on the courts to have insured that the issue would at least have been brought to a vote. Excepting Kane-Abbel (which had "lined up on the 'wrong' side"), however, Cibola's large economic units had refused to become enmeshed in so heated a controversy which appeared to them little relevant to *their* continued and successful operation.

At the completion of my field work, Cibola's expansion quandary remained unresolved, and its leaders confused and uncertain as to what the next course of action should be. They realized that Big Bend had become a nearly integral part of the community; without it, most of them said, no annexation plan would make sense or "pay for itself." Their attitudes ranged from the slender optimism of James Forme ("Oh, I think things will eventually work themselves out — in maybe five to fifteen years. . .") to the more prevalent pessimism of James Taylor ("if we don't lick this thing soon, we're going to have a dying old city here. . .") Even Grant Moseley, III, usually a vigorous adversary of community ills (as he saw them), had finally withdrawn from the battle, having resigned as mayor "in disgust over the whole annexation mess." He spoke about the problem with resignation:

Frankly, I'm beginning to doubt if the men of my generation will ever be able to solve this thing. It's dragged on too long; too many feelings have been hurt; too many threats have been made; too many men have got their fingers burned trying to handle the problem. After so long, you know, you feel more discouraged than anything. . .

The Dilemma of Community Leadership. For roughly fifty years Cibola has been struggling to adjust to the status of a satellite community — sometimes vigorously, sometimes blindly, always rather reluctantly. World War II and its aftermath served to sharpen and intensify this struggle, and it was in the charter and annexation episodes that recent local efforts at adjustment were in large measure reflected. In our necessarily abbreviated review of these issues and their attempted resolutions, we have tried to discern the community control structure in motion, to see how power "really worked" in Cibola. Although complex, extended, scientifically uncontrolled events do not lend themselves to nice summary nor to the neat testing of theory, the ones described nevertheless suggest the growing dilemma of leadership in this satellite community.

Superficially, the data seem to reveal that there had occurred a *tri-* rather than a *bi-furcation* in Cibola's power structure. Careful analysis of our findings indicates, however, that there were, in fact, but *two* significant power types in the community: the absentee-firm economic dominants and the public leaders. The local-firm dominants appear rather as anachronisms in the control structure. They represented industrial and financial units too small and unimportant to give them decisive economic power; likewise, most of them had been too little responsibly involved in the public life of the community to have acquired much civic-political power. The influence of a local-firm dominant such as Grant Moseley III primarily stemmed not from the fact that he was an economic heavyweight as his father and grandfather had been, but from the fact of his active commitment to the maintenance of Cibola as a viable social-political system. It is suggested that local-firm dominants of the future will figure significantly in the community power structure only if they participate actively in the civic and political life of Cibola — only, that is, if they become sufficiently involved to be accorded the status of public leader.

Manifestly, the charter and annexation episodes revealed that the initiators and directors of important programs of community action were the public leaders, the men who actively endeavored to preserve the community as a significant area of life organization and personal indentification for Cibola's inhabitants (including themselves). While they tended to be persons of some economic substance, they were not men who occupied key business positions, nor could they meaningfully identify with the large and powerful units in the local industrial and financial complex. It may, in fact, have been as one economic dominant stated:

I get the feeling that for these men [the community leaders], running [Cibola] is sort of equivalent to what, for some people, is a sex substitute. Don't the psychologists say that if you don't have a satisfactory sex life, you can adjust by taking it out in some other area? Well, I think that's kind of what the bigwigs in [Cibola] have done. They know they can't make a real success of their own businesses or jobs — either the businesses are too small or the jobs aren't important enough. So they get their satisfactions in community affairs.

That the public leaders could not operate in a vacuum, that they had to take account of a variety of community groups was apparent. That their power derived largely from the withdrawal of the economic dominants from community involvement seems true enough; yet the evidence also suggests that the dominants themselves had limited options. Immersion in community affairs and maintenance of economic power in regional or societal networks appeared increasingly incompatible. To this extent, the economic dominants, if they wanted to remain dominant, perhaps had little choice but to dissociate themselves from the functions of community leadership.

But although they made the major determinations in the area of community action, the public leaders' effectiveness was increasingly challenged and vitiated. From "below" there were once subordinate elements of the population, now organized and demanding a larger voice in the direction of community affairs. Of negligible importance in the period prior to 1940, the Negro sub-community and the labor unions had grown in size and, more significantly, were steadily fusing their efforts through the Democratic Party. Likewise, the community's voluntary associations had proliferated, and some of them were beginning to question the traditional prerogatives of the Chamber of Commerce-Rotary-Kiwanis clique. In an effort to stem the tide of these local competing centers of power, the public leaders resorted to an assortment of tactics. Sometimes they offered direct and indirect support to the less aggressive and more compliant sub-leaders, thus fostering disunion within the control structures of the out-groups; sometimes they extended their own voluntary associational memberships in an effort to "join and maneuver" — though there were limits to how thin they could spread themselves and yet have time and energy sufficient for the control of the key associations; sometimes they granted policy concessions in what seemed to be peripheral matters; and sometimes they relied on co-optation — letting a few of the leaders of minority opinion gain access to the higher echelon of local decision-making.

None of these manipulatory efforts, however, promised to be indefinitely effective — perhaps because it was apparent that none involved a genuine readiness to broaden the base of local power. With the growing fusion of the Negro and working-class sections of the community, in particular, the public leaders were convinced that to foster widespread sharing in the process of decision-making would be to invite a Trojan horse into their ranks. Basically therefore, the "old crowd" attempted to close ranks, not to open them.

The formal organization through which the public leaders endeavored to "run" the community was the Chamber of Commerce. That association might indeed have been regarded as public leadership institutionalized. And in that fact lay its strength and its weakness, as well as much of the strength and weakness of the public leaders.

The usual community control procedure was for the public leaders to make initial, tentative policy decisions in informal friendship groups. These were then discussed with William Houston and other Chamber officials, whose task it was to "feel out" the key economic units and the potentially concerned voluntary associations. Thereafter, if the programs appeared feasible, the necessary engineering of consent and co-ordination of action was supposedly handled in and through the offices and committees of the Chamber.

This, in general, was the control process followed in both the city charter and annexation episodes. In both instances, however, the Chamber found itself confronted with two largely incompatible tasks: it was supposed to be the spearhead of effective community action, but at the same time, it was responsible for conciliating and holding together the various elements in Cibola's power structure. Consequently, the pursuit of present objectives was usually tempered by the need to maintain personal and organizational incentives in the future. This dilemma was well reflected in the charter issue. The failure of the initial campaign was in part the consequence of the Chamber's reluctance to alienate certain segments of Cibola's leadership cadre. Likewise, the Chamber's intensive concern to heal the breach which the charter fight eventually caused tended to compromise the objectives of that fight: bringing the vanquished elements "back into the fold" meant that persons unsympathetic to the municipal setup were allowed to assume positions of authority in the community.

To the extent that the Chamber of Commerce was obliged to serve an accomodative function, its efforts to assume a positive and dynamic leadership role constantly faced the danger of being watered down. The concern to close ranks made it difficult to move forward, and ultimately, therefore, the Chamber — like the public leaders themselves — found itself waging a series of holding operations.

The major dilemma of public leadership, however, was the growing "neutralism" of the absentee-owned corporation units in the community area, and the public leaders' ill-defined relationship with the representatives of these largest and most powerful "out groups."

Although programs of community action might be originated, planned, and directed primarily by the public leaders, it did not follow that they could be effected in the face of economic dominant opposition or indifference. As a group, the public leaders represented control of Cibola by business-oriented interests, yet they were painfully discovering that they could not count on *big* business to commit its men or its resources to the solution of pressing local problems.

The large corporations — and this was especially true of such behemoths as U.S. Motors and Wade Motors — had grown to a stature resembling societal institutions. It was, I think, their very sensitivity to political determinations at the regional and national levels which militated against their involvement in these matters at the level of the local community. Meaningful involvement in a community such as Cibola was primarily regarded by these corporations as entailing risks to their operations and to their positions in the larger social system. First, there existed the possibility that participation by their executives in local affairs would induce conflicting loyalties; secondly, decisive involvement in critical and potentially controversial community decisions posed the threat of alienating significant superiors and publics at the extra-community level.

In general, the role of large economic units in the community control process had become a negative one. In those rare instances in which local decisions conceivably could prove significant to their well-being, absentee-owned corporations might covertly endeavor to veto or subvert programs of community action. Thus, in the annexation episode, Kane-Abbel Corporation abandoned its usual posture of indifference, and helped scuttle Cibola's ambitious plans for expansion. Kane-Abbel, however, was highly atypical of large corporations; it was a consistently unstable and financially unsound operation. Far more illustrative of the emergent attitude of huge economic units was U.S. Motors' policy of "neutralism."

The reluctance of Daniel Porter, the Hall Products' general manager, to "get involved in things here," and the assertation of U.S. Motors' Harold Leeds that "We're playing it strictly hands-off!" represented a theme which pervaded the interviews with the absentee-firm dominants. Harry Sherlock, the general manager of the Grove Manufacturing plant, summed up his attitude:

One sure way to give [Grove] a black eye would be for me to get myself into things so deeply in town that no matter what I did I'd end up alienating a lot of people.

The effort to avoid community involvement was reflected by the fact that but two of the top ten executives in the Wade plant lived in Cibola, and none of the ten highest officials in the local division of U.S. Motors were community residents. Albert Larmee, the U.S. Motors general manager, indicated that he frequently drove to Tappan — a town some twelve miles from the Big Bend plant — for lunch, but later added that he had "almost never" eaten in Cibola — less than three miles from his office. Larmee's assistant, in charge of personnel and community relations, commented:

Sometimes I get my hair cut in [Cibola], but outside of that I don't show my face any more than I feel I absolutely have to in order to convince them that we have some interest in the community. The people at the Chamber of Commerce seem to fall all over themselves trying to do anything we want — but the point is, we don't really *want anything* there except for people to have a good opinion of us. But mostly due to this placating attitude of the town's leaders, I'm afraid to say much or be around much.

But, of course, this was not the face which the corporations' public relations experts turned toward the community. Thus, U.S. Motors' full-page ad in the *Beacon's* 50th anniversary issue proclaimed:

WE'RE SURE GLAD TO BE HERE. . .

We can understand the pride the [*Cibola Daily Beacon*] must have in its 50th anniversary of service to this community.
For any company that makes itself a real part of the progress of [Cibola] is bound to feel a little pride as well as a lot of deep-down satisfaction. Take ourselves.
We've only been here at [Big Bend] turning out [gear mechanisms] about a year. . . .
Yet even in this short time — and busy as we've been — we've managed to catch the spirit of you folks here in [Cibola]. This certainly is one up-and-coming community. And we're glad to be part of it. . .

Despite folksy press releases, the evidence overwhelmingly suggested that the large corporations most certainly did not desire to be a "real part" of Cibola. They were, to be sure, interested in "Making Friends for (U.S. Motors) in the Local Community," but every one of them was coming to regard "making friends" and "getting involved" as inconsonant.

This does not mean that the large corporations tended to refrain entirely from certain kinds of initiatory action in Cibola. Total abstention from local participation would have been hardly less inimical to "sound" public relations than injudicious involvement. Thus, the top policy committee of U.S. Motors had formally pronounced that ". . .every corporation and divisional executive has an obligation to help maintain the position of (U.S. Motors) as a good responsible citizen of the community." This positive commitment, however, appeared limited largely to the performance of non-controversial rituals of the "good works" variety. The nature of Wade Motors' directive was indicated by Cal Lamkin:

It's pretty well cut and dried by company policy what we can and can't do in town. For example, we can't contribute or help support activities of a rather narrow nature — like particular churches. If you were the minister of the Episcopal Church here in town and came to me for money for a kids' ball team the church was sponsoring, I'd have to tell you, "No." The Boy Scouts, the Community Chest, Junior Achievement — things like that, "yes." But it's always got to be more or less interdenominational, inter-racial and so forth. Sort of for everybody.

Thus, at U.S. Motors' instigation, a "Little League" was founded in Cibola. Likewise, in 1954, Cal Lamkin suggested that it might be well for the community to have a "Boys' Club — a service and recreation center for Cibola's underprivileged youth." A public leader commented:

Now what the devil we needed a thing like that for was beyond most of us. We've already got Scout troops and quite a few Junior Achievement "companies," plus the regular city recreational facilities. Maybe there's a need for Boys' Clubs in places like Chicago or Detroit, but we couldn't see it here in [Cibola]. Whatever real juvenile delinquents we've got probably won't join anything like this anyway.

And on top of things, we already had the Community Chest budget all figured when [Lamkin] came up with this idea. But you can't very well say, "No," to [Wade Motors]. So we went ahead, changed the allotments around at the last minute, and set aside $5000 for the project — though it'll take at least $15,000 to get the thing really going. . . . Maybe if the project doesn't fall through before then, [Wade] will kick in a club-house or something.

Faced with pressing problems of municipal control and community expansion, the public leaders of Cibola found an ever-growing number of economic dominants unwilling to commit themselves in matters more contentious than "Boys' Clubs" and "Little Leagues."

It's gotten anymore that when we try to bring up something really tough like annexation [said public leader Paul Warne] the big outfits say they don't want to interfere with local politics, that is, assuming we can get in to talk it over with them in the first place.

To the public leaders, no less alarming an element of the large corporations' neutralism than their indifference was the relative inaccessibility of their managers. If the dominants usually turned deaf ears to the central problems of Cibola's leaders, most of the time they were beyond hearing range altogether.

There was at least one further and significant consequence of these developments — one not sharply apparent, yet more than faintly discernible during the course of this research. James Taylor's withdrawal from the city council; the resignation of Grant Moseley III as mayor; Norbert Johns' complaint that "under the old system you had more prominent people. . . in the city government"; and the lament of a Chamber of Commerce official that "it's been getting harder these last few years to find top men willing to run for Chamber president" — all of these were perhaps indicative of a certain discouragement and disenchantment among the public leaders *themselves* insofar as sustained community leadership was concerned.

It seemed, at any rate, that the other public leaders were increasingly willing to delegate responsibility for the management of community affairs to William Houston, the executive secretary of the Chamber of Commerce, and John Milan, the city manager. Furthermore, Houston's perception by all control segments interviewed as the *top* influential in Cibola, together with the common judgment that Milan was among the top local leaders, suggests that these two men were considerably more than mere functionaries or "errand boys." Yet unlike the rest of the public leaders, they were *professionals* in the administration of municipal and civic affairs. Consequently, their orientations and associations were, in some measure, extra-communal[68], and there was ever present the possibility that they, like the corporation managers, might some day — next month? next year? — "move on."

Meanwhile, few Cibolans doubted that Houston and Milan were able — if somewhat cautious — administrators. What many of them refused to recognize, however, was that in their increasing reliance on these men, the community's civic and political direction was perhaps becoming the province of "outside" professionals, much as had its economic life some years earlier.

Some Conclusions. In general, the Cibola research confirmed the three broad hypotheses which it had been designed to test. Historically active in its civic and political life, its economic dominants appeared indeed to have withdrawn both their interest and their participation from community involvement. Furthermore, the bifurcation process had resulted in the presence of two crucial power types, clearly distinguishable in terms of formal and informal patterns of local attachment. And finally, a considerable measure of autonomy had accrued to the public leaders in the initiation and direction of community affairs.

What I had failed sufficiently to anticipate, however, was a major outcome of these several developments. In Cibola, they did not stimulate a genuine civic revival, nor a grass-roots democratization of community decision-making. Rather, it seems to me, they frustrated local civic and political leadership.

In earlier ("pre-bifurcation") periods, the goals of maintaining Cibola's economic and civic-political systems were easily perceived as twin objectives because the two systems were so thoroughly interwoven. With increasing urbanization, however, the common goal, like the control structure itself, split. But notwithstanding their appreciable degree of autonomy, the public leaders by no means *replaced* the economic dominants in the community power structure, nor was their power in local affairs comparable to that once held and wielded by the dominants. For despite their "civic sterilization," the economic dominants were still "around." Their *potential* for control remained considerable, even if their actual exercise of power was superficial, sporadic, or largely dormant. And this potential hung, like the sword above Damocles, over the heads of the public leaders, undermining their confidence, rendering their decisions uncertain and unsure, and serving generally to vitiate local efforts to confront effectively the many problems faced by Cibola midway in the twentieth century.

If this *ex post facto* analysis is plausible, it perhaps suggests the one-sidedness of a much-mouthed and much-cherished bit of "conventional wisdom." For too long, perhaps, we have been inclined to concede Lord Acton's classic dictum too readily, failing adequately to recognize that *power unused is also power abused*. It may be suggested that in a social system in which legitimate potential for determinative action is afforded the occupants of certain statuses, refusal to commit that potential (or its erratic use) serves to frustrate direction of group life hardly less than does the corrupt utilization of power.

But I suppose that before we venture to use the present research as a spring-board for pretentious extrapolation, we must face up to the prior question: to what extent may we generalize at all from the study of this single, small Midwestern community?

Some recent sociological research seems to indicate that the Cibola findings are by no means typical of other American cities. Both Hunter's study of "Regional City," and Miller's of "Pacific City" suggest that in these large Southern and Far Western communities, men of considerable economic substance have *not* withdrawn from participation in local power structures.[69] Even more relevant is the Pellegrin and Coates finding that absentee-corporation executives played active roles in the community decision-making processes of "Bigtown."[70]

While none of these studies viewed the economic dominants as a category, nor attempted to chart historical changes in the nature and extent of the dominants' local involvements, they nevertheless indicate that the withdrawal-bifurcation trend may not be apparent in the *central cities* of large metropolitan areas. To the extent that home offices and/or major segments of the subject economic units were concentrated in these central cities, however, the Hunter, Miller, Pellegrin, and Coates findings are not necessarily contrary to the theory advanced in Section I. In such instances, community policy determinations may be highly relevant to the operations and well-being of the concerned corporations. But assuming that the trend toward the concentration of economic, labor union, and governmental organization at the national levels continues (together with the high horizontal mobility rates characteristic of the managerial personnel of large bureaucracies), our theory would suggest that even in large communities such as "Regional City," the importance of local political decisions for huge economic units will greatly diminish, and concomitantly, that the community involvements of economic dominants will decline.

However compelling these possibilities, I do not want to have to argue, like the Marxist, that "if what we've predicted hasn't yet happened where you live, just wait — it will." Given the existing fund of community power structure research, it is perhaps more sensible to suggest that the Cibola findings may have primary relevance for smaller communities, and especially for those which are *satellites* of large metropolitan centers. The studies of Rossi and his associates in "Bay City" and in several Midwestern communities, and of Agger and Goldrich in two Far Western cities are thus more comparable to the present research.[71] In "Bay City," Rossi found that the 19th century was a period of local industrialization in which political hegemony was exercised by the community's industrial and mercantile elite. Beginning with the first decades of the 20th century, however, political power in

"Bay City" shifted to the middle classes as local politics declined in economic relevance to the community's industrialists. And in "Boomtown" — a city having even closer resemblances to Cibola[72] — Agger and Goldrich report that "the economic dominants and top leaders [the latter, reputationally-defined] were for the most part two separate groups."[73]

We must conclude, nevertheless, that the role of economic dominants in the structures and dynamics of power in American communities have lately been discerned and analyzed somewhat differently by different students. The immediately important thing, I suppose, is that this question — investigated so effectively by the Lynds some twenty years ago — is again being explored.

In particular, I hope that the Cibola study raises some questions provocative for our understanding of the evolving role of large corporations in American community life. The nature of that role, as the Fund for the Republic has recognized, is one of the crucial issues confronting our society. "How do the political habits formed by members of corporations fit with the habits that republican forms of government have developed in their citizens heretofore?[74] The present findings would appear to support Scott Buchanan's conjecture: "It may be that the corporation is the school of political prudence in which we learn not to practice what the political republic has always preached."[75] And thus is created what Professor Berle has called "the great lacuna in the economic power system today."[76] The economic dominants' abnegation of civic responsibility and accountability has perhaps done more than undermine their own claims to legitimacy. Very possibly, their withdrawal from responsible involvement threatens to subvert the viability of community life as well.

Appendix A.

Criteria for Categorization of Persons as Economic Dominants

Persons were classified as economic dominants by historical periods. As the community's industrial and financial base expanded, it was obviously necessary to alter (raise) the criteria. Occupancy of the following statuses served to categorize individuals as economic dominants in the four periods:

1823–1860 Period:
    a. prominent position (i.e., owner, partner, or president) in *two or more* banks or industries; or
    b. major property-owner—defined as being among the ten largest property-owners in the township in addition to being in a prominent position in at least one business in the village.

1860–1900 Period:
    a. prominent position (owner, partner, or president) in one or more banks, or in one or more industrial units employing at least 25 workers or having capital worth (or assessed valuation) of $20,000 or more; or
    b. officer or director in *two or more* units described in a, above; or
    c. major property owner, as defined for 1823–60 period.

1900–1940 Period:
    a. prominent position (owner, partner, president, or general manager) in one or more banks, or in one or more industries employing at least 10 workers or having capital worth (or assessed valuation) of $50,000 or more; or
    b. officer or director in *two or more* units described in a, above.

1940–1954 Period:
    a. prominent position (owner, partner, president, or general manager) in one or

more banks or in one or more industries employing at least 75 workers or having capital worth (or assessed valuation) of $100,000 or more; or
b. officer or director in *two or more* units described in a, above.

No size or capital worth criteria were set for the earliest (1823–60) period because available data on these variables were inadequate. While none of the banks or industries (e.g. mills) of this period appears to have sizeable operations, it is doubtful that any which did exist failed to be cited in at least one of the several sources consulted. It further appeared that economic dominance throughout this period attached less to particular units, and more to individual men involved in a multiplicity of economic activities. Therefore, the definition of dominant was drawn to include those men who occupied prominent positions in *two or more* known banks or industries.

While in the most recent two periods (1900–40, and 1940–54), control of banks or industries has been defined as the principal determinant of economic dominance, these types of units appear to have been either too unstable or too small to serve as the sole determinants in the two earlier periods. Consequently, land ownership was also used as a basis for categorizing individuals as economic dominants in the 1823–60 and 1860–1900 periods. Until almost 1900, however, the county tax records failed to differentiate clearly between assessed properties located in Cibola and those located in the surrounding township. It was my judgment that individuals who had sizeable land holdings in the township, but no direct ties with economic units in Cibola itself should not be included among the community's economic dominants. Therefore, the largest property owners of the first two periods were classified as dominants only if they were also prominently associated with an economic unit known to have been located in the village or city.

(As it happened, very few persons in either the 1823–60 or 1860–1900 periods were classified as dominants on this basis alone; that is, almost all of those who were among the largest property owners in the township were also the heads or partners of banks or industries in the community, and therefore, would have been categorized as economic dominants even had they owned no township property. It should be added that while the ownership of property *per se* was not regarded as a sufficient basis for classification as an economic dominant in the 1900–40 and 1940–54 periods, its inclusion as a qualifier would have resulted in no changes whatever in the roster of economic dominants as otherwise defined. Since 1900 the largest banks and industries in Cibola have consistently been the largest property-owners in the entire township.)

No person was classified as an economic dominant in more than one of the four time-periods. An individual was placed in that period in which the largest portion of his career as an economic dominant was encompassed. The efficacy of the period limitations employed was perhaps reflected by the fact that there were very few cases in which it was difficult to decide into which period an individual should be placed.

Appendix B.

Questions Used to Determine the Public Leaders of Cibola

1. "Suppose a major project were before the community that required decisions by a group of leaders that nearly everyone would accept. Which people would you choose, regardless of whether or not you know them personally?

2. "In most cities, certain persons are said to be influential 'behind-the-scenes' and to have a lot to say about programs that are planned, and projects and issues that come up around town. What persons in [Cibola] are influential in this way?

3. "If a decision was to be made in the state capital that affected Cibola, who would be the best contact man to get in touch with state officials (besides the local members of the Legislature)?

4. "Who [besides local members of Congress] would be the best people to get in touch with federal officials in [Metro City] or Washington?

5. "Are there any other people with whom these leaders work that have not been named so far and should be included in a list of community leaders?"

Since the object was to determine a *general* community-leadership-power-group, the responses to the five questions were combined in the final tabulation. Previously, however, the association heads' responses to each of the questions had been tabulated. Regarding questions 1 and 2, it was found that all but one of those 18 persons subsequently defined as public leaders ranked among the top 19 in both the "major project" and the "behind-the-scenes" questions. Furthermore, eliminating nominations in questions 3, 4, and 5 influenced the total scores and the rank order of public leaders, but had little effect on the overall composition of the public leadership segment.

NOTES TO CHAPTER I

1. I wish to thank Morris Janowitz for providing the initial guidance and continuing stimulation for this study, and Leonard Blumberg for the opportunity to share in his ground-breaking research on the Cibola power structure. For help and counsel, I am also indebted to Robert Cooley Angell, Gerhard Lenski, Horace Miner, Amos Hawley, David Varley, Howard McClusky, H. Clever Bald, and, of course, the many respondents and informants in Cibola. My greatest debt, however, is owed my wife, Suzanne Sims Schulze, for her contribution to every stage of this work, and for her unflagging encouragement and forebearance. The quotation comes from Herbert Kaufman and Victor Jones, "The Mystery of Power," *Public Administration Review,* 14 (Summer, 1954), 205.

2. Drucker is one of the few scholars who has acknowledged this point directly and clearly. See Peter F. Drucker, *The Future of Industrial Man,* New York: John Day, 1942, 93.

3. Harold D. Lasswell, "The Garrison State," *American Journal of Sociology,* 46 (January, 1941), 455-68; Harold D. Lasswell, "The Elite Concept," in H. D. Lasswell, Daniel Lerner, and C. Easton Rothwell, *The Comparative Study of Elites,* Stanford: Stanford Univ. Press, 1953, 6-21; C. Wright Mills, *The Power Elite,* New York: Oxford University Press, 1956.

4. J. K. Galbraith, *American Capitalism and the Concept of Countervailing Power,* Boston: Houghton, Mifflin, 1952; David Riesman, *The Lonely Crowd,* New Haven: Yale University Press, 1950.

5. The Lynds presented a graphic summary of the contemporary (1930's) involvements of the "X's" in Middletown's social structure. Their concern, however, was primarily with this *one* family. Their passing mention of the inactive "Y" family clearly suggests that the "X's" pattern of local activity was probably not representative of the involvements of all economic dominants in Middletown. See Robert S. and Helen M. Lynd, *Middletown in Transition,* New York: Harcourt, Brace, 1937, Chapter 3.

6. The research of Peter Rossi and his associates in Bay City is the notable exception, but their focus of study was the political and educational leader rather than the economic dominant.

7. The present research is reported in considerably greater detail in Robert O. Schulze, *Economic Dominance and Public Leadership,* microfilmed Ph.D. dissertation, University of Michigan, 1956.

8. Hans H. Gerth and C. Wright Mills, eds., *From Max Weber: Essays in Sociology,* New York: Oxford University Press, 1946, 180.

9. See Herbert Goldhammer and Edward Shils, "Types of Power and Status," *American Journal of Sociology,* 45 (1950), 171-82; Robert Bierstedt, "An Analysis of Social Power," *American Sociological Review,* 15 (1950), 730-8; Talcott Parsons, "A Revised Analytical Approach to the Theory of Social Stratification," in Reinhard Bendix and Seymour M. Lipset, *Class, Status, and Power,* Glencoe: The Free Press, 1953, 92-128; Hans H. Gerth and C. Wright Mills, *Character and Social Structure,* New York: Harcourt, Brace, 1953, 195.

10. Floyd Hunter, *Community Power Structure,* Chapel Hill: University of North Carolina Press, 1953, 2-3: "Power is a word that will be used to describe the acts of men going about the business of moving other men to act in relation to organic or inorganic things."

11. Communities, like societies, are, of course, examples of the former type, while small, contrived (laboratory) groups and larger bureaucratic organizations are illustrative of the latter type. See Talcott Parsons, *The Social System,* Glencoe: The Free Press, 1952, 190.

12. In view of my earlier assertion about the desirability of conceving power in terms of statuses within groups, I realize that the public leader definition employed here re-

quires some justification. Admittedly, the public leader status does not constitute an official position within a formally organized group — as does the status of economic dominant. I believe, however, that as defined, it may legitimately be regarded as designating a sociological status within the community, no less "positional" because it is informal, nor because it is determined by subjective techniques. Small group sociologists often employ a comparable procedure in designating occupants of leadership-influence statuses. Cf. Cecil A. Gibb, "Leadership," in Gardner Lindzey, ed., *Handbook of Social Psychology*, Cambridge: Addison-Wesley, 1954, 877–920.

13. Harold D. Lasswell and Abraham Kaplan, *Power and Society*, New Haven: Yale University Press, 1950.

14. Robert S. Lynd and Helen M. Lynd, *op. cit.* Also see Professor Lynd's "Foreword" to Robert A. Brady, *Business as a System of Power*, New York: Columbia University Press, 1943, vii-xviii and his essay, "Power in American Society as Resource and Problem," in Arthur Kornhauser, ed., *Problems of Power in American Society*, Detroit: Wayne University Press, 1956, 1–56.

15. W. Lloyd Warner and Paul S. Lunt, *The Social Life of a Modern Community*, New Haven: Yale University Press, 1941.

16. It is not suggested, however, that these two are the *only* important sets of power statuses in the urban community, but that they are the *most* significant to the overall life of the community. In addition, for example, there may be technicians and professional personnel who exert influence because of their specialized skills. While their power, according to the research of such students as Lynd and Hunter, does not appear to be very considerable in most communities, it may well assume increased significance at the large metropolitan and societal levels.

17. W. Lloyd Warner and J. O. Low, "The Factory in the Community," in William Foote Whyte, ed., *Industry and Society*, New York: McGraw-Hill, 1946, 35.

18. The Lynds and Warner noted this trend in both Middletown and Yankee City. That the Lynds regarded it as a tendency common to communities other than Middletown is suggested by their statement: "One can classify American small manufacturing cities into two groups: those in which the industrial pioneers or their sons still dominate the local business scene, and those in which 'new blood' has taken over the leadership..." (*Op. cit.*, 76.) The "new blood" was in most instances, of course, also "outside, non-local blood."

19. Lasswell makes something of the same point, although he sees the "withdrawal" of the economic dominants occurring at a later stage of urbanization than is here suggested: "So long as the scale is no greater than a trading city, businessmen can combine the direction of their private enterprises with the guidance of diplomacy, strategy, and propaganda. In many cases they can keep the support of the general public by part-time activities, such as doing good works, the handling of ceremony, and the maintaining of personal ties.

"It is a different story when the city grows into a vast metropolis, and develops complex ties with a large hinterland, or with a number of auxiliary regions. Business enterprises grow more complicated at the very time that the scope of top community decisions is enlarging." (Harold D. Lasswell, "The Elite Concept," in Lasswell, Lerner, and Rothwell, *op. cit.*, 19.)

20. That a similar need is experienced at the sub-community level within the large metropolis is indicated in Morris Janowitz, *The Community Press in an Urban Setting*, Glencoe: The Free Press, 1952.

21. This, it seems to me, is a possibility which has been insufficiently explored by those students who continue to document the preponderance of persons in business and related occupations in community power structures. See, for example, Hunter, *op. cit.*, and Delbert C. Miller, "Industry and Community Power Strutcure," *American Sociological Review*, 23 (February, 1958), 9–15.

22. Peter H. Rossi, "Community Decision Making," *Administrative Science Quarterly*, 1 (March, 1957), 438–39.

23. S. A. Stouffer and his associates at Harvard's Laboratory of Social Relations have recently undertaken a series of pilot studies, presumably preparatory to the initiation of a large-scale comparative community power structures survey.

24. See especially Leonard U. Blumberg, *Community Leaders: The Social Bases and Social Psychological Concommitants of Community Power*, microfilmed Ph.D. dissertation, University of Michigan, 1955.

25. See Amos H. Hawley, *The Changing Shape of Metropolitan America*, Glencoe: The Free Press, 1956; Leo F. Schnore, "Metropolitan Growth and Decentralization," *American Journal of Sociology*, 63 (September, 1957), 171–80.

26. For another report on the utility and reliability of using city directories in his-

torical reconstructions, see Sidney Goldstein, "City Directories as Sources of Migration Data," *American Journal of Sociology,* 60 (September, 1954), 169–76.

27. It is suggestive for the fate of local "holdouts" against absentee absorption to note that this company had employed as many workers within a decade after its founding, 90 years earlier, as it did in 1954.

28. As already noted, the criteria for economic dominant classification for each of the periods in Cibola's history are presented in Appendix A. Complete listings of all economic dominants, 1823–1954, including the economic and public statuses which they held, are contained in my dissertation. *Op. cit.,* 109–12, 127–31, 154–60, and 171–74.

29. These and all subsequent figures pertaining to reciprocal economic ties are based only on occupancy of official statuses in the dominant economic units, specifically, on partnerships and fellow officer and directorships. Although I was not able to obtain information on additional economic associations stemming from investment and/or credit relationships, these must have been numerous. Insofar as the quality of business links among the economic dominants of each period are concerned, therefore, the figures given represent the bare minima.

30. Until Cibola's incorporation as a city, its chief official was the village president; after incorporation, mayor.

31. The evidence does not indicate that possible differences between the two blocs were reflected in divergent party affiliations. Thus, both Moseley I and Kemphill, for example, were well known as Democrats, while Stover and Barth were active Republicans. But despite the surface heat generated in political campaigns in those days (Stover, for instance, is reported to have decorated his Cibola Dress Stay Manufacturing Company with a huge quantity of Chinese lanterns in celebration of Benjamin Harrison's election to the presidency in 1888), it must be remembered that until the rise of Bryanism shortly before the turn of the century, the differences between the two parties (in the Midwest) was not great. Nevertheless, the foregoing suggests that, in historical terms, at least, there may be a need to re-examine Coleman's claim that in small towns political control tends almost inevitably to be of the one-party variety. Cf. James Coleman, *Community Conflict,* Glencoe: The Free Press, 1957.

32. The fact that roughly twice as many persons qualified for economic dominant classification between 1900 and 1940 than between 1860 and 1900 reflects both the rapid growth of industry in Cibola in the 20th century and the accelerated rates of individual turnover and mobility. On the other hand, the abrupt decline in the proportion of dominants in public office was *not* a consequence of the fact that the number of dominants increased at a rate greater than the number of available offices. As documented elsewhere, changes in the number of dominants throughout the four periods were very closely paralleled by proportionately similar changes in the number of available public offices. See Robert O. Schulze, "The Role of Economic Dominants in Community Power Structures," *American Sociological Review,* 13 (February, 1958), 5, Table 2.

33. I do not mean to suggest that this marked withdrawal of the economic dominants from public life was solely the result of the sharply-waning interest in local affairs. Since it was partly coincident with the Great Depression, it perhaps also reflected popular disillusionment with business leadership in the community. Nevertheless, if such repudiation in fact occurred, it was implicitly recognized rather than explicitly demonstrated. Grant Moseley II told me that "after the depression, I couldn't have been elected dog catcher in this town." Yet the facts remain that he did not run for any public office after the 1920's, and his son, who did, was several times a successful candidate.

34. Although their predecessors, as we saw, "went under" during the depression, the present two banks occupy the same buildings and, with but slight variation, have adopted the same titles as their financial forebears. The earlier Cibola Savings Bank was reorganized in 1932, while the old Cibola National Bank was replaced in 1934 by a new group, the National Bank of Cibola. Its directors included several men who had lost heavily in the failure of the original National. The new bank's first president told me: "I think my *main* qualification was that I'd had *nothing, nothing* to do with what happened to the old (National)."

35. It should be pointed out that slightly more than half of these absentee-firm dominants did not reside in the city (nor within Pottawatomie Township), and were therefore legally ineligible to hold public office. But this in no way detracts from the significance of the preceding finding. The very fact that it had become feasible for key members in Cibola's economic life to live elsewhere in the metropolitan area is highly relevant to our understanding of the shifting relationship between economic

dominance and local public leadership. And the further fact that so many of them have taken advantage of this "opportunity" — whether because of personal choice, corporation pressures, or for other reasons — is even more suggestive.

36. The mean number of offices occupied by the dominants of the two eras were 1.7 and .52, respectively; the mean number of years in office were 6.6 and 2.5, respectively.

37. Some theoretical and methodological considerations involved in this approach to community power are discussed in Robert O. Schulze and Leonard U. Blumberg, "The Determination of Local Power Elites," *American Journal of Sociology*, 63 (November, 1957), 290–96.

38. Specifically, these included industrial plants located within either the city or surrounding township which employed seventy-five or more workers, and banks having total assets of one million dollars or more. Persons serving on the boards of directors of two or more of the foregoing units were also defined as economic dominants.

39. Despite the great size of this plant, the Metro Gear Division of U.S. Motors Corporation, its presence in the area did not mean that Cibola was a "one-industry town." The "Big Bend" plant, as it was called, was located some two miles beyond the city limits. Since it first went into operation in 1942, it had been "run" by three different corporations: Wade Motors, Kane-Abbel Motors, and U.S. Motors. And finally, as of 1954, only about 7 per cent of its employees resided in Cibola.

40. Concretely, the top officers representing 83 per cent of the white adult associations known to exist in Cibola were interviewed, and their perceptions of the most influential persons in the community were determined, using the questions contained in Appendix B. Of the thirty-four association heads whom we were unable to locate and interview, none was perceived by the 153 interviewed as influential in Cibola, nor were the organizations they represented regarded as influential. Blumberg, *op. cit.*

41. Specifically, both the economic dominants and the public leaders nominated as most influential 72 per cent (thirteen out of eighteen) of those already so designated by our initial procedure. Furthermore, of the ten persons most frequently considered top influentials by both of these categories of men, nine had in fact been operationally defined as public leaders. Again see Schulze and Blumberg, *op. cit.*

42. For purposes of subsequent summarization, data on Moseley III and Rogers have been tabulated in both categories.

43. The principal occupation of two public leaders was governmental, although neither of them were politicians in the usual sense of that term. One served as city manager, the other as circuit judge. A third public leader, while he had devoted rather sustained attention to local, county, and state politics for the past decade or more, derived his major income from a law firm in which he was senior partner.

44. Only one of the seven absentee-firm dominants resided in Cibola in 1954. However, none had held public office in the communities in which they were currently residing. In addition, I found that since joining the corporations by which they were employed, only one had ever held public office in *any* community of previous residence. (This lone exception had served a single term as a school board member.)

45. Neither the public leaders nor the economic dominants were technically split, as the latter apparently had been in earlier periods, by formal partisan cleavages. All of the current economic dominants and all but one of the public leaders were Republicans. One public leader was chairman of the County GOP Committee, and another had recently been state chairman of that party. The single "deviant case" among the public leaders did not broadcast the fact that he was a Democrat, nor was he active or influential in the local councils of that party. So solid and taken-for-granted was the Republican affiliation of Cibola's elites that several respondents were highly incredulous when, in the course of our interviews, I happened to mention that the Moseley family had been Democratic throughout the earlier periods of their prominence in the community.

The local Democrats, however, were by no means dormant. As might be expected, their following consisted mostly of working class and Negro elements in the population, both of which were rapidly increasing in numbers, and slowly gaining in political organization and effectiveness. Although elections to the city council have been "officially" non-partisan since 1947, a small minority of its members have lately been Democrats.

46. Between 1934 and 1954, for example, 137 persons held regular elective or appointive offices in the city government of Cibola.

47. And here the problem of residence did not arise. Membership in most local associations was not restricted to persons living in the city, and therefore economic

dominants residing elsewhere in the metropolitan area could and did belong to such organizations as the Chamber of Commerce, Rotary, and the Pottawatomie Country Club.

48. The voluntary association heads, the public leaders, and the economic dominants were asked to name the most influential organizations in Cibola. By considerable margins, all three categories designated the Chamber of Commerce as most powerful. And although there were slight differences in rank orders, all three categories likewise named the JCC and the three service-luncheon clubs — Rotary, Kiwanis, and Lions — as the next four most influential associations in the community.

49. And again, the lone dominant who had served as Chamber president was Grant Moseley III, also regarded as a public leader.

50. Among other things, this revealing little episode offers support to a suggestion made in Section I: that a long record of civic dormancy tends to undermine an economic dominant's public leadership base, making it increasingly difficult to cash in on any potential for popular support in the community. On the other hand, it clearly does not indicate that the economic dominants are therefore without means to "get what they want" locally.

51. Previous familiarity with the *Beacon* had suggested that "important" local news was invariably printed on page one.

52. It should not be inferred, however, that the comparative magnitude of this coverage made any considerable contribution to the fact that these persons were perceived as top influentials in the community. Of the twenty-five individuals most frequently mentioned in the newspaper in connection with local events, only eight were public leaders. In other words, an appreciable number of "other" local citizens received greater press coverage than did the majority of the public leaders.

53. The names of all individuals were alphabetically-arranged, thus "mixing" the public leaders and economic dominants. The scale designations ranged from "close personal friend" to "never heard of him."

54. Despite the seeming crudeness of the scaling device, the summary tabulations suggested that it was pretty reliable. It was possible to check overall reliability by comparing the reciprocal scores of the various elites: thus, the composite score reflecting the public leaders' perception of the closeness of their relationship to the economic dominants was compared with the composite score reflecting the dominants' judgment of their degree of familiarity with the public leaders. Similar comparisons were made between the mutual perceptions of the public leaders and the local-firm dominants, the public leaders and the absentee-firm dominants, and the local-firm and absentee-firm dominants. The total possible range of scores extended from 1.00 to 9.00. The differences in mean scores within each of the four paired comparisons were quite small: .01, .04, .19, and .59, respectively. (See Figure 6.)

55. The singular is used here because in both cases the absentee-firm dominant was Wade Motors' general manager, Cal Lamkin, the only absentee-firm dominant who resided in Cibola.

56. It should be added that during the summer of 1947, and thus by the time of the second vote on the charter, the Savings Bank had been "swung into favorable line," as had certain key leaders (and their followers) in both the Negro and working-class sections of the city.

57. Neither John Milan, who became city manager, nor Cleveland Chapman, president of the local college, lived or worked in Cibola until 1948.

58. Earlier in the company's history, Wade Motors, largely in the person of Harry Bender, old Luther Wade's right-hand man, had "strong-armed" its way into the civic control structures of several communities in the Metro City area. A major result of these forays had been much unfavorable publicity for the company. The Cibola charter episode, however, occurred some years later, shortly after the young and civic-minded grandson of Luther Wade had assumed the company's presidency and "given the ax" to Bender. Thereupon, a company-wide community relations committee was formed (with Lamkin among its members), and, *for a while,* executives were apparently encouraged to participate openly and responsibly in local affairs.

59. Kane-Abbel Corporation had made a dramatic (and abortive) entry into the automobile manufacturing field in 1946. Until 1953, the corporation's main plant was located a short distance from Cibola — in the buildings presently occupied by U.S. Motors.

60. At the time this remark was made, the only public leader on the council was Robert Drew.

61. This plant was operated by Wade Motors from 1940–1946, by Kane-Abbel from 1946–1953, and by U.S. Motors from 1953–present.

62. Hawley has shown that (in large communities) the costs of municipal government are more closely related to the size of the population living in the built-up areas adjacent to the city than to the population within the city. See Amos H. Hawley, "Metropolitan Population and Municipal Government Expenditures in Central Cities," *Journal of Social Issues,* 7 (1951), 100–8.

63. Burns, alone, was not regarded by the association heads as among the community's top influentials. (See Table 6.)

64. At various times, township residents filed bills of complaint and obtained temporary injunctions, thus consistently forestalling the efforts of Cibola's leaders to bring annexation proposals to a popular vote.

65. It should be noted that throughout its long history, the Moseley-controlled Pottawatomie Carton Company had "conveniently" (for the Moseleys) gone unannexed; for many years, in fact, the city limits had remained drawn just short of its property. By 1950 the company was paying the township approximately $4,000 per year in property taxes. Yet despite the fact that annexation to the city would have boosted Pottawatomie's tax load at least three-fold, the carton company was included in all annexation proposals. Although Grant Moseley III admitted that he was "not exactly overjoyed by the prospect of an appreciable tax increase," the fact that he was among the most vigorous leaders in the annexation efforts suggests that his commitments as a public leader in the community were apparently more compelling than were the pressures for economic expediency.

66. As I have already indicated, this firm's bold entry into the automobile manufacturing field had been both late and abortive. In the face of intensive competition from the entrenched "Big Three," plus strong union pressures for maintenance of the high wartime wage scales, Kane-Abbel's financial position remained consistently precarious. That the corporation was able to "hold out" in the automobile field as long as one decade was mainly attributable to the fact that it had been granted large contracts by the federal government.

67. The "substitute proposal" mentioned would not have included the Big Bend plant in the annexation. It provided instead for a series of gradual and more modest additions to the city. The Kane-Abbel plan failed to win the support of Cibola's leaders, and did not get beyond the "blueprint" stage.

68. Both Houston and Milan, for example, belonged to a greater number of nonlocal organizations than did the "average" public leader.

69. Cf. Hunter, *op. cit.,* and Miller, *op. cit.,*

70. Cf. Roland J. Pellegrin and Charles H. Coates, "Absentee-Owned Corporations and Community Power Structure, *American Journal of Sociology,* 61 (March, 1956), 413–19.

71. Cf. Rossi, Freeman, and Shipten, *Politics and Education in Bay City,* op. cit., and Robert E. Agger and Daniel Goldrich, "Community Power Structures and Partisanship," *American Sociological Review,* 23 (August, 1958), 383–92.

72. "Boomtown" was a fast-growing community with a population of approximately 16,000; it was located near "Big City," and most of its industries were absentee-owned. *Ibid.*

73. *Ibid.,* 389.

74. Scott Buchanan, *The Corporation and the Republic,* New York: The Fund for the Republic, 1958, 28.

75. *Ibid.*

76. A. A. Berle, Jr., *Economic Power and the Free Society,* New York: The Fund for the Republic, 1958, 16–17.

The Impact of Party Organization
in an Industrial Setting

BY *PETER H. ROSSI*

AND *PHILLIPS CUTRIGHT*

THE POLICY-MAKING ACTIVITIES of local government rest ultimately, if somewhat indirectly, on the consent of an electorate which periodically registers its preferences for candidates and parties in local elections. Centered on the influencing of this consent are the organized political parties.

Viewed comparatively against the contrasts provided by parties in other countries, the major American political parties are almost unique. There is little ideological coherence within each party and little difference in this respect between them. Party unity within administrations, within legislatures, and within party officialdom appears to be a fragile thing, easily broken, hard to reassemble, and achieved rarely. The boundaries of the parties are so permeable that membership carries little in the way of commitment of affect and less in the way of finance. The formal organizations of the parties are partly defined by custom and partly determined by statute, both varying considerably from place to place.

Perhaps the most important structural feature which underlies and favors these characteristics is the fact that ultimate jurisdiction over the designation of party officialdom and party candidates is centered at the local level. The lowest level of party officials are elected and candidates for the lowest offices are universally nominated in popular primaries open to all who wish to designate themselves as party members. Once elected in a primary a party official or a candidate is primarily constrained by self-interest to co-operate with other candidates or other party officials. Self-interest is a weak source of motivation to bind together a slate and its full exploitation requires a continual exchange of support, favors, and benefits, Once elected, an official has again primarily self-interest to motivate him to co-operate with other members of his party and a similar exchange of benefits and support occurs within administration and legislatures. Some degree of party unity is achieved but at the price of considerable negotiation and compromise.

The research reported in this paper is a study of the organizations developed by the two major parties in a Midwest industrial city to which we have given the pseudonym, Stackton. Our concern will be to show how the organizations developed by the Republican and Democratic parties have been conditioned by the structural characteristics described above and how party organizations are maintained under them.

The organization of political parties may be studied on a number of levels. Our concern here will be primarily with the lowest level as represented by the precinct committeeman. While we recognize that much of importance occurs at the higher party levels of the city or county committee or among the leading party figures, as far as influencing the electorate is concerned, a major portion of party activities takes place on the precinct level. Furthermore, the higher levels of the party can be effectively studied only by comparing several communities while the variety of precincts to be found within a single community makes this lower level more appropriate to a study of a single community.

Specifically our analysis will be concerned with the following questions:

How are individuals recruited to political work and how is their activity sustained?

What are the relationships between the party worker and the local constituency which he both represents and influences?

What are the relationships between party workers, candidates and public officials which hold the party together?

What is the effect of party organization on the electorate?

How do precinct committeemen affect the outcomes of elections?

What are the differences between a majority and a minority party?

The data upon which the analysis is based are derived from three sources: First, interviews were made with 307 precinct workers, members of the city committees of the two parties, and other party officials. These interviews focused primarily on the activities of committeemen in their precincts and their relationships to other party workers. Second, the Census materials for the city of Stackton were reworked to provide social and economic descriptions of each of the city's 109 precincts by aggregating block statistics into precincts. The Census data were supplemented by data on the ethnic origins of the populations in each district, derived from ratings made on samples of the names of registered voters. Finally, data were collected on the votes of primary and general elections. The interview data were obtained during the summer of 1957 and the voting records of each precinct extend from 1952 to 1958. The specific content of these interviews will become more apparent from the analysis to be presented.

Stackton

Stackton, the community whose political parties are to be scrutinized is a Midwestern, industrial city. This pseudonym was employed to preserve the anonymity of our respondents and the individuals of whom they spoke. In 1950, Stackton had a population in the vicinity of 150,000. More than a third of Stackton's residents were Negroes. Another third derived from recent immigrant stock, largely of Slavic and Eastern European origin. The remaining third derived from the older immigrant stocks of Anglo-Saxon or Germanic origin.

Stackton is a manufacturing town, with a much larger than usual percentage of its working force employed in manufacturing activities. A very large proportion of the working force is employed in the plant of a large firm, American Metals, in one of the basic metal industries. Stackton comes as close as any city of its size to being a "company" town, at least insofar as the dependence of its population on a single firm is concerned. Indeed, the land on which most of the city now stands was once owned by this company, and the original subdivision of the city was laid out by company engineers in the early part of this century.

Stackton is part of a great metropolitan complex spreading out over three states. Less than forty miles from Stackton's city hall is the downtown center of the central city. Some portion of Stackton's population works in the central city, and some of the central city's population gets its livelihood primarily from Stackton. Because of its role in the economic web of the metropolitan region and in the national economy, Stackton cannot be considered an independent urban place. Indeed, the connection between the city and the nation can be seen most dramatically by the sensitivity of unemployment compensation rolls in Stackton to the recent recession. When the recent recession hit basic metals, the city felt it most directly.

In contrast to Stackton's dependence on and sensitivity to the national scene in its economic life, it is relatively independent politically. A mayor-council form of government, popularly elected, and an appointed school board administer and determine municipal affairs. Political fortunes wax and wane in Stackton without too much regard for the trends in either state or nation. Indeed, the political complexion of Stackton and the county surrounding it has been Democratic since early New Deal days, while the state government has been controlled, in the main, by Republican office-holders.

It is hard to say whether Stackton has a "good" or "bad" city government. The city provides, with some degree of efficiency, the usual municipal services, run by civil servants who are largely exempt from civil service regulations.

Stackton is a union town. A militant CIO union organized the big plants of American Metals in the 1930's. The building trades and Teamsters have strong locals in Stackton, and there are few of the minor firms that can claim an open shop. Along with the growth of unions the climate of opinion toward Labor has changed drastically from the early days of unionization. The CIO fought a hard and sometimes bloody battle to obtain recognition, but nowadays, when the big plant is closed by an infrequent strike, landlords and merchants liberally extend credit to the strikers. The local police are neutral, but mainly "neutral against" the company.

Stackton is not a beautiful city. Its lake front boundary holds the huge and smoky plants of its metal industry. The central business district contains far from fashionable stores whose cheap wares advertise the working-class tastes of the population of Stackton. Spreading out from the center are street after street of small individual homes, among which are dispersed two-flat structures and a small number of larger apartment houses.

In sum, Stackton is a middle-sized industrial satellite of a large Midwestern metropolitan complex, politically independent, dominated economically by a single industry, with a strong labor movement, and a perennial Democratic majority.

Channels of Recruitment to Precinct Work

On the precinct levels of the party organizations in Stackton, there are 436 positions to be filled; each party has a precinct captain in each of the 109 precincts who are aided by vice-committeemen. The captain represents his party in the district, and although in law he is only charged with the overseeing of ballotting, he also performs many other functions for his party and for the voters in his precinct. On election day, he is present in the polling place aided by election workers whom he appoints. Before election day, he has been busy canvassing his precinct and persuading voters to vote for his party. In between elections, he acts as a mediator between voters and those party candidates who are in power. He is the link between the central party and the local constituency, providing two way communication between these two levels.

However useful a function for the party may be played by the precinct workers, it is nevertheless a problem for the parties to recruit individuals to these positions and to motivate them to perform the tasks properly. More than two hundred persons in Stackton have to be persuaded to run for precinct committeemen and, when elected, the captains have to persuade others to serve as vice-committeemen.

The formal structure of the parties in Stackton contains no specification of the duties of a precinct committeeman. Yet each party has definite images of the ideal precinct captain and the optimum performance of this role. These images have arisen over the years of experience with the running of the two parties and have been widely diffused through the party organization and to some degree to the voters themselves. In Stackton, each party wants to have a hard-working, loyal, and widely known person representing it in each of the 109 precincts. Loyalty to the party is a prime and highly desired attribute, but of equal importance is the precinct committeeman's breadth of acquaintance with the voters in his precinct. Both city chairmen expressed the view that a principal characteristic of a good captain is a wide circle of acquaintance and friendship among neighbors.

Although recruitment of party workers is a problem to both parties, it is a much more serious one for the Republicans whose chances for success in Stackton are slight. The contrasts between the two parties in how their workers are recruited will provide many insights into motives which bring individuals into party work and which sustain their interest in performing political tasks over time.

The Legal Framework of Party Organization

Both parties operate under the election laws of the state. Although it is clearly impossible to trace all of the consequences of these laws, our data do shed some light on the possible relations between certain of these laws and the maintenance of the party system.

The law provides that in each precinct in the state the precinct committeeman representing each party will be elected by the voters of that precinct for a two-year term. In the event that one or both parties do not have an elected committeeman, the county chairman appoints a resident voter to that position.

The elected committeeman then appoints his vice-committeeman, and these two persons are the official representatives of their party in their precinct until the time of the next election. Shortly after the election of precinct committeemen, a county-wide meeting is held, and the county organization elects a county committee, and, if the county comprises a state district, the organization also elects a district committee. In these elections, the committeeman and his vice-committeeman each have one vote. This district committee represents the county on the state central committee. With each county, the members of the city precinct organization meet and elect the members of their city committee.

There are two points that should be remembered throughout our discussion of the organization of the political parties in this city. First, the members of the precinct organization are *elected* by plurality vote of the voters in each precinct. They are *not* appointed by a ward boss. Second, these committeemen determine the organization of the county committee and, ultimately, the state central committee. Another way to phrase the second point is that the person or clique that controls the precinct organization controls the county, city, and district organizations.

The time of greatest interest in the life of the political party is election day itself. A host of rules shape the conduct of the election, from the opening of the polling place to the final tabulation of the vote. The law also designates who is to be inside the polling place as well. Each political party is required to have a sheriff, a clerk, and a judge, and the party which obtained the majority of the votes in the previous election throughout the county is given an additional representative called an inspector. In reading these sections of these laws of our state, one is struck by the implicit assumption that it will always be possible to find at least four persons willing to work for each party on election day in every precinct in the state. Without these workers, the polling places would not be open.

One of the consequences of these requirements is that the precinct committeeman has at least four patronage appointments in his precinct and can reward the loyal, and usually needy, party workers in the precinct. Another consequence is that in those precincts where interest in a party is small, the precinct committeeman, ward captain, or even city chairman, is required to scout around and find four persons willing to serve on the precinct election board.

In this city, the electorate has favored the Democratic Party in nearly all elections since the early 1930's. State patronage, which might bolster the minority Republican Party, is no match for the variety and quantity of city and country patronage jobs available to Democratic workers. Further, the disproportionate shift of voters to the Democratic ticket in primary elections results in very small numbers of registered Republicans in many precincts in the city. For example, several precincts will have a vote, in general elections, about 70 per cent Democratic, but this figure climbs to 90 per cent Democratic in primary elections. Many Republicans attribute this drop-off in the Republican vote in primary elections to the unwillingness of small businessmen and professional people to declare themselves as Republicans in a city controlled by Democrats. Be this as it may, the problem of recruitment of party workers in these heavily Democratic areas is a difficult one for the

Republican Party, and, in fact, the Republicans complain that even in a majority precinct it is difficult for them to recruit workers. However, the structure of the election laws forces the Republicans to recruit polling place workers, regardless of whether the precinct is Republican or Democratic.

Our interviews with the committeemen document the heavier emphasis which the Republican party placed on polling place work as a step towards political work. For example, one Republican became a committeeman through his wife who was needed to work on an election board. Following this experience, she told her husband about certain irregularities in the polling place. He decided to take a more active interest in the next election. When the city chairman came around to ask his wife to work on the board again, the husband was persuaded to run for precinct committeeman and was elected in an unopposed contest. As a precinct committeeman, he took his responsibilities seriously and managed, he said, to clean up existing malpractices. At the date of our interview, he had been a precinct committeeman for ten years.

Work in a polling place as a member of an election board as a step towards becoming a precinct worker is cited fairly often by workers in both parties as a reason for becoming a precinct committeeman. But while only about a fifth of both white and Negro Democrats cited prior work in a polling place as a reason for their involvement as precinct workers, slightly more than a third of both white and Negro Republican precinct workers did.

Republican difficulties in recruitment of committeemen are also apparent in the proportions of those who specifically mentioned that they were persuaded — many somewhat reluctant — into party work by higher party officials. Twenty-four per cent of the white Republicans and 9 per cent of the Negro Republicans indicated that they were reluctant committeemen, while only 6 per cent of the white Democrats and none of the Negro Democrats revealed reluctance — further evidence to support the notion that Republicans have a greater recruitment problem than do the Democrats, and that the existing structure of election laws results in pressures on responsible party officials to fill these unwanted positions.

While active solicitation and polling place work brings to political work some portion of the committeemen, others are brought in by the other activities of the electoral process. Candidates in the primaries or in general elections in Stackton strive to recruit persons to work directly in their behalf. Indeed as we shall see in our analysis of the primary elections, the "private" political workers represent in toto a group larger than the official party organization. There was consensus among our respondents that a good many of these "private" political workers are paid for their services, particularly in the Negro areas of the city. In addition, especially around election time, the parties may often recruit workers to help precinct committeemen, such workers being usually paid for their services.

A good proportion of the committeemen had entered the political scene first as "private" political workers or had been recruited for electioneering (not election board work) by the party apparatus. About 40 per cent of all groups except Republican Negroes had been first drawn into political work in this fashion. Among Republican Negroes, this proportion reaches a very high 70 per cent expressing perhaps the commonly held opinion that in the very heavily Democratic Negro areas of the city only money will recruit workers in behalf of the Republican party.

The control the Negro committeeman has over the vote in primary elections in his area presents a glittering attraction for any candidate seeking party nomination. If the candidate can outbid his opponent in committeeman support, and if he is generally acceptable to the mayor (or in the case of the Republicans, top party leaders), he is usually assured of very heavy pluralities in the Negro areas.

One of the consequences of this control over the vote is that candidates have a tendency to spend their money in Negro areas where it will do them the most good and rely on other means to get the white vote. Negro committeemen in our interviews emphasized that they work in campaigns in which money is spent and do not work in campaigns where the candidates are "cheap." In short, a strong expectation of being paid for political work exists in the Negro areas. This seems to explain the high percentage of Negro Republicans who entered party work as paid and not as volunteer workers. The Negro Republican is attracted to active party work by the money involved in working for candidates.

A different pattern of economic motivation operates for the Negro Democratic committeeman. Among this group, the economic rewards of party work are not only in being paid for supporting particular candidates but also in being offered patronage jobs on the city payroll. As we shall see later on in this section, patronage played a strong role as a motive in this group. In any event the density of patronage is high among Negro committeemen, 56 per cent holding patronage jobs in city government.

Although both parties have recruitment problems which they meet with some degree of success by active solicitation, some precinct committeemen become involved in party work through a search for the solution of group or individual goals. Some seek to advance the positions of their nationality, racial or religious groups; others to advance the interests of their immediate neighborhoods or their class. Nor are conceptions of general or public interest lacking as goals; some committeemen entered party work to work for a general improvement in the standards of local government. Finally, there are committeemen who saw party work as a means of advancing their personal careers through rising in the political hierarchy or through the effects party work might have on their non-political occupations. Such responses as these are shown in Table 1.

Table 1 shows striking differences between the Republicans and Democrats and between white and Negro committeemen. White Republican committeemen emphasize heavily the general goals of improving the tone of *local* government: note that the emphasis is on *local,* not national or state government. In contrast the white Democratic committeemen emphasize group and self-interests, with one out of every four concerned with personal advancement and another one out of every five concerned to advance the cause of his class or of the labor movement.

Both Republican and Democratic Negro committeemen emphasize understandably the interests of their racial group and their neighborhoods (in Stackton neighborhood and race are coterminous). In addition, Negro

Democrats resemble their white counterparts in according some importance to class and personal goals.

Table 1

PROPORTIONS CITING SELF-ACTIVATING MOTIVES AS REASON
FOR ENTERING POLITICAL WORK

Reasons Cited	White Republican	Democrat	Negro Republican	Democrat
Race, nationality or religious group interests	2.2%	7.3%	17.4%	16.3%
Union or class interests	0.0%	19.8%	0.0%	23.2%
Local neighborhood interests	1.1%	3.5%	15.2%	32.6%
General local government goals (e.g. "clean govt.")	31.5%	3.5%	6.5%	9.2%
To get ahead in business or politics	5.5%	23.5%	2.2%	14.0%
100% =	(91)	(85)	(46)	(43)

The distribution of self-activating motives further highlights the difference between perennial majority and minority parties. Republican committeemen see realistically little personal gain to be derived from their participation in party work and phrase their goals in community-wide moral terms. Party workers for the majority Democratic party seek personal and group goals soft-pedalling general community interests, reflecting the greater ability of a majority party to distribute political benefits.

In many ways, the Republican committeemen who seek to advance the general welfare and the Democratic counterparts who seek to advance class or labor interests are somewhat similar in stamp. Both groups are the most issue-oriented of the committeemen in Stackton. Democratic committeemen motivated by class or union goals cite more local issues and considerably more national issues than other Democratic committeemen in response to a question asking them to recall the issues which were being debated over the previous year in the newspapers or other public places. Republican committeemen who sought to advance the "clean government" campaign were similarly differentiated from their fellows. The ideologically committed Democrat then seeks to advance the interests of the working class while the ideologically committed Republican seeks to improve the management of local government.

The recruitment of individuals to political work is aided by the existing network of friendships and kinship. This network provides means by which, on the one hand, active political workers may draw upon others to join them in their work, and, on the other hand, ways in which the citizen who desires to enter political work may be apprised of the available opportunities and how to take advantage of them. Candidates seeking nomination or election feel that it is proper to call upon their friends and kin to help and precinct committeemen lean heavily on their own social circles as recruiting grounds for election board workers and canvassers. Of course, this pattern of recruitment is aided by the political homogeneity of friendship and kinship groups.

An important facet of recruitment is the network of social ties. Forty-eight per cent of the white Democrats and 44 per cent of the white Republicans were brought into precinct work through the requests of friends or kin. A wide range of specific circumstances is represented in these figures. Some of the female vice-committeemen were appointed by their husbands who were elected to the committeeman post. (This applies primarily to the Republicans; the Democrats frown on husband-wife teams in their precincts.) Others were approached by their high-school classmates who were candidates in an election to provide support and subsequently ran for committeemen. Still others were called on to help a brother or cousin in his attempt to win political office. Among a little less than half of the white committeemen, circumstances like these played some role in their recruitment to political work.

Among Negro committeemen relatively few were recruited in this fashion, around a third of the Republicans and about 16 per cent of the Democrats. To some small degree this finding may reflect the less integrated character of Stackton's Negro community with its high mobility and high proportion of newcomers, whose friendship and kinship networks may not be as well developed as those of the white community. But, in larger measure, the explanation is more that there are and have been few Negro candidates for public office in Stackton. The white candidates who seek support in the Negro community rely on money and not social ties to enlist workers in their cause. While the Negro precinct committeeman may rely on his social ties to pursue his work of persuasion, these ties are not used as frequently as among his white counterparts as means for recruitment of his fellows to political work.

Although the data we have presented in this section are obviously crude, they do reveal some of the ways in which committeemen are recruited to political work. Different patterns obtain for the two parties and, within each party, for the party organizations in white and Negro areas, representing partly the differences in the social positions of the populations involved and partly the differences in the political positions of the parties.

The Republican party, cut off as it is from the municipal patronage and with only a meager allotment of state patronage at its disposal, has the more severe recruitment problem. If we believe our respondents, few white Republican committeemen volunteer for their jobs: they prefer rather to say that they were pressured into their jobs or brought slowly along step-by-step from pollwatching to canvassing to precinct committeemen positions. A large proportion are motivated in their work by the goal of raising the tone of local government. Republican committeemen in the white areas of Stackton as a group come closest to being concerned with municipal government as such.

Some contrast to this portrait is presented by the white Democrats. The steady control exercised by the Democratic party over the local government makes recruitment a serious problem. A good proportion of the committeemen are seeking, through their political work, to advance their personal careers either through patronage or achieving public office. Even among the ideologically committed precinct committeemen, being in the party which is in power means being concerned with achieving specific ends for specific groups, mainly class and labor unions.

Both Democrats and Republicans rely heavily on existing friendship and kinship networks to continually bring new persons into political work. "Machines" like those in Stackton rely, to some degree, on stable and integrated subcommunity life to provide the social matrix for influence and the manpower for their organizations.

In the Negro areas of Stackton, both parties rely heavily on money incentives to recruit and motivate precinct workers. Republican and Democratic candidates pay for the support that party workers give them and the Democratic party, in addition, liberally dispenses patronage jobs to its Negro committeemen. (These are jobs which are much more desirable to Negroes than to whites because of the generally low occupational level of the former.) The idcological goals of the Negro committeemen are to advance the social position of their race and neighborhood.

The Committeemen and Their Constituents

From the viewpoint of the top-level party official, the ideal committeeman is one who is thoroughly a part of the web of social life in his precinct and a person of influence among his constituents. A man or woman so situated can best fulfill his function to produce for his party the necessary election day pluralities. This reasoning is quite accurate for, as we have shown elsewhere, a precinct worker who approximates this ideal does manage to produce significantly more votes for his party.[2]

Crucial to the efficient functioning of a political party is its ability to establish and maintain contact with the electorate. While contact with voters is perhaps more immediately crucial at election time, the building up of good will toward the party on a day-to-day basis may be even more important in the long haul.

Accordingly, precinct committeemen tend to be a fairly gregarious bunch, partly because this is not the activity which might attract an introvert and partly because the parties seek to recruit persons whose social horizons are wide. Table 2 documents the committeeman's sociability indicating that the average committeeman talks to about ten of his constituents on an average day. In the aggregate this average represents about 2,500 to 3,000 individuals who are seen daily out of a total of around 100,000 voters, or about 3 per cent of the electorate. While there is undoubtedly a good deal of repetition from day to day in the contacts made, this rate of interaction appears to mean that most of Stackton's voting population has some sort of contact wih the party apparatuses.

The better coverage of the Democratic party is clearly shown in Table 2 where it is shown that both white and Negro Democrats see about five more persons per day than their Republican counterparts. In addition Negro committeemen appear to be much more sociable than their white counterparts, both Republicans and Democrats seeing about five more persons per day. Indeed, the gregariousness of the Negro Democratic committeemen who talk to an average of sixteen persons per day would seem fantastic were it not that a stroll through Stackton would easily verify that the amount of interaction among the residents of the Negro sections is considerably greater than in the white areas.

To a very large degree the sociability under discussion here does not represent contacts with a primarily political purpose. Indeed, some committeemen deliberately avoid "political talk" between elections, as Table 3 indicates. Interestingly, the Republicans who have the smallest social horizon use it least often for political purposes, while the Negro committeemen with their very wide acquaintance range are least hesitant to discuss politics between elections.

Table 2

AVERAGE NUMBER OF PERSONS IN THE PRECINCT CONTACTED DAILY

		Republicans	Democrats
White		7.0	11.5
	N =	(91)	(85)
Negro		11.9	16.3
	N =	(46)	(43)

All told, the Democratic party seems much more firmly imbedded into the ongoing web of social life in Stackton, a fact which to some degree redounds to its benefit.[3] To be sure, this advantage may stem in large part from the ability of the Democrats to select from among a reservoir of candates for their precinct workers while the minority party may have to take whomever may be available.

In any community, an important context for meeting persons is provided by voluntary associations. Indeed, the folklore of the practical politician gives a heavy weight to associational activity as a means of increasing one's visibility to the electorate and obtaining followers. The precinct workers in Stackton also subscribe to this aspect of the folklore of politics and every respondent belonged to at least one non-political organization and most were members of several. (Surveys of organizational membership in the general population usually show that around 50 per cent of the adult population do not belong to any organizations.) Many of our precinct workers were active members and some had been or were presently officers of the organizations to which they belonged.

Table 3

PROPORTIONS OF COMMITTEEMEN WHO AVOID POLITICAL TALK BETWEEN ELECTIONS

		PERCENTAGES AMONG	
		Republicans	Democrats
White		63%	56%
	100% =	(91)	(85)
Negro		24%	25%
	100% =	(46)	(43)

How important were these organizational memberships to the pursuit of the party's goals of influencing the electorate is hard to evaluate. Many of the organizations to which the workers belonged were city-wide in scope. Perhaps the heavy incidence of membership expresses more the sociability of the workers than it reveals an important means by which the workers performed their political tasks.

Be that as it may, the distribution of organizational attachments is shown in Table 4. An organizational score was computed for each committeeman giving a weight of one for each membership, an additional weight of one for each active membership, and a further weight of one for each organization in which the individual had ever been an officer. The numbers in Table 4 are the average scores for the groups indicated. Again the superior sociability of the Democratic committeemen is shown. The typical white Democratic committeeman received a score of 8, indicating, typically, active membership in three or four organizations, while his Republican counterpart had only two active memberships. The Negro committeemen of both parties had fewer organizational ties than their white counterparts, expressing perhaps the slighter density of associational opportunities in the Negro community.

Of greater significance to the political life of Stackton are those contacts between voters and committeemen which are directly political in content. The respondents were asked to estimate the number of persons in their precincts who had come to them for aid during the previous month. Table 5 presents the resulting data.

Table 4

MEAN ORGANIZATIONTAL ATTACHMENT SCORES*

	Republicans	Democrats
White	6.1	8.2
N =	(91)	(85)
Negro	5.8	5.9
N =	(46)	(43)

*Scores were computed by giving weights of one for each membership, each active membership, and each officership ever held. Only non-political organizations were counted.

Table 5

MEDIAN NUMBERS OF PERSONS SEEKING THE AID OF
COMMITTEEMEN IN A MONTHLY PERIOD

	Republicans	Democrats
White	0.6	2.2
N =	(95)	(85)
Negro	2.2	13.4
N =	(46)	(43)

Providing the committeemen can satisfy these demands, these are the kinds of contacts which presumably build a network of obligations of the voters to the organization. In this table we see, again, the reflection of the difference between a party in power and one out of power. Virtually no one asked white Republican committeemen for help. In large part this is simply a matter of the inability to satisfy the voters' demands for jobs, street repairs, temporary relief work, and the like.

The frequency of business contacts between white voters and their committeemen pales beside the numbers of Negroes seeking aid from Negro Democratic committeemen. Roughly one person every two days asked a favor of some kind from each member of the Negro Democratic organization. By comparison, requests directed toward Negro Republicans seem small indeed. In fact, some Negro Republicans refer these requests to the Democrat in the precinct. Since there were 43 Negro Democratic respondents, their average number of aid requests, when translated into a monthly total, becomes 776 persons. About 100 persons sought out the 46 Negro Republicans we interviewed. Since the Negro population numbered some 50,000, about 2 per cent of the Negro population had made requests of their committeemen during a month. At the time of our interviewing, the 1957 recession had already reached Stackton and these figures seem quite reasonable.

Unlike the number of persons contacted in the day-to-day social life of the committeeman, these aid requests are probably not repetitions of the same contacts. In short, the party in power, by virtue of being able to satisfy the demands of the voters, attracts to it persons in need and thus enables the precinct committeeman to establish contacts with persons within the precinct he might otherwise not meet. Negro Democratic committeemen emphasize the importance of the obligations these services engender, but this aspect of the relationship is not emphasized as openly by white respondents.

Aside from having a larger number of requests for aid, the kind of aid requested by Negroes differs from the requests by white constituents. Negro requests are for (1) jobs, (2) relief money from the township trustee or welfare agency, or (3) aid in dealing with law enforcement agencies. In a majority of white precincts, the requests are for (1) a summer job with the park district for a high-school age son, or (2) information about how to contact the city government agencies. The problems Negroes bring to their committeemen are usually pressing: Often the applicant is hungry, and several precinct workers (all Democrats) said that they had paid grocery, electric, and other bills out of their own pockets on occasion. No white committeeman reported he himself had given aid of this sort or had ever been asked for such aid.[4]

The committeeman-voter contacts described above constitute the ordinary day-to-day interaction. Around election time, the tempo increases and the contacts become more specific in objective. The activities which make up a primary election in Stackton can begin as far as two years in advance of the election. The earliest moves are limited, for the most part, to incumbent office-holders who are looking far ahead to their fight for re-election. On the precinct organization level, the primary gets underway about sixty days before polling day. Each precinct committeeman is supposed to finish a poll of his precinct thirty days before the election. No voter can be registered after that time. In taking his poll, the committeeman ideally covers every dwelling unit, asks persons whether they are registered to vote and, if not, volunteers help in registering. This provides the committeeman with opportunities to meet every voter in the precinct on a "non-partisan" basis.

Do the committeemen take advantage of this opportunity to meet their constituents? While 80 per cent of the white Democrats and 90 per cent of the Negro Democrats take their polls, Republicans, generally speaking, do not bother. (Republicans say they poll their precincts before the general election, however.) In 1956, virtually all the precincts in the city were polled by the Democratic organization, but only a third of the white precincts and about two-thirds of the Negro precincts were polled by the Republicans.

There is a qualitative difference between the polling of the two parties. When a Republican says he has polled his precinct, he usually means that he has made certain that those persons whom he knew or felt were Republicans were registered. In contrast, the official Democratic policy was to pay the committeeman twenty-five cents for each registration, regardless of the party the person registered in. This policy of the Democratic organization is based on the assumption that two-thirds of all unregistered voters will vote Democratic, if they can be registered. This assumption is probably well-founded. Republican officials urged the organization to poll before the primary, but did not emphasize that they should talk to everyone. Several Republican ward captains commented that they only went to "sure" Republicans, that is, persons with "old immigrant"⁵ names who were not previously registered.

After the polling period is over, each party comes to some agreement on which candidate it is going to support in each campaign. At this point the job of the precinct committeeman is to persuade the voters to endorse the organization's choice at the polling place. This job requires contact between the voter and his committeeman. Highly active may be considered those persons who knocked on doors on behalf of candidates in the 1956 primary, or who went out of their way to talk to friends about a candidate, distributed his literature in the precinct, or gave a house party for a candidate in the precinct.

The more extensive activity of the Democratic party organization is again evident in the data. Some 51 per cent of the white and 88 per cent of the Negro Democrats tried to influence the votes of their constituents in the primary elections while only the Negro Republicans made strong efforts (72 per cent as against a mere 24 per cent of the white Republicans). We will see later on how this activity affected the character of primary elections in Stackton.

With respect to the relationships between party organization and voter, we have seen that both parties are composed on the precinct level of persons whose ties into the informal and associational lives of the community are strong. In addition, the Democrats, especially in the poorer Negro sections of Stackton, still perform the role of social work that characterized the "machines" of the large cities before the advent of full-employment.

The Internal Organization of the Political Parties

The formal structures of the political parties in Stackton provide only a weak and fragile structure for sustaining the parties through the month-to-month routine of maintaining contact with the electorate and for mobilization of additional effort around election time. Mechanisms which help to supplement party structure include patronage and favors, which give the precinct worker a role in the political process and reward him personally, and the growth of an informal organization centering around the party. Indeed, if the formal structure were alone necessary the two parties in Stackton would be equally energetic and equally capable at their tasks of influencing the electorate, and the data presented in the last section heavily contradict such a portrait of equality.

Party activity at the grass roots level is sustained by several factors: first, when in power, the party workers become essentially part of the political machinery of the state providing means of access to office-holders and governmental bureaucrats. Patronage to the precinct workers may mean a job for himself (an important goal for the Negro committeemen) and/or a supply of jobs for others. The favors that the committeeman can dispense earn a place of importance for himself in his neighborhood. Even for the minority party the sense of participation in the political process is not lacking.

A second factor which sustains inter-election activity is the informal organization which grows up around the party framework. Party workers through frequent contact among themselves and with party officials and office-holders diffuse a consensus over goals and methods and sustain in each other a sense of the importance of their activities. Indeed, perhaps the function of the old fashioned neighborhood political club was along these lines of inducing solidarity through providing an enduring context for sociability.

In this section we will consider the informal organizations of the two parties in Stackton.⁶ The basic data consists primarily of measures of the frequency of contacts among the rank and file and party leaders or public officials. In order to measure the amount of contact, each committeeman was given a list of party officials and of the other committeemen within his ward (around twenty names), and asked to indicate the number of times he had talked to each of the individuals on the list during the previous month.

The proportion of all committeemen within a ward who acknowledge having contact with a particular committeeman yields for the latter his acknowledged "coverage" within his ward. The average coverage percentages for the two parties are shown in Table 6. There are several salient tendencies

Table 6

PROPORTIONS OF COMMITTEEMEN HAVING CONTACT
WITH EACH OTHER

	REPUBLICANS		DEMOCRATS	
	Committeemen	Vice-Committeemen	Committeemen	Vice-Committeemen
White	24%		52%	
		14%		27%
100% =	(61)	(37)	(74)	(31)
Negro	46%		62%	
		22%		27%
100% =	(36)	(14)	(30)	(16)

apparent in these percentages. First, committeemen are much more drawn into the informal organization of the parties than vice-committeemen. Second, Negro committeemen show almost uniformly a higher level of contact than whites. But the strongest differences appear between the parties: Democratic committeemen are much more in contact with each other than their Republican counterparts, this higher degree of integration undoubtedly sustaining the higher morale and effectiveness of the Democratic party.

Each precinct committeeman was also given a list of names of party leaders and recent candidates, and asked to indicate how many times, if any, he had contacted or been contacted by each official in the previous thirty days. For Republicans, there were thirty-three names on this list; Democrats were given a list of forty-five names (a larger number of candidates running in the Democratic primary). The data show clearly the different pattern of contacts among the several groupings of party workers. Excluding vice-commiteemen, we find that Republican committeemen contacted over a period of a month about 15 per cent of the party figures on their list, while Democrats contacted around 30 per cent.

Are Democratic party officials so much more active than Republicans, or is this a matter of the precinct committeemen seeking out these officials? An answer to this question is provided partially in Table 7, which contrasts the contact in the two parties with comparable party posts, the city chairman and the district chairman in each party. The somewhat strong party differences tend to soften but not disappear. At least two-thirds of the white Republicans see either the city chairman or district chairman, while about 80 per cent of the Democrats were seeing these same officials. Among Negroes, about the same proportion of Republicans as Democrats had seen their city chairman, although more Negro Democrats had contacts with their precinct chairman than Negro Republicans.

Almost without exception, we can say that the lower levels of the Republican organization are, during a between-election period, at least, in rather limited contact with party leaders. A Republican committeeman will, in a month's time, see two or three of his official party leaders and one or two other party leaders.

Table 7

PERCENTAGE OF COMMITTEMEN WHO SAW SELECTED
PARTY LEADERS*

| | REPUBLICANS | | DEMOCRATS | |
	White	Negro	White	Negro
City Chairman	66%		83%	
		67%		70%
District Official	75%		83%	
		58%		73%
100% =	(63)	(31)	(61)	(29)

*Vice-committeemen excluded.

The higher levels of contact of the Democratic precinct organization with its officials are primarily the result of having elected officials to office. Of the possible people to see, office-holders are the ones that are seen. Another way of stating this is that while 42 per cent of the persons on the list presented to Democratic committeemen were elected officials or members of the city or county committees, only 18 per cent of the persons on the Republican list were in these categories. Democrats have, in other words, more local party figures to whom they can go for a favor or a discussion of what's going on in local politics.

The Role of Political Organizations in Primary Elections[7]

One of the major functions of a political party is to present to the electorate a set of candidates for public office. The device for their selection specified in the state laws covering Stackton consists of a series of primary elections. In theory the primary election is the ultimate authority over the party, but in practice, party organizations necessarily play a strong role in influencing their members. The description and evaluation of this role is the subject of this section.

The manifest function of a primary election is to select who shall be the party's candidates in the next general election. Given the normal stability of the relative strengths of the two parties in many elections, the decisions as to who shall occupy a wide range of political offices are made, in effect, in the primaries. This is obviously true for state and local offices in the one-party South, and holds for a wide variety of offices on similar levels in Northern communities like Stackton where the normal balance of strength between the parties is one-sided.

Despite this importance, few studies have been made of primaries, in contrast with the many made of general elections. To be sure, Key's[8] justly famous studies of Southern states have made the Southern primary very well known, but the ordinary "run-of-the-mill" primary election in other areas has not been the subject of much research. It is true that primary elections are not the most dramatic of political phenomena, and much research has been directed toward that most glamorous of American elections, the election of a President. But there are additional obstacles in the way of the study of primary elections which have hindered research on this topic. For one thing, primary elections occur within each major party. Each party is a relatively homogeneous group, as compared with the variation in a variety of socio-economic characteristics between parties. Hence the factors which help to account for so much of the variation in the support garnered by each candidate in a general election do not apply or apply with less force in primary elections.

To illustrate this point, Table 8 presents the correlations found between selected demographic characteristics of precincts and the precinct vote in three elections. In the two primary elections, the correlations are uniformly much smaller in size than in the general election. Table 8 indicates that we have to look to a considerably different set of variables for the explanation of the vote in primary elections.

Our plan of analysis is to relate the activities of party workers to the support received by candidates in primary elections from the voters. In the course of interviews, each respondent was asked to report on what occurred in his precinct during the 1955 and 1956 primary and general elections. He was questioned about the support which he personally gave to different candidates and about other support received by the same candidates in their precincts. The specific primary campaigns studied were selected on the basis of two criteria: First, only primary campaigns were used in which the "official" party organization was divided in its support of candidates. Second, the campaigns studied were characterized by active competition between two or more candidates seeking nomination. These criteria assured that there would be variations in the support for candidates from place to place within Stackton.

Table 8

CORRELATIONS BETWEEN DEMOGRAPHIC VARIABLES
AND THE VOTE IN PRIMARY AND GENERAL
ELECTIONS: 1955*

Selected demographic characteristic	General election for mayor: % Democratic	Republican mayoralty primary	Democratic city judge primary
Per cent "Old immigrant"**	—.919	—.356	—.074
Median rental	—.874	—.426	—.105
Per cent Negro	+.729	+.532	+.249

* In the Republican mayoralty primary, the dependent variable was the per cent of the two candidate vote for the winning candidate. In the Democratic primary, it was the per cent of the five candidate vote received by the winning candidate. The signs of the coefficients are arbitrary and depend on which candidate's vote was taken as the dependent variable. Correlations are between the vote and the demographic characteristics of clusters of precincts.
**"Old Immigrant" comprises persons of Anglo-Saxon, German or Scandinavian descent.

For each race, precinct workers were asked which candidate they supported, how many workers each of the candidates had in the precincts, and how many house parties each of the candidates attended in the precinct. The committeeman was also asked what he did in the thirty-day period preceding the primary, and his responses to these questions were coded on a scale from inactive to active participation in the primary campaign.

For each candidate in each campaign we now have three measures of the "inputs" he had in each precinct: the degree of precinct captain support, the number of other workers, and the number of house parties he attended. A fourth variable we used measures the notoriety of each candidate. A sample of residents in each of the city's six wards was given a list containing the names of our candidates. The percentage of the sample who recognized his name gives us a measure of the candidate's notoriety in the ward.

Party Activity in Primaries

Party activity in a primary election takes place on several levels. In the top political circles in the community, there is much jockeying for the support of major party figures and for the support of the central party organization in the community and at the higher organizational levels of county and state. At the lower organizational levels, with which we are primarily concerned, candidates attempt to gain the support of precinct workers and to have other persons in the precinct drum up sentiment in their favor. The candidates also attempt to reach the voters directly through campaigns in the mass media and through house parties. The latter are devices which are financed by the candidate, conducted by his workers in a precinct, and are designed to bring the candidate face to face with voters in an informal context.

Table 9 presents a measure of the intensity of the partisanship of the precinct captains in the two parties. A little more than a third of the precinct captains engaged in door-to-door campaigning for the candidates which they supported in the primary. Another third talked only to friends and people whom they knew well in their precincts. The remaining third only revealed their own choices if asked, or did nothing at all. Note that the two parties contrast strongly, with the Democratic precinct workers being considerably more partisan than their Republican counterparts. The effect of this difference, as we will see later on, is to lessen the weight of the party workers in the Republican primaries.

Table 9

INTENSITY OF PARTISAN CANDIDATE SUPPORT BY PRECINCT CAPTAINS IN 1956 PRIMARY ELECTIONS

Intensity of support	Democratic	Republican	Total
No support	1%	16%	9%
Minor support: Told voters whom he supported if asked; handed out literature at polling place	23%	38%	31%
Medium support: Talked to friends and people he knew	35%	20%	27%
Strong support: Went door to door campaigning for candidates	46%	27%	36%
100% =	(100)	(116)	(216)

Table 10 presents data on the number of political workers (other than precinct captains) available to the candidates in different primary elections and the number of house parties held in the same elections. It must be remembered that these are estimates provided by the precinct workers and are of unknown accuracy. If, however, we take these reports as given, in the usual contested primary race, some 500 individuals, outside of the 200-odd precinct captains, become involved in the face-to-face attempts at influencing voters in the primary. Thus if there are five contested primary races within each of the two parties in an election, some 2,000 to 3,000 individuals may become involved in the task of influencing the vote, or about 2 per cent to 3 per cent of the total electorate. Table 10 also indicates that more of the citizenry become involved in the Democratic primaries than the Republican, showing again the difference between the majority and minority parties.

To give concrete meaning to the data on house parties is somewhat harder. We know little about these social affairs in ways that might enable us to evaluate their worth — for example, the number of voters attending them. We may note again, however, the expected differences between the parties, with Democratic candidates having more house parties than Republican candidates.

The consistent differences between the two parties reflect in part the greater popular interest in the majority party primaries. This can be seen most dramatically in the proportion of voters in each party who turn out for the primary elections: in the white and Negro precincts respectively 56 per cent and 46 per cent of the Democratic voters in the 1956 general election turned out in the previous primary, while for the Republican party the correspond-

Table 10

NUMBER OF POLITICAL WORKERS AND PRECINCT HOUSE PARTIES: BY PARTY AND PRIMARY CAMPAIGN

A. DEMOCRATIC	County Surveyor	County Commission (A)	County Commission (B)	City Judge
Year:	1956	1956	1956	1955
Number of workers	234	359	237	353
Number of house parties	127	145	115	170
Number of reporting precincts	(78)	(81)	(80)	(80)

B. REPUBLICAN	Congress	County Commission	Mayor	City Judge
Year:	1956	1956	1955	1955
Number of workers	114	122	310	140
Number of house parties	76	90	179	127
Number of reporting precincts	(84)	(84)	(87)	(83)

ing percentages are 20 per cent and 23 per cent. These differences also reflect the amount of money which candidates spent in their campaigns. By and large, Republican precinct captains and workers are unpaid volunteers in the areas of the city occupied by whites. A very large proportion of the precinct captains and workers in the Democratic primaries are paid for their support by the candidates. Or, at least, such are the accounts our field workers heard from both sides.

Turnout in Primary Elections

In a city like Stackton in which one of the parties maintains a majority almost consistently from election to election, the primaries assume considerable importance. Nomination for local office in the Democratic primaries almost assures election, particularly in those years when national and state contests heighten voter interest in the general elections. Yet despite their importance, far fewer voters turn out to the polls in primary elections as compared with the subsequent general elections. In 1955, for example, in the average precinct about half the number of voters turned out for the Democratic primaries that voted for the leading Democratic candidate in the subsequent general election. Understandably, the corresponding proportion, one in five, for the Republicans is much lower.

That there is some interest in the primary elections is, in part, a credit to the competition for nomination among would-be candidates. The party organization strives to get as many people who would support its slate to the polls as possible. In addition, those citizens who follow closely the world of local affairs can be counted on to provide some of the voters who will appear at the polling places on primary election day.

Although the proportions of the voters turning out in primary elections referred to above are low, there is considerable variation among precincts: in some, only a handful of the voters come to the polls; in others, almost as many as would appear to vote in a general election make their appearances. In part, the differences among precincts are a function of the kinds of voters to be found there; in part, the differences depend on the activity of the party in that precinct. The relative contributions of a number of factors to turnout in the primary elections of 1955 can be seen in Table 11, where we show for the white precincts of Stackton the regression of a number of such factors on the turnout. Note that these factors account for about 38 per cent of the variation among precincts in the Democratic primaries and for about 51 per cent in the Republican primaries, the differences between the two primary elections possibly being accounted for by the greater activity of the "private" party workers in the former election.

Table 11

THE MULTIPLE REGRESSIONS OF PRECINCT CHARACTERISTICS
AND COMMITTEEMAN ACTIVITY ON PRIMARY TURNOUT*
IN THE 1955 STACKTON PRIMARY ELECTIONS
(White Precincts Only)

Variable	DEMOCRATIC PRIMARY (N=71)		REPUBLICAN PRIMARY (N=59)	
	Beta Weights	Proportion of variance explained	Beta Weights	Proportion of variance explained
Per cent home ownership	.309	11%	−.410	12%
Rental level	.207	3%	.499	25%
Per cent "Old immigrants"	−.287	6%	.328	4%
Precinct Committeeman activity*	.361	14%	.294	8%
Patronage density*	.166	5%	(not used for Republicans)	
Totals	R = .62	39%	R = .71	51%

*Turnout in the primary election was defined as the proportion of the voters in a party's primary election to the vote for the leading candidate of the party on the subsequent general election. Committeeman activity was measured as a combination of the number of persons the committeeman talks to daily in his precinct and the intensity of his activities in the primary election. The N's for the correlations consist of all white precincts in Stackton whose committeemen were interviewed.
Patronage density was measured as the ratio of patronage city employees in a precinct to the total number of registered voters in the precinct.

In the Democratic primary, about 14 per cent of the variation among precincts is accounted for by differences in the activity of precinct captains. Where a precinct captain is well integrated into his neighborhood and has been active in soliciting his constituents to appear at the polls, the precinct is likely to have a high turnout. Next in importance in the Democratic primaries is the proportion of home ownership in the precinct — the higher the home ownership, the greater the turnout. The other factors considered, proportion of "old immigrants," the density of patronage, and the average rental level of the precinct, account, in that order, for the remainder of the variation from precinct to precinct. In short, in areas which are inhabited by stable and fairly well-to-do descendants of recent immigrants and where the precinct captain is active in stirring up interest in the primary, the turnout is the heaviest.

A considerable contrast is provided by the Republican primary. Here the weightiest factor is the socio-economic status of the precinct: the higher the average rental in an area the more likely there is to be high interest in the primary, this variable accounting for 25 per cent of the variation from precinct to precinct. Next in importance is the proportion of home ownership, but in this case, the relationship is opposite to that in the Democratic primaries. The higher the proportion of home ownership, the lower the turnout in Republican primaries! It appears that high primary turnout for the Republicans is in the high rental apartment house precincts of Stackton. No easy explanation for this finding comes to mind. Precinct captain activity counts for little in the Republican primaries, explaining less than 9 per cent of the variation among precincts. Finally, a small weight must be given to the presence of "old immigrants" in the precinct.

Organizational Determinants of the Primary Vote

In order to assess how activities of precinct committeemen affected the outcome of primary elections, we shall present the correlations between each of the different types of support and the votes received by a candidate. The correlations are taken over clusters of precincts and refer to votes obtained by each of the candidates in a particular race.[9] Eighteen clusters of precincts are used in the Democratic primary races and nineteen in the Republican, each cluster consisting of a group of contiguous precincts.

Each candidate in a particular race was given a score on each of the variables derived from the precinct captain's reports. These scores were then made relative within each race by computing the ratio this score represented to the highest score received by any candidate in any precinct cluster in that race. The ratios so computed remove the differences between races and between parties, the differences between the score values obtained by candidates being primarily a function of his support.

Table 12 presents the correlations for one primary election among the measure of support and of each support measure with the primary vote. Note that the measures of support obtained from the precinct captain's reports — variables 1, 2, and 3 — are correlated highly with each other and also with the vote. The notoriety of a candidate — the ability of a candidate to obtain recognition from a sample of voters — is poorly related to measures of support and the vote. Note that among the support measures it is best related to the number of workers a candidate had. Similar tables of intercorrelations were computed for each of the eight primary races under study. In order to conserve space, we shall not present these additional tables. The pattern of relationships shown in table 12 obtains for all of the eight campaign races, except that in the Republican primaries the values of the coefficients for measures of support with the vote were less.

Table 12

CORRELATIONS AMONG CANDIDATE INPUTS AND CANDIDATE VOTE: DEMOCARTIC COUNTY COMMISSIONER A PRIMARY: 1955

	(1) Committeeman Support	(2) Workers	(3) House parties	(4) Notoriety	(5) Candidate vote
Committeeman support	----	.69	.69	.31	.86
Workers		----	.73	.49	.80
House parties			----	.34	.72
Notoriety				---	.52

In order to assess the joint contributions of these variables to the success of a candidate in a primary election, we have resorted to multiple correlation analysis. In Table 13, we examine the beta weights (not the regression coefficients) and R for each of the Democratic campaigns. R ranges from .9 to .90. At least 80 per cent of the variation in the votes among candidates in each Democratic campaign has been accounted for by the four predictor variables.

Table 14 presents the rank order of the beta weights *within* each campaign. The rank order of these beta weights are almost consistent from race to race. The support of the committeemen is first, followed by workers, notoriety, and house parties. The single deviation from this pattern (city judge) is interesting, but we cannot account for it.

Beta weights and R's for Republican primaries are presented in Table 15. As compared with Democratic primaries, R tends to be much smaller, and the amount of variation in the vote among the candidates that is related to our input variables ranges from a high of 79 per cent to a low of 28 per cent. The rank order of the beta weights maintains a certain degree of consistency with those previously examined, as shown in Table 16. In spite of the rather wide fluctuations in multiple R, the beta weight rank order of house parties and notoriety remains the same for each of these Republican campaigns. The fluctuation in the importance of support and workers is of considerable interest to us, but the best we can say about this at the present time is that either one *or* the other is the most important of the four beta weights. The reasons for this fluctuation remain unknown.

Table 13

MULTIPLE CORRELATION AND BETA WEIGHTS: DEMOCRATIC CAMPAIGNS

Campaign	Number of Candidates	Support	Workers	House Parties	Notoriety	$R_{y.1234}$
City Judge	5	.187	.292	.020	.559	.96
Commissioner [B]	5	.484	.411	−.055	.321	.90
Commissioner [A]	4	.579	.269	.060	.193	.93
Surveyor	4	.492	.354	−.014	.237	.93

Table 14

RANK ORDER OF BETA WEIGHTS
DEMOCRATIC CAMPAIGNS

Campaign	Support	Workers	House Parties	Notoriety
City Judge	3	2	4	1
Commissioner [B]	1	2	4	3
Commissioner [A]	1	2	4	3
Surveyor	1	2	4	3

Table 15

MULTIPLE CORRELATIONS AND BETA WEIGHTS:
REPUBLICAN CAMPAIGNS

Campaign	Number of Candidates	Support	Workers	House Parties	Notoriety	$R_{y.1234}$
Congress	3	.758	—.054	—.157	.422	.89
Mayor	2	.913	—.070	—.423	.400	.68
City Judge	3	.277	.461	—.089	.339	.67
Commissioner	3	—.066	.442	—.108	.390	.53

Table 16

RANK ORDER OF BETA WEIGHTS:
REPUBLICAN CAMPAIGNS

Campaign	Support	Workers	House Parties	Notoriety
Congress	1	3	4	2
Mayor	1	3	4	2
City Judge	3	1	4	2
Commissioner	3	1	4	2

Comparison of tables 14 and 16 shows that for both the Democrats and the Republicans house parties consistently carry less weight (and in a majority of cases, a small negative weight) than any other variable. Thus, although the zero order correlation of house parties with the vote is moderately strong, or even high, this correlation partials out when the other variables are added. Perhaps another way to think about house parties is as a measure of individual candidate activity, as opposed to mass activities on the behalf of the candidate by others.

A second comparison of considerable interest is the shift in the importance of notoriety; it assumes a more important role in accounting for the vote in Republican primaries than it does in Democratic primaries. This observation seems to be in line with the previously observed differences between the two parties which indicated that the Democratic precinct organization is far more active in primary elections and that, in general, Democratic campaigns involved more political workers and more candidate activity in the form of house parties. Given this higher level of party and candidate activity in the Democratic party, a relative difference in the importance of the notoriety of candidates might be expected.

A third comparison between the parties shows that either workers or support occupy the first rank in seven out of eight primary elections, the support variable being in the first place five out of eight times. In two of the three cases where support was dislodged from the first position, its place was taken by workers. In other words, it is the doorbell-ringing, face-to-face contact which appears to win primary elections in this city.

Patronage and the Primary Vote

The Democratic Party through its control over the major local government offices has almost seven hundred patronage jobs to distribute (exclusive of police, firemen, and school crossing guards). Patronage employees are supposed to help the party remain in power in return for their job. In a primary election, of course, the party is by no means a completely undivided organization. Different factions and cliques vie with each other for nomination.

The patronage employees of Stackton participate in this internecine warfare, primarily on the side of the faction that controls the distribution of patronage jobs. This means that when the mayor and the public officials who are associated with him endorse a candidate for nomination, the white patronage employees act as a sort of "machine" to produce pluralities in favor of these candidates in the precincts where patronage is especially heavy. Table 17 illustrates this point by presenting the differences in residuals between heavy and light patronage areas in Stackton. Candidates who are favored by the mayor get additional votes over and above the support they received in those areas from precinct workers and persons working directly for the candidates in question.

Those areas of Stackton which have a high density of patronage jobs are not all in the heavily partisan Democratic areas, but tend to be in middle and high income areas, middle and high *old* immigrant areas, while three of the five low-patronage areas are also high on the number of voters seeking aid. In short, patronage is distributed, not through areas where the voters "need it the most," but in areas where the *party* needs it the most. Table 18 also makes it clear that patronage is not distributed in vain, but does have a sizable effect on the vote for party-supported candidates in the primary elections we have studied. In addition, if the committeemen are split into those high and those low on primary election activities, 43 per cent of the less active group are in high patronage areas, while only 18 per cent of the very active group are in high patronage areas. Similarly, 21 per cent of the less active committeemen are in areas with little patronage, while 22 per cent of the most active committeemen are in the low patronage areas. In short, in white areas patronage is in those areas which have the less active committeemen. From this point of view, patronage is allocated to these areas of the city where it is needed to make up for the less active members of the party organization.

Patronage has quite a different effect in the Negro areas of Stackton as table 18 indicates. The gain of heavy patronage over light patronage areas does not obtain. This probably is a reflection of the difference in the relations of patronage employees to committeemen in white and Negro areas. In Negro areas of the city, the precinct committeeman is the person who gets a city job for his constituent. In white areas, job applications still must be signed by the committeeman, but a patronage employee most frequently gets the job through his contacts with the mayor or friends of the mayor. The committeeman is essentially bypassed, and the loyalty of the patronage employee is to the mayor and not to the committeeman. This difference in the relations of the patronage employee to the committeeman between white and Negro areas is also reflected in the difference of the ties between white and Negro constituents and their committeemen. The Negro voter goes *through* the committeeman to get his favors; the white voter frequently bypasses the committeeman altogether and goes directly to the officeholder. The Negro voter, be he a city employee or not, still looks to the precinct committeeman for direction of his vote.

Since the Republican party in Stackton has no patronage to dispense a similar analysis with this party was not possible.

Table 17

DIFFERENCES BETWEEN HEAVY AND LIGHT PATRONAGE AREAS OF STACKTON IN SUPPORT RECEIVED BY CANDIDATES FAVORED BY THE MAYOR

(WHITE AREAS ONLY)

| | GAIN OF HEAVY PATRONAGE PRECINCTS OVER LIGHT PATRONAGE PRECINCTS | |
Primary Race	Candidates Favored by Mayor	Candidates Not Endorsed by Mayor
Commissioner [A]	+9.95	−4.08
Commissioner [B]	+6.30	+3.14
Surveyor	+2.71	−0.76
City Judge	+6.34	−2.91

Table 18

DIFFERENCES BETWEEN HEAVY AND LIGHT PATRONAGE AREAS OF STACKTON IN SUPPORT RECEIVED BY CANDIDATES FAVORED BY THE MAYOR

(NEGRO AREAS ONLY)

| | GAIN OF HEAVY PATRONAGE AREAS OVER LIGHT PATRONAGE AREAS | |
Primary Race	Candidates Favored by Mayor	Candidates Not Endorsed by Mayor
Commissioner [A]	− 6.70	+6.03
Commissioner [B]	−11.50	−2.67
Surveyor	+ 7.65	−6.80
City Judge	+ 7.04	−6.86

The Party Organization in a Presidential Election[10]

While the primary elections are important to a party in the sense that they define both the officers of the party and the slate which the party will present to the voters, it is still the general election which authoritatively defines success or failure. Of course, the party may succeed or fail on many levels, depending on the offices in contest. Although the local party centers its attention on the local governmental structure, there is enough connection in the voters' minds and in fact between different levels of government to make the local party organization concerned with a wide spectrum of offices. Despite the remoteness of the President's office from the local scene in Stackton, it is important symbolically to the local party organizations to pile up pluralities for its presidential aspirant, and it is important in a practical sense to connect the candidates for local office to the presidential candidate to cash in on the latter's wider notoriety and prestige.

In one sense, the problem faced by a party organization in a general election is a more difficult one than it faces in a primary election and, in another sense, it is an easier one. In a primary election, it is necessary to convince voters to support the aspirations of particular men who are united by their membership in the same party but divided primarily by their personal aspirations. There are no clearcut lines of cleavage within the supporters of a particular party to which candidates may appeal. Hence the party is in the position of influencing choices among alternatives which are not clearly defined. It is apparent from our previous discussion that the cues supplied to the voter by the party organization are effective in the primaries.

In contrast, in a general election, the party is faced with altering the long standing loyalties of voters on the opposite side of a fence and of reinforcing the similar loyalties of its own supporters. To win over some voters from the opposite side is a difficult task, but it is easy to reactivate the sentiments of the party's traditional sources of support.

Hence we can expect that, in a general election, "history" will count for more than party organization. By "history" we mean the long standing cleavages within the electorate along class and ethnic lines. Party organization and party activity certainly played a role historically in building up these loyalties, but it is unlikely that the organization can produce radical shifts from election to election.

The researchers on voting behavior in Presidential elections which have received so much deserved praise have paid little attention to the roles played by party organizations. In part, this neglect stems from the employment of a methodology which is focused on the individual voter. The discernment of the influence of party workers on the voting decisions of the individual voter is so hazardous that it is understandable that the voting behavior studies which have employed the techniques of the sample survey have been unable to study party effects. In fact, the neglect of party organizations in research on voting behavior stems from an inability to solve the problem of how to separate out the effects of party activity from those effects produced by the other factors at work in a particular election. It is important to see this methodological problem clearly. To say, for example, that the Democratic party was effective in obtaining a given vote for its candidate in a particular precinct involves assessing somehow what the Democratic candidate would have received in that district *without* the activity of his party. Because of the way voters divide along ethnic and class lines in most general elections, either one of the parties has a rather large pool of "natural" Democrats or "natural" Republicans whose party vote is assured regardless of the activities of the party in the campaign period. Thus the base line for measuring how much impact a party organization has upon a district is the way in which that district's vote for the party exceeds what is to be expected on the basis of the longstanding predispositions of the voters.

In this section, we shall attempt an analysis of the effects of party activities in the 1956 Presidential election in Stackton. The strategy of the analysis is as follows: The voting records of seventy-four precincts inhabited primarily by whites are analyzed in terms of the social characteristics of the precincts. A multiple regression equation links together the voting records and the precinct social characteristics, providing an estimate of how each precinct would vote if its social characteristics were the only factors at work. The demographic variables to be used include the proportion of the precinct's registered voters that were "old immigrants," the estimated rentals, and the proportion of owner occupied dwelling units in the precincts.[11] An account of the sources used in obtaining this information was given earlier in this paper.

By correlating each of these three variables of social composition with each other and with the proportion of the vote received by Stevenson in the 1956 Presidential election, a regression equation was computed which then was used to obtain an estimate for each precinct of the Democratic vote to be expected on the grounds of its social composition alone. The correlations among these variables and the resulting regression equation are shown in Table 19.[12]

In Table 19, it is important to note that the precinct characteristics are poorly correlated with each other, but each is fairly strongly correlated with the vote for Stevenson. This situation led to a very high multiple correlation with the vote: — .908, indicating that about 80 per cent of the variation in vote among precincts could be accounted for by the differences among precincts in these three social characteristics.

The regression equation shown in the bottom line of Table 19 indicates the weights that should be applied to each of the precinct characteristics to obtain a "best" estimate of the vote for each precinct. This regression equation was used to obtain an estimated Democratic vote for each of the seventy-four white precincts. The estimated vote for a precinct represents a "best" estimate of what the vote should be in that precinct if only these three social characteristics were involved in the vote of a precinct. The residuals, differences between the actual vote and that estimated for a precinct, then represents random fluctuations and the effects of factors not yet taken into account. These residual differences are the focus of our analysis. We try to account for the way in which a precinct departs from its estimated vote by considering the degree of party activity within that precinct.

Before proceeding to the analysis of residuals, it may be worthwhile to consider the difference between a Presidential and a local general election. In Table 20 we compare the differences between regression analysis of the 1956 Presidential vote and the 1955 Mayoralty campaign in Stackton. To begin with, we may note that the demographic variables account for more (83 per cent as compared with 75 per cent) of the variation among precincts in the Presidential as compared with the local election, indicating that the activities of the parties may have been more effective in the latter election.

Second, the role played by ethnicity in the mayoralty election is stronger (accounting for more of the explained variance) while the role played by class factors, such as homeownership and average rental, is greater in the presidential election.

Table 19

INTERCORRELATIONS AMONG PRECINCT CHARACTERISTICS AND PRECINCT VOTING RECORDS:

White Precincts

		(1) Proportion "Old Immi- grant"	(2) Estimated Rental	(3) Proportion Owner- Occupied Dwellings	(4) Proportion Democratic 1956 Presi- dential
Proportion "Old immigrant"	(1)	....	+.33	+.10	—.76
Estimated rental	(2)		....	+.15	—.67
Proportion home owners	(3)			....	—.35

$R_{4.123} = -.908$

Regression equation of precinct characteristics on the Democratic vote:

$Y = -.422X_1 - .724 X_2 - .112X_2 + 108.23$

Table 20

REGRESSION ANALYSES OF THE VOTE BY PRECINCTS IN THE 1955 MAYORALTY AND 1956 PRESIDENTIAL ELECTION

(WHITE PRECINCTS ONLY)

Precinct Characteristic	1955 MAYORALTY		1956 PRESIDENTIAL	
	Beta Weights	Proportion of Variation Explained	Beta Weights	Proportion of Variation Explained
Proportion "Old immigrant"	.643	49%	.590	45%
Average rental	.362	21%	.446	30%
Proportion home ownership	.103	2%	.350	8%
Totals	R = .86	74%	R = .91	83%

The "Breakage" Effect

Although we are concerned primarily with ferreting out the effects of party organizations on the precinct level, we must also consider whether these residuals may not have been generated by other kinds of differences among precincts.

Several recent studies[13] have indicated that a political party gains an added advantage whenever it is able to obtain a very large majority in an area. A large majority of voters supporting a particular party produces a "political atmosphere" which results in a larger than expected vote for that party. This has been called the "bandwagon" effect, or, more recently the "breakage" effect.

Table 21 shows that the "breakage" effect may be present in the precincts we have studied. If we divided precincts into those with heavy, medium, or light Democratic votes, we see that, on the average, in heavily Democratic precincts the party receices 2.6 per cent more votes than expected and in light Democratic precincts about 2.5 per cent less than expected. This is a spread of five percentage points, representing a considerable increment to the party in some areas of the city.[14]

The Measurement of Party Organization at the Precinct Level

Our approach to the measurement of the activities of the two political parties at the precinct level was to question precinct committeemen about the ways in which they individually went about their precinct duties. Admittedly, there are other types of party activity going on during a campaign which do not involve the precinct committeemen — the speeches, advertisements, and so on which appear in the mass media. Presumably these mass media effects are not segmented by precincts, but are common to all precincts. The organizational efforts which we studied are primarily those involving face-to-face contacts with voters on the neighborhood level. As we have seen in several earlier sections, the Democratic committeemen have a considerable edge over their Republican counterparts in their contacts with voters both between and during election campaigns.

Despite the better showing of the Democrats as a group, there is still much variation among them, as well as considerable variation among the Republican workers. This variation in performance is the subject of the remainder of our analysis. In other terms, the question may be put as follows: How many percentage points advantage does a party obtain by having a good precinct committeeman on the job? Conversely, what does the party lose by having a worker who does not perform well?

Table 21

AVERAGE RESIDUALS IN PRECINCTS OF DIFFERENT
DEMOCRATIC PARTISANSHIP

	Light Democratic Vote (44% or less)	Medium Democratic Vote (45-55%)	Heavy Democratic Vote (56% and over)
Percentage Gain or Loss For Democratic Candidate	−2.46	+0.19	+2.63
Number of Precincts	**[26]**	**[22]**	**[26]**

In Table 22, we take up the analysis of the differences in characteristics of committeemen in terms of the amount of daily contacts the Democratic committeeman has with persons within his precinct between elections. The twenty-three precincts in which the committeeman talked with only 0–10 persons daily show an average loss of 1.2 per cent, while the fifteen precincts in which the committeeman talked with 21 or more persons daily gained, on the average, about 1.8 per cent for the Democratic candidate.

Much the same relationship holds for Republican committeemen, with the twenty-nine precincts in which the Republican committeemen were low in daily interaction showing a loss of about 0.5 per cent, while the eleven precincts in which the Republicans were high in daily interaction show a gain for the Republican candidate of about 2.5 per cent.

In Table 23, we return briefly to a breakdown of precincts into areas which give light, medium, or heavy support to either party. The gain for the party in precincts with more energetic committeemen is especially large in those precincts with uneasy majorities for either party — the difference for both Republicans and Democrats being about 6 per cent. Thus we can see that the efforts of the party organizations are particularly important where the election outcome can be easily affected. Perhaps this effect may also be discerned on the level of large geographic districts, wards, congressional districts, and the like.

The popular idea that patronage is extremely important in getting out the vote for a party is investigated in Table 24. Since there are no Republicans employed by the local government, this table is limited to Democratic committeemen. While we cannot tell from these results alone whether the better precinct workers are rewarded by patronage jobs or whether those precinct workers with city jobs are more committed to their precinct work, it is clear that the party does gain additional support from those precincts led by patronage committeemen, and also that it loses votes in those precincts where the committeemen are not employed by local government.

Up to this point we have shown how a number of different variables singly contributed to the way in which a precinct exceeded or fell short of its estimated vote. If we add some of the more effective precinct committeemen characteristics together to form an overall index of the "goodness" of precinct workers, we may see how much a "good" party worker is worth to his party. In Table 25 we see that for both the Democrats and the Republicans the difference between "good" and "poor" committeemen is about four per cent.

These findings provide important clues concerning the ways in which party organizations, through their grass roots representatives, may affect the popular vote. The effective party worker is one who is embedded in the social life of the area he serves. He knows personally many of the residents, is

Table 22

PRECINCT ACTIVITY AND PERCENTAGE GAIN IN PARTY VOTE: 1956 PRESIDENTIAL ELECTION*

A. DEMOCRATIC COMMITTEEMEN	NUMBER OF PERSONS TALKED WITH ON AN AVERAGE DAY		
	0-10	11-20	21 and over
Average percentage gained by Democratic candidate	−1.21	−0.24	+1.78
	[23]	[14]	[15]

B. REPUBLICAN COMMITTEEMEN	NUMBER OF PERSONS TALKED WITH ON AN AVERAGE DAY		
	0-10	11-20	21 and over
Average percentage gained by Republican candidate	−0.56	+1.91	+6.92
	[29]	[10]	[1]

*Residuals in this table were adjusted to remove "breakage effect."

Table 23

PERCENTAGE GAIN IN PARTY VOTE IN PRECINCTS
WITH DIFFERENT PLURALITIES*

A. DEMOCRATIC COMMITTEEMEN	PERCENTAGE GAINED BY DEMOCRATIC CANDIDATE IN PRECINCTS IN WHICH THE DEMOCRATS OBTAINED OF THE TOTAL VOTE:		
Number of Persons Talked with on Average Day	Less than 45%	Between 45% and 55%	56% or More
10 or Fewer	−2.98	−2.99	+2.49
	[8]	[8]	[7]
11 or More	−2.66	+3.55	+2.47
	[8]	[11]	[10]

B. REPUBLICAN COMMITTEEMEN**	PERCENTAGE GAINED BY REPUBLICAN CANDIDATE IN PRECINCTS IN WHICH THE REPUBLICANS OBTAINED OF THE TOTAL VOTE:		
Number of Persons Talked with on Average Day	Less than 45%	Between 45% and 55%	56% or More
5 or Fewer	−5.30	−3.85	+2.29
	[4]	[5]	[10]
6 or More	−0.66	+1.57	+3.75
	[7]	[10]	[4]

*Residuals in this table were not adjusted to remove the "breakage effect."
**If Republicans are divided at the 10 or less, 11 or more line (as were the Democrats), the same relationships hold as are seen in this table; however, the distributions of cases is pathetically small for some cells.

Table 24

GOVERNMENT EMPLOYMENT AND GAIN IN THE
DEMOCRATIC VOTE*

	Employed by Local Government	Not Employed by Local Government
Percentage gained by Democratic candidate	+1.45	−1.02
	[18]	[39]

*Democratic committeemen only.

similar to them in group memberships, and actively seeks to reinforce the bonds of acquaintance and friendship in the interim between elections and especially at election times. From our qualitative interviews with precinct committeemen and observation of these individuals in action, we have learned that the *content* of the contacts with voters need not necessarily be primarily political. Run-of-the-mill contacts, built up into a relationship of trust, provide channels for the influence of party headquarters to be felt on the precinct level.

Table 25

PERFORMANCE RATINGS OF PRECINCT COMMITTEEMEN
AND GAIN IN PARTY VOTE

A. DEMOCRATIC
   COMMITTEEMEN

	PERFORMANCE SCORES*			
	+4 or Better	+3 or +2	+1, 0, or —1	—2 or Worse
Percentage gained by Democratic candidate	+2.34	—0.20	—0.52	—1.61
	[8]	[14]	[28]	[8]

B. REPUBLICAN
   COMMITTEEMEN

	PERFORMANCE SCORES			
	+4 or Better	+3 or +2	+1, 0, or —1	—2 or Worse
Percentage gained by Republican candidate	+1.44	+0.99	+0.05	—2.67
	[3]	[12]	[26]	[6]

*Scores were constructed by giving a precinct committeeman a + 1 for each of five items if his answer was in the direction of a "good" performance, a zero if no answer, and a — 1 if the answer was in the direction of a "poor" response. For Democrats, the five items were daily contact within the precinct, party partisanship, time spent as committeeman between elections, evaluation of "party support" in the last election, and whether or not he was employed by local government. For Republicans, the last item was necessarily replaced by an attitude question on the role of the committeeman.

An Overview

The overall portrait of the party organizations in Stackton that has emerged in the preceding pages presents some familiar features and others which may turn out to be idiosyncratic. The familiar features are those which are held in common by cities of this size, composition, and economic base: Stackton is an industrial satellite of a large metropolitan center in the Midwest. Other characteristics of the political parties of Stackton appear to mark out the city as unique. Indeed this is one of the hazards of case studies, for any individual city is always partly an illustration of the general laws of urban development and partly a unique manifestation of the particular time, population, and ecological exigencies involved.

Certainly, the formal structures of the Republican and Democratic parties in Stackton are very familiar. Many of our cities operate under the same rules concerning primaries, the designation of party officials and the conduct of elections. While in some cities, the precinct captains are appointed by ward captains rather than elected directly in primaries, in all cities party primaries are the source for the authority wielded by party officials.

Yet despite this rather common formal structure to the parties in Stackton, they do appear to be cut to an old-fashioned pattern which is probably a deviant one among American cities. Civil service reform has yet to make inroads on the traffic in city jobs and municipal favors and there is no large block of municipal jobs which is not under the control of the top elected public officials. As a consequence, jobs are one of the goals of the party workers and municipal employees are very sensitive to the demands made upon them by party officials and by those in higher public office. For this reason the organization of the Democratic party in Stackton is probably stronger than in the more usual city. The precinct workers are more sensitive to the wishes of party officials and a set of sanctions are available to the latter to keep some semblance of unity within the party.

Cut off from access to city hall, the Republican party shows what might be considered a more normal pattern. From our interviews with party leaders, it is apparent that there is no central focus to the party in the same way that the highest elected local official, the mayor, is the central figure for the Democrats. Indeed, the Republican Party seems to be more fragmented and less coherent than their opponents with the central figures being patronage appointees in state government agencies serving Stackton.

The differences between the two parties conditioned by the control which one exercises over the apparatus are dramatically reflected in the more solidary appearance and greater effectiveness of the Democratic Party. How differently this would appear in another community where the "spoils system" has been undermined by civil service reform is a question which awaits further studies to provide an answer.

Whatever eventual judgment emerges as to the representativeness of the patterns of party organization in Stackton, it does seem likely that in other places systems of recruitment into, and maintenance of, participation will be found resembling those in Stackton in at least gross features. In this connection our study has uncovered several important mechanisms. To begin with, a party in power has an edge over the party out of power in its ability to recruit party workers and to maintain their interest over time. Practical individuals seeking to advance self and group interests are more easily recruited into the party in power and are sustained in their party work by some degree of success in attaining these goals. As a corollary the party officials when elected to office can foster solidarity and spur activity by dispensing benefits and wielding sanctions in relation to the goals held by party workers.

In contrast, a minority party has a less tangible hold on its workers. It must rely on activating motives for participating which cannot bind individuals closely to their party. In addition, having few or no party leaders in office means that the party has few individuals who could provide rallying points for the organization.

A second set of findings refers to the roles played by party workers in elections. In primary elections, a very heavy weight must be accorded to the precinct committeemen and the loyal followers of aspirants for nomination. Their face-to-face contacts with the voters within each party determine the party slates. Only where the party workers are slack in their efforts, as in the Republican party of Stackton, do the reputation and popularity of persons seeking nomination come into play. This characteristic of primary elections further strengthens the positions of party members who have been elected to office, for their control over favors and patronage affects strongly where the support of the party workers will go.

In a Presidential election, the heaviest weight must be given to what must be considered historical factors. It is the traditional loyalties of the electorate plus some element of economic interest which determines the greater part of the balance between the parties. Yet, even here, the party workers do make a significant contribution. In a precinct where the party committeeman is embedded within the existing social organization of the neighborhood and where he makes an effort to influence his neighbors, the party to which he belongs dóes better than in a precinct in which there is a less active committeeman.

In our studies both of the primary and general elections, what stands out is the importance of the precinct committeeman's being a part of the social organization of his neighborhood. Where the committeeman has many friends among his neighbors, actively canvasses his constituents, the party fares very well at the polls. Nor need his efforts be directed specifically at persuasion; his presence as a member of the informal neighboring circles counts more than his proselytizing efforts.

There was much evidence, albeit indirect, that the relationship between local government, political parties and voters can best be conceptualized as a system of *quid pro quo* with the benefits and services of the municipal government being distributed by the party in power to those areas of the city where they might do the most good in garnering support for the party. In fact, the next step in research on party organization might be to look more systematically into local politics as an exchange of benefits and support between local government and the electorate with the political party serving as a middleman exacting a broker's profit on the way.

NOTES TO CHAPTER II

1. The research reported in this paper was supported by a grant from the Committee on Political Behavior of the Social Science Research Council whose aid is gratefully acknowledged. This paper represents part of the efforts of a research team which studied the power structure of the community as well as the topics which are discussed in this paper. The team consisted of the authors of this paper and the following individuals: Warner Bloomberg, Jr. (Syracuse University), Victor Hoffmann (Valparaiso University), and Thomas Thompson (Indiana University).

2. P. Cutright and P. H. Rossi, "Grass Roots Politicians and the Vote," *American Sociological Review*, 23 (April, 1958).

3. If we assume that the friendship and kinship circles of Stackton are politically homogeneous, as many studies have shown, and that therefore committeemen see primarily persons of the same political persuasion as themselves, then the Republicans may have a smaller social horizon because of their smaller numbers in Stackton. Hence the Republicans may have as good or perhaps better coverage of their party members than their rivals.

4. The party organization in the Negro precincts resembles strongly the organizations described by earlier studies undertaken in the 'thirties. See especially H. F. Gosnell, *Machine Politics; Chicago Style*, University of Chicago Press, 1937. Considering the poverty and incidence of unemployment among the Negro population of Stackton, perhaps this is the contemporary group which is most similar in life situation to the working class during the depression.

5. An "Old immigrant" is defined as a person of Anglo-Saxon, German, or Scandinavian descent.

6. The method of analysis employed in this section is based on suggestions made by Prof. James S. Coleman of the University of Chicago, whose aid is gratefully acknowledged.

7. A preliminary analysis of the findings of this section was presented in P. Cutright and P. H. Rossi, "Party Organization in Primary Elections," *American Journal of Sociology*, 64 (November, 1958).

8. V. O. Key, Jr., *Southern Politics in State and Nation*, New York: A. A. Knopf, 1949.

9. Precincts were clustered in order to raise the reliability of the reports of precinct captains — each captain's reports being pooled with those of four or five others — and in order to raise the reliability of the vote, since the vote for a particular candidate in any one precinct may be a very small number, especially in those precincts where turnout was very slight. Thus the N for any primary race correlation is the number of clusters, times the number of candidates, in that race. A three-candidate Republican primary race is thus based on an N of 57.

10. An earlier presentation of some of the findings reported in this section may be found in P. Cutright and P. H. Rossi, "Grass Roots Politicians and the Vote," op. cit. The data on precinct organization in this section was collected by questionnaires distributed to precinct committeemen in the Summer of 1956. Because only a few Negroes returned this questionnaire, our analysis is limited to white precincts. Also note that we are working with a smaller number of committeemen in our analysis of Presidential election residuals than was the case in our analysis of primary elections.

11. The terms "Old immigrants" and "New immigrants" coincide largely with religious groups as well, the "Old immigrants" being largely Protestant and the "New Immigrants" largely Catholic. Had it been possible to employ measures of the religious composition of precincts in the computation of the regression equation, perhaps more of the total variance would have been accounted for. However, since the correlation of ethnicity with the vote is so high, it is not likely that a religious composition index would have done much better

12. No variables beyond the ones shown in table 33 were considered, primarily because these were the only ones available and because the resulting multiple correlation coefficient was so high.

13. Bernard Berelson et al., Voting, Chicago: University of Chicago Press, 1954.

14. Statistically, the "breakage" effect indicates that the relationship between the vote and the social characteristics of the precincts is slightly curvilinear.

Leadership Hierarchies and Political Issues in a New England Town

BY *HARRY SCOBLE*

IN *Community Power Structure,* Floyd Hunter sought to identify community leaders by interviewing his "panel" via general questions as to who were the leaders. The purpose of this research was to identify community leaders in the context of *specific* disputes and decisions in *different* policy subject matter areas. Once community leaders were so identified, the question was asked: Was there any evidence of a ruling elite?[1]

The research was carried out in Bennington, Vermont, during 1953-54. At the time of the study, Bennington had a population of about 12,500. As in most New England towns, its population has grown steadily but slowly — at less than the national average and with an increasing "aged" distribution. Again, as in most northern New England towns, Bennington's Yankee Protestantism has given way numerically to Catholicism of Irish, French-Canadian, and more recently, Italian origin.

The town is located in the extreme southwest quadrant of Vermont. It serves as a trading area for a number of satellite townships (that is, rural hamlets and villages) located in an area cutting also into Massachusetts and New York. Situated thus, Bennington is in many ways independent of the rest of the state. While its dairy interests pull it toward the Boston milk market, an increasing "rurban proletariat" orients Bennington toward the better job markets of Pittsfield and North Adams, in Massachusetts, and of Albany-Schenectady-Troy complex, in New York. Within the township, the industrial sector of its economy has changed in the last half century from a few, relatively large, domestically-owned, textile employers to present-day diversification and absentee-ownership.

The regular formal media of communication within Bennington are two: an afternoon, daily-except-Sunday newspaper (the *Bennington Banner*) and a daylight-hours AM radio station (WBTN). These are supplemented by regular and special public meetings and by public forums (the latter usually sponsored by an active local unit of the League of Women Voters).

Governmentally, Bennington serves as one of the two county seats of Bennington County. It is also a prime example of a unique feature of local government in New England: the multiple-overlay of local governmental (taxing) units. At the time of study, Bennington proper included the town government entire, the governments of three separately incorporated villages (of Bennington, Old Bennington, and North Bennington), and the governments of four separately incorporated school districts (an elementary district coterminous with the Village of Bennington; an all-grades district coterminous with the Village of North Bennington; a Rural Schools, Incorporated, providing elementary education for Old Bennington and for the unincorporated rural "outside" area of the township; and a Union High School District recently formed and containing the first and third of these).

Politically, Benningtonians live in the state exhibiting the most durable one-party system in American history: in 1954, it could be said that no non-Republican had won a statewide office or achieved a statewide winning plurality in Vermont for almost a century. Within Bennington, as befits the state's third largest community, the Democratic party fares better: *local* candidates bearing that label have been elected with some frequency (see below) and an occasional statewide Democratic candidate has carried the town. Since Bennington is a small New England town, if it seems possible to extend the subsequent generalizations of this study at all beyond Bennington, then it is necessary to do so with severe limitations — to the region, to the size, type, and function of the community, and to the time period.

Two assumptions were made which guided the research design. First, if political power existed in Bennington, it could be observed in an attempt to "solve" an actual dispute. (This was assumed to avoid defining only a generalized structure of attributed power *potential*.) And, second, if "leaders"[2] existed in the community, the degree to which they acted as a cohesive group could be determined only by observing their behavior in two or more such disputes.

The first step, therefore, was to determine a number of issues which could be used as the framework for empirically identifying the leadership. Employing public documentation, participant observation, informal interviews, and other available sources, an initial list was reduced to three "issues" which best satisfied the criteria of having (1) extended over a considerable period of time, (2) involved substantial numbers of active individuals, and (3) just ended (or being then still in the process of decision).

The first "issue" selected was the general "process" area of nominations and elections to public office.[3] The remaining two, more specific, "subject-matter" issues were as follows:

Consolidation of the municipal governments of Bennington. As early as 1935, various individuals in the township had concerned themselves with the problems resulting from multiple and overlapping units of local government. Interest in consolidation was dormant through World War I, in part because informal consolidation was achieved through both the township and the central village hiring the same individual as their separate "half-time" manager. By the late 1940's, the demands of an increased population for better or new services made some form of consolidation seem attractive to several active members of the community. Repeatedly during the period of 1948 to 1951, efforts at consolidation were blocked. In 1952, the issue lay dormant, but during the period of the study it was again revived; the proponents of consolidation gained further approval of their study and work by votes of 1,132 to 847 in 1953 and 1,453 to 635 in 1954. Meanwhile, in this period, a majority of the board of trustees of Bennington Village had instructed the village president to appoint a Village Committee on City Government, for studying this alternative form of action.

Formation of a Union High School District and construction of a new high school building. In 1945, the Vermont Legislature passed permissive legislation for the formation of "union" districts (i.e., of two or more towns) at the high school level. In June, 1952, after numerous attempts, the annual meetings of the districts of Bennington Village and of the rural, "outside" town voted 613 to 458 and 105 to 46, respectively, in favor of joining in a union district. The new Union High School District of Bennington was organized in November, 1952, and its Directors were authorized by a vote of 201 to 129 to borrow $35,000 for the purchase of a site and the employment of an architect to prepare preliminary plans for a new building.

In April, 1953, members of the union district voted 1,784 to 1,245 *not* to authorize their Directors to construct the new building and 1,772 to 1,242 *not* to authorize the negotiation of bonds to cover a proposed cost of $1,250,000.

At the time of the study, efforts were being made to gain a successful second "new building" vote, amid increasing rumors of a decision to build a central Catholic High School in Bennington and other rumors of a move to get the legislature to authorize a vote to dissolve this first Union High School district in Vermont.

While the two issues selected for identifying leadership are obviously closely related, they are different in that they involved different formal governmental mechanisms and different non-governmental organizations. Moreover, one involved a substantial change from the past way of doing things in Bennington, whereas the other involved primarily a substantial expenditure of money.

The second step of the study involved identifying the leaders and administering to them the Leadership Interviews which were informal and focused, making use of a wide variety of specific and general open-ended questions and lasting just under two hours on the average. Forty-two persons were given the Leadership Interview. The first ten were selected because, from documentary data and informal interviews then available, they seemed best to satisfy the criteria: (1) they had been active for a period of time that, as nearly as possible, coincided with the "life" of one or more of the three issues; (2) they had been active at the level of participating in the formulation of attempted policies; and (3) they had taken different public positions on the issue(s). Thirty-two additional respondents were then selected from the referrals made by the first ten, again attempting to preserve balance among the three issue areas and between or among the two or more "sides" within each issue.[4]

The third step of the study was undertaken simultaneously with the second, by interviewing each new nomination of a leader by way of a schedule of 107 items, requiring roughly an hour and a quarter.[5] In this fashion an attempt was made to complete a General Interview census of all individuals nominated as leaders by the Leadership Interview respondents.[6]

Tabulation of the nominations made by these forty-two respondents produced the following separate lists:

1. A total of twenty-seven individuals were named as leaders ("important in work-ing for or against") in the over-all Consolidation issue, by two or more respondents.

2. A total of twenty-one individuals were named as leaders ("important in work-ing for or against") in the formation of the Union High School District and the unsuccessful new building vote, by two or more respondents.

3. A total of forty-three individuals were named as leaders in "politics" in response to questions asked (a) about leaders (same definition) in the two nominations and elections studied *or* (b) generally posing the question, "If you wanted to run for local office in town or if you were a candidate for statewide office, who would be important to have backing you or not against you in town?" (A cut-off of nomination by at least *four* respondents was employed in this policy area, to reduce an initial list of eighty-six names to more manageable proportions.)

4. A total of twenty-seven individuals were named as "general leaders" in response to the generally phrased, concluding question — "In any issue of this sort, in-volving a substantial expenditure or a significant change from past ways of doing things here, who would it be important to have working for or against the policy?" (Nomination by two or more respondents.)

When these four lists of names were analyzed for duplications, they reduced to a total of sixty-nine individuals. Of these, fifty-eight were administered the General Interview schedule.[7] This sample of fifty-eight leaders (occasional data are available on all sixty-nine), identified via influence attributions by individuals themselves active in three different policy areas in Bennington, provides the basis of this analysis.

The Structure of Power

A. *Generalization-Specialization.* Having identified a total of sixty-nine leaders in Bennington, the first question is whether the twenty-seven among them named as "general leaders" are, in fact, identified as leaders in the policy areas. Table 1 indicates that 47 per cent of all those nominated as Union High School issue leaders were nominated for that policy area alone; this same proportion was 37 per cent for "politics"; and for the Consolidation issue it was 22 per cent. Viewing the total group of sixty-nine leaders, thirty-two (46 per cent) were nominated as leaders in only a single one of the *three policy areas.* Rearranging the data of Table 1, those who were also identified as general leaders comprise: 38 per cent of the total leaders of the

Table 1

EXTENT TO WHICH LEADERS NAMED IN ONE AREA ARE ALSO NAMED ON OTHER LISTS OF LEADERS

	General Leaders	UHS Leaders	Consol. Leaders	Politics Leaders
% named to 3 other lists	15	19	15	9
% named to 2 other lists	33	5	30	21
% named to 1 other list	37	29	33	33
% named this list only	15	47	22	37
Number =	**27**	**21**	**27**	**43**

UHS list; 44 per cent of the total Consolidation list; and 46 per cent of the total Politics list.

The initial significance of these data on specialization is this: two of these policy areas compete for control of the tax resources of Bennington;[8] therefore, if a cohesive leadership group exists within the community, it must seek to control and co-ordinate the actions of a relatively large number of individuals whose power and/or interest is apparently confined to a limited area of community action. Also, since no formal governmental mechanism exists for reconciling conflicting budgets, such control and co-ordination would have to be achieved infomally if at all.

Turning next to the twenty-seven general leaders, it is to be noted first that four were named to this list *only*. This may reflect a time-lag in the political perceptions of the Leadership Interview respondents; or it may indicate the essential arbitrariness of social research when a "bottom" line has to be drawn somewhere, for three of these four received the bare minimum of nominations (two). At this stage of leadership research, this fact was deemed less important than the facts that: (a) 85 per cent of the general leaders were named to at least one of the three policy lists; (b) no individual was named to all three policy lists who was *not also* named as a general leader (but four general leaders were nominated to all three of these lists); and (c) of another eighteen leaders named to any two of the three policy lists, nine were *also* identified as general leaders.

Given this greater amount of actual policy "overlap" by general leaders, it was initially presumed that the core of any cohesive leadership group, if it existed, would be found among the general leaders; for the easiest means of achieving co-ordination of separated policy areas in the community would be through identical or significantly overlapping personnel.

This presumption was further strengthened when amounts and types of public office holding were examined. For example, data on all sixty-nine leaders indicate that 51 per cent of the general leaders as against 38 per cent of the other leaders were currently holding office in Bennington. Furthermore, 33 per cent and 21.5 per cent, respectively, had held past office. On the other hand, only 15 per cent of the general leaders compared with 40.5 per cent of the other leaders had never held elective or appointive office locally. In this sense, the general leaders were relatively more "visible" in the community.

Although there is no precise quantitative way to show it, the general leaders also held formal positions of power over wider areas or greater numbers of people, of greater policy (rather than ministerial) orientation, or of higher status. Qualitatively, for example, the only county-wide offices (of clerk and senator) held by these Bennington leaders were held by general leaders; so too for the judicial positions and town representative. On the other hand, the only "honorific positions" (i.e., cemetery trustee, justice of the peace), or elective civil service positions (i.e., the village and town clerks, the commissioners of the water board), and most of the minor policy-making positions (e.g., road commissioner, village corporation counsel) were then occupied by other leaders.

Multiple-office-holding within a single governmental unit or between municipal and school governments also buttressed the presumption. Multiple-office-holding was more prevalent among the general leaders; five of fourteen general leaders (36 per cent), as against only three of sixteen other leaders (19 per cent), were presently holding two or more offices at the time of study. Qualitative analysis again heightens the disparities in formal power positions. For example, the ninth-ranked general leader was both Municipal Judge and Town Representative in the lower house of the Vermont legislature, while the second-ranked general leader was then Town Agent, Moderator of the annual town meeting, Moderator of the Union High School District, and legal adviser to the Rural School District.[9] (He was also then a member of both the Town and County Republican Committees and Moderator of the Republican town caucus; previously he had served as Corporation Attorney for Bennington Village, as State's Attorney, Town Representative, and State Senator.)

We can assume that men who have both the power and the desire for cohesive control (co-ordination) will act in the most, rather than the least, efficient way. Thus, the easiest means of co-ordination in Bennington would be through identical or significantly overlapping personnel distributed among the different major policy areas. Having "responsible agents" in the key policy-making offices in the different major policy areas would be a direct pre-condition to co-ordination in Bennington. And since such office holding is more characteristic of the general leaders than of the other leaders, we turn to examine them with more detailed reference to the ruling group concept in the next section.

Summarizing, the argument of this section is as follows: (1) policy-making involves competitive claims for limited resources; (2) co-ordination of such claims is a pre-condition to the existence of a ruling group; (3) no institutional mechanism exists in Bennington for such co-ordination; (4) co-ordination would thus have to be achieved informally, through occupancy of policy-making positions in the separate policy areas by an identical or significantly overlapping personnel; and (5) since (a) they were more frequently nominated as leaders in these separate policy areas, (b) they were more frequently present (and also past) office holders, (c) they were more frequently holders of more powerful, more policy-oriented offices; and (d) they were more frequently holding multiple offices, *therefore* the tentative conclusion was that the general leaders — rather than the other leaders — was the logical point for beginning a detailed investigation of the existence of a ruling group.[10]

B. Tests of the Existence of a Ruling Group. Political scientists have for some time been in general agreement that, whereas all communities and societies have power aggregates (the most powerful of whom have been termed "elites"), the factors which distinguish different forms of rule are (1) the manner in which the elite is recruited and (2) its relations with the non-elite (i.e., the manner in which it exercises its power).[11] In particular, in order to show that an elite — or, as used here, leadership aggregate — were also a ruling group, the investigator would have to determine that (a) the elite controlled recruitment into its midst and that (b) the values of the elite were those of the society at large.

i. Elite Recruitment in Bennington. In Bennington, there were two essentially independent routes by which a leader could come to power. One route was via election to public office; the other, by having one's "ideas" on issues accepted by effective majorities of those exercising the legislative function of the community through the meeting.

Detailed examination of nominations and elections revealed few, if any, formal obstacles to candidacy or success. Procedural requirements for nomination as Democrat, Republican, or independent, were minimal. Informally, election campaign costs in money and time were small. It was theoretically equally possible for any individual to disseminate his "ideas" for public acceptance. There was evidence of both financial and content control of the two formal media (by a somewhat overlapping group drawn from the general leaders and their business associates); yet only three of fifty-eight leaders indicated that they relied exclusively, and only nineteen others said they relied even partially, on such formal media as their source of information about local affairs. Meanwhile, every leader willing to name his "two best friends" also indicated that he discussed "local problems and issues" with at least one of these; and it is presumed that such informal conversational networks provide a flow of information *from,* as well as a source of information for, these leaders.

In short, access to situations in which leaders may be designated by the community seemed initially free and open. More detailed examination of formal and informal recruitment processes then indicated a number of institutional and structural limitations.[12]

A poll-tax requirement (averaging $10) annually excluded some 6.5 per cent of the potential electorate from participation in local voting. Presumably, this most affects those for whom the marginal utility of a dollar is highest. Furthermore, public "business" meetings most frequently occur in Bennington during morning hours; this obviously disadvantages potential leaders of wage workers or mothers of the young. Once at such a meeting, dissemination of ideas is limited to those willing and able to walk the hundred-odd feet from the back of the Armory (where most citizens stand) to the microphone at the front. Since the Bennington custom of deciding on these business items is normally by voice or division, this presumably inhibits those most strongly preferring a secret ballot.

Analysis of the primary occupations of the general leaders indicates further limitations. Of the twenty-four presently employed, eight were owners of independent business, commercial, or manufacturing establishments, seven were lawyers, two bankers, one an orchard owner, one an editor-publisher, and one a minister. Only four could be classified as having relatively fixed sites and hours of (non-self) employment.

Father-son intergenerational career mobility emphasizes these structural limitations. Analyzing all fifty-eight, the leaders were primarily stationary; their over-all mobility rate was only half that of the non-leaders (19 and 38 per cent respectively); but the upward mobility rate of leaders was almost twice that of the non-leaders (83 and 45 per cent); and whatever mobility had occurred among the leadership was entirely upward. Of course, in this community, as elsewhere in American politics, there is an observable biasing in the recruitment process in favor of those with the time, talent, and interest to make use of formally equalitarian access.[13]

ii. Intra-Leadership Conflict over Values. While Bennington's leadership aggregate may not consciously control admission to its rank,[14] the structure of the community clearly limits the sources of leadership. But to demonstrate that this elite is a ruling group requires a further demonstration that "the values of the elite are those of the society at large." This statement actually contains *two* precedent conditions — the first is that the elite be *agreed* upon the values it seeks and the second, that these values be sought and *gained*. This section focuses upon the first problem, the extent to which the leadership aggregate is agreed upon policies; the second problem, that of the extent to which such policies are enacted, is treated as one measurement of power and is accordingly reserved for the concluding section.

Cohesion (i.e., regardless of success or failure) was tested by treating interview data as roll-call data and thus employing the Rice-Turner indices of "cohesion" and "likeness."[15] The first tests the internal unity of behavior of an aggregate group; the second is an external or comparative measure of the extent to which two aggregates or groups are similar in behavior. If one assumes the equal importance of two or more issues, then indices of either cohesion or likeness may be averaged. A cohesion index figure of 1.0 denotes unanimity, of 0, complete disunity; a likeness index figure of 1.0 denotes identical behavior, of 0, complete dissimilarity.

The data tested are positions taken on three different categories of issues. The first (termed "two major local" issues) is positions taken by *involved* leadership on the Union High School and Consolidation issues. ("Involved" refers to those among the fifty-eight who had been nominated as leaders in one or both issues by the respondents in the Leadership Interview.) In addition, from the General Interview questionnaires, there were data for all fifty-eight leaders with regard to "four minor local" issues[16] and with regard to 1952 presidential and gubernatorial votes (termed "two state-national" issues). And the standard employed was cohesion indices of .60 or higher in all three sets of issues. (This would mean average voting, by the members of an hypothesized group, at a rate of four-to-one, permitting active opposition of as much as 20 per cent. It does not seem an arbitrarily high test of the meaning of cohesive behavior or of ruling group.)

Initially it was noted that only six leaders — four general and two other leaders — had been designated as leaders involved in *both* major local issues. (Fifteen leaders "joined" them in the Union High School issue and twenty-one different leaders "joined" them in the Consolidation issue.) These six "overlapping personnel" were examined first, relative to their cohesion. Their average cohesion was *zero,* and they have been eliminated (as a possible group) from the further analyses summarized in Table 2. Most briefly, following down the list of variously hypothesized groups of leaders examined for their cohesion in Table 2:

(1) Testing *all* fifty-eight leaders confirmed Madison's paraphrased prediction that the larger the aggregate, the greater the disagreement. Furthermore, the first line of Table 2 indicates that Bennington's leaders achieved their greatest cohesion on the least important issues.

(2) Testing the twenty-two *general* leaders versus the thirty-six *other* leaders (item 2 of Table 2) indicated that the general leaders were *less* cohesive than the other leaders on the more important issues and that neither achieved a consistently high degree of unity (even 75 per cent or better voting together) on the three *or* on the two more important sets of issues.

(3) Lastly, a variety of smaller "synthetic" and "political" aggregates were tested for their cohesion (items numbered 3 on Table 2): the twenty general-*and*-politics leaders were compared with the twenty-three *non*-general politics leaders; the fewer numbers of these two aggregates who had been *involved* in the two major local issues were next compared (that is, there were thirteen general-*and*-politics leaders and seven non-general politics leaders who had been nominated leaders in the school and/or the Consolidation issues and these were separately tested for their cohesion); and lastly the total fifty-eight leaders were *synthetically* categorized according to whether they had been "winners," or "losers," or residually "uninvolved" in the outcomes of the two major local issues[17] and these were then tested for their cohesion in the two remaining categories of issues examined. Among these "synthetic" and "political" headings, no sub-aggregate that was then tested is characterized by a "high" (.60 or better) degree of cohesion on all three sets of issues or on the two more important sets.[18]

Table 2

COMPARISON OF AVERAGE COHESION ON THREE TYPES OF ISSUES OF VARIOUS SUB-STRUCTURES OF BENNINGTON'S LEADERS

Selected Sub structurings of Leaders	(N)	AVERAGE INDEX OF COHESION Types of Issues		
		Two Major Local (Involved)	Four Minor Local (All)	Two State-National (All)
1. All leaders	(58)	.24	.39	.20
2. General leaders	(22)	.33	.58	.32
Other leaders	(36)	.41	.47	.43
3. Synthetic				
Winners	(26)	(1.00)	.45	.55
Losers	(15)	(1.00)	.67	.33
Uninvolved	(17)	(——)	.51	.44
Political				
General-and-politics	(20)	.30	.49	.30
Non-general politics	(23)	.83	.47	.42
7 involved politics	(7)	.83	.50	.55
13 involved generals	(13)	.33	.42	.25
Factional*				
Isolates	(9)	.27	.50	.45
Thorndyke	(16)	.67	.65	.06
Bailey-Ford	(17)	.36	.47	.71
Darby-Masters	(10)	.47	.35	.60
Outsiders	(6)	1.00	.30	.00

* These leadership factions are identified and analyzed in the next section of the text.

To recapitulate, the argument of this section has been that a second, separable attribute of a ruling group is agreement upon the values it seeks. "Values" was roughly translated as preferred events in terms of policies or candidates. And "agreement" was then measured in terms of cohesion on these.

The major conclusions of this section are that Bennington's total leadership was disunified during this period and that no imaginable sub-aggregate of that leadership was consistently and "highly" cohesive over the range of political issues that arose. This finding is of especial importance with regard to the general leader category, because so much initial evidence supported the hypothesis that the core of a cohesive ruling group would be found within it.

These findings furthermore cast doubt on the universality of an assumption underlying Hunter's analysis of the power system of Atlanta that "likes attract" — where Hunter measures "likeness" both by type of power base (economic) and by amount of power (high). But the data of this section on cohesion indicate that "likes do *not* attract" in Bennington politics. (There is some evidence that "likes" among the leadership do in fact attract socially — in the one Country Club, in the "better" residential area of Old Bennington, in the higher status churches — in Bennington as in Atlanta.) Stated differently, a conclusion of this section is that substructuring within the leadership aggregate of Bennington does not occur along horizontal lines (of type and amount of power). The following sections thus will be directed, in part, to the question of whether consistent internal substructuring of Bennington's leadership occurs along vertical lines or perhaps not at all.[19]

The recurrent appeal of the "ruling group" concept may lie in the fact that, like politically subversive thought, it is exceedingly difficult to prove it does not exist. As against this the present section on recruitment, cohesion, and (partially) success has attempted a statement of available objective tests which would permit one to accept the existence of a ruling group. Neither the entire leadership aggregate nor any reasonably defined portion of it has met such tests. Motivation may exist, but achievement has not been demonstrated.

Moreover, it is difficult to conceive of the conditions that would have to arise in Bennington to permit the activation and success of a cohesive group desiring to dominate policy-making. Presumably, the issues studied — and those that normally occur — are negligible issues which do not produce strong cleavage based on conflicting social values.

The immediate impact of the emergency conditions presented by natural disaster or foreign attack and/or invasion might stimulate cohesion (without necessarily involving value conflicts);[20] the emergency conditions presented by mass unemployment — the only threat of total social disintegration that Bennington has experienced in this century, with its relatively much slower impact, would seem to be the sole situation seriously testing cohesion based upon important social values. Examination of newspaper accounts, election statistics, and recollections of older Leadership Interview respondents indicated that the most recent emergency of such a nature in Bennington — between 1931 and 1937 — produced a very slow realignment of leadership and a new majority which included a new age group come to power out of dissatisfaction with the old.

C. Intra-Leadership Factions in Bennington. In the General Interviews, respondents were asked to nominate a single individual, whom they knew well enough to speak to, and whom they considered worth listening to, with regard to local politics. Sociometric analysis of the leaders involved in the

UHS and Consolidation issues indicated that those in favor on the given issue tended to nominate the same few leaders *who had taken the same position as the nominator;* that those in opposition had gone "outside the system" (to nominate as leaders individuals not involved in the issue) or "across the line" (to nominate as leaders, general leaders opposing them on the issue) as much as they had made nominations from among themselves. Furthermore, of the forty-nine in the total leadership sample who were willing to nominate someone under this question, forty-six (94 per cent) nominated one of themselves, mainly general leaders (who received forty-one, or 84 per cent, of the "votes" cast).

A full analysis of the fifty-eight leaders, undertaken in terms of this nomination-of-local-leader question, produced five aggregates as follows:

1. Nine leaders, labeled "Isolates," who nominated no one.
2. Fifteen leaders who make up the "Thorndyke" faction since they either nominated him or other leaders who in turn nominated him.
3. Fifteen leaders centering around Bailey and Ford since these either nominated one of these two law partners or they nominated other leaders nominating one of these partners.
4. Eight leaders who joined with Darby and Masters to constitute another group, since these either nominated one of these two directly or else they nominated other leaders nominating one of these two.
5. Six leaders, labeled "Outsiders," who nominated anyone outside of the Thorndyke-Bailey-Ford-Darby-Masters "system," even including an "Isolate."

The Leadership Interviews had already provided fragmentary evidence of this structure, since various individuals readily identified themselves as members of "more or less permanent factions" which "worked against" other "factions" in local politics. Thus, two of the other leaders in politics separately identified themselves with, and were identified by, two general leaders ranked 4.5 and 14.5, in frequently working *with* the general ranked 3 (Thorndyke) and *against* the general leaders ranked 1 and 2 (Bailey and Ford). And they confirmed this by designating Thorndyke a local leader when they were administered the General Interview. That is, prior to the above analysis, there was partial evidence of a sub-structuring of Bennington's leadership along vertical (factional) rather than horizontal lines.

The three largest of these factions (hereafter termed, "the central factions," or referred to by specific names of factional leaders) were then examined with reference to the four local issues and the two state-national issues previously described. When average indices of cohesion were computed, no one of these factions was characterized by a consistently "high" (.60 or better) cohesion on the three sets of issues or on the two more important sets (Table 2). And when average indices of *likeness were computed on the four minor local issues* for successive pairs of these factions, the ranges extended over the same narrow distribution, the average indices were high and similar (between 80 and 90 for all three factional pairs), and these ranges and indices were very similar to those previously figured for the general and other leader aggregates.

Do the leadership *factions* exist in any more real sense than did the possible sub-categories previously examined and discarded? Despite the relative infrequency of direct electoral tests of factional position, these factions do exist as groups with "closely interlocking social roles" and with "shared norms."

   i. Factional Basis I: Occupational Co-operation. For some factions more than others, and for some members of each faction more than others, these factions exist because their members make better livings by working together. The Bailey-Ford faction is the most diversified and extensive in this sense.

   Joseph Bailey is president of one of the two statewide agencies seeking to develop Vermont's economy; he chairs its Industrial Committee and consequently knows what firms might be contemplating relocation within the Bennington area. A co-operating "active" ally heads the parallel committee within the local Chamber of Commerce, to which the town and central village governments have long contributed tax funds and in which Bailey has held many formal offices. Bailey and his law partner, Hubert Ford, are both able to close title on any land deals and to handle local corporate affairs (especially inventory appraisals, municipal services, and "labor") on a retainer basis. A third member of the faction owns, or has options on, most of the remaining potential industrial sites within the township. A fourth is director of one of the two main banks — the "progressive" one and one always anxious to expand its industrial accounts. Another "active" ally — younger brother of Bailey — is an industrial contractor. A fifth member of the faction is a heating-plumbing contractor; a sixth, editor-publisher of the local newspaper, interested in expanding its advertising accounts. A seventh member, Pelham, is a junior member of the Bailey-Ford law firm.

   This Bailey-Ford faction operates as a service agency, organized along the specialties of its main members. It has not only depth within Bennington but also breadth — key members such as Ford and Bailey tie in with other factions in the area beyond Bennington and also work with what might be termed "confederations" within the state. The other two main factions in Bennington, while similar in organization, are not so interlockingly diversified.

   The Thorndyke faction is the second largest and most active. Its main members have occupational interests which can be served through co-operative political action — for these are the interests of independent realtor, lawyer, department-store owner-manager, and of two smaller commercial establishments. When the occupations of other factional members are added to these — newspaper reporter, union president, textile dyer — it is evident that the Thorndyke faction gains part of its identification in serving as one relatively permanent base of opposition to the Bailey-Ford faction, which had tended to dominate locally and which, with other groups in the state, had tended to dominate the recent political and economic history of Vermont.

   The third and smallest of the central factions is headed by Darby and Masters. Darby, a lawyer, identifies himself (and was identified by others) as an independent force in Bennington politics — which he explains as resulting from his relatively high paid and protected tenure status as clerk of the County Court. Masters, an official of the more "conservative" of the two banks (as is a third member of this faction), was also identified as a local leader who had established his record independent of either the Bailey-Ford or the Thorndyke faction.

   These leaders might well be active in politics even without their factional memberships. The factions form, apparently *after* the politicization of individual leaders, in order to perfect service functions, for even local government is both regulator and especially promoter of the economy. If the town, as a matter of both law and practice, must maintain a ready-cash account, then one bank or the other will benefit (in use of the funds, prestige, etc.); or if major manufacturing units are managed by non-natives, then retention of a local lawyer is necessary to represent corporate interests vis-à-vis "the government" on taxation, water, other public services, and so on.

In one sense, the total leadership aggregate of Bennington is a protective league of the business, commerce, financial, and professional interests as against other latent or actual interests in the community. But such "economic government" is modified and weakened to the extent that factions exist within the leadership. That is, at some point the success of one faction necessarily entails a relative decline in standards of living and prestige of members of other factions. A particular event of "greediness" re-crystallizes factional lines, giving the "out-party" new strength and unity of purpose; such as occurred in a 1953–54 industrial tax appeal case handled by the Bailey-Ford firm. A legal member of the opposing Thorndyke faction commented that they were "very, very definitely abusing their privilege on these appraisals; they were giving false appraisals and they were paying way, way less than anybody else. In other words, *you didn't mind if they cheated a little but they were hogs about it.*" (Emphasis added.) Delegations from opposing factions "met with" the chairman of the Board of Listers — a man identified as an "other" leader but not as belonging to any faction.

The various appeals boards, in the main, upheld the upwardly revised inventory appraisals by the Board of Listers; Leadership Interview respondents agreed that the Bailey-Ford firm "lost" the case. When the editor-publisher of the "defeated" faction refused to handle the news item "straight" (i.e., as a "victory" for the Board and "good government"), the "outraged" Thorndyke faction relied on its other means of communication. When the reporter who had covered the story disputed its ultimate treatment with his editor and threatened to resign, key members of the Thorndyke faction, to which that reporter belonged, "talked him into staying because — he was a valuable asset to us and we didn't feel that we wanted to lose him; we felt that he should pocket his pride and continue on there; we felt he could do more on there than he could off."

Personal interest is only the first of the observed bases of factional substructuring of Bennington's leadership. Within the broad consensus, these same factions maintained positions that were durable and consistent in relation to one another, in their responses to the state, national, and international issues that tended to divide Americans during this period.

ii. Factional Basis II: State-National Issue Alignment. In Tables 3 and 4, the leadership factions have been compared by means of their positions on a variety of state, national, and international political issues and attitudes. In each instance, the data are recorded so that the conventionally defined "conservative" position comes at the top, and the "liberal" position comes at the bottom, within the given issue or index (except, of course, for the "All other" and "No answer" categories).

The overall consistency of alignments is significant. On all four single issues (Table 3) and on the two indices summarized in Table 4, the "center

of gravity" of the Thorndyke faction is *lower* than, and therefore by definition to the "liberal left" of, that of the Bailey-Ford faction. The consistency
of these liberal-conservative positions was also maintained on two additional
single questions (on evaluation of McCarthy's methods and on overall appraisal of McCarthy) and on three additional indices (of domestic economic
liberalism-conservatism, of a modified authoritarianism-equalitarianism, and
of aggressive-interventionism), which have not been included in Tables 3
and 4 for lack of space.[21]

Furthermore, the Darby-Masters faction, in terms of its center of gravity,
is higher than, and to the "conservative right" of, the center of the Bailey-
Ford faction on three of the four single issues, falling lower than, and thus
to the left of, what might be termed the "moderate conservative" position on
the Eisenhower vote (Table 3). With regard to the indices of freedom of
speech-press and of isolationism (Table 4), the Darby-Masters faction is
again higher than, and to the political right of, the Bailey-Ford faction.

In addition to the above consistent positions of the central factions, the
"Isolates" have been placed on the left in this identification of leadership
factions, because they shared several positions (on the three related McCarthy
questions, on the indices of Table 4, and on two of the three indices not re-
produced in that table) with the Thorndyke faction; but on single issues or

Table 3

RELATIVE POSITIONS OF BENNINGTON'S LEADERSHIP FACTIONS ON VARIOUS STATE AND NATIONAL CANDIDATES AND ON SINGLE NATIONAL ISSUES

	Isolates	Thorndyke	Bailey-Ford	Darby-Masters	Outsiders
1. 1952 Gubernatorial:					
H. Harding	67%	25%	71%	80%	50%
H. Olds	11	12	12	10	----
J. Connelly	11	44	12	10	33
AO answers	11	18	6	----	17
2. 1952 Presidential:					
Eisenhower	78%	56%	100%	80%	50%
Stevenson	11	37	----	20	33
AO answers	11	6	----	----	17
3. Taft-Hartley					
Good	55%	31%	47%	80%	50%
Good with bad	33	50	41	10	50
Bad	11	19	----	10	----
AO answers	----	----	12	----	----
4. McCarthy—activities:					
Strong favor	11%	25%	35%	40%	84%
Mild favor	22	19	29	40	----
Mild oppose	11	6	19	20	17
Strong oppose	44	50	23	----	----
No answers	11	----	----	----	----
N	**9**	**16**	**17**	**10**	**6**

indices in which the "Isolates" did not share center-of-gravity positions with the Thorndyke faction, they were most similar to the centerist Bailey-Ford faction. The "Outsiders," meanwhile, have been located on the far right, because the majority tended to express radical-reactionary views. (On the three McCarthy questions, on the two indices included, and on the authoritarian index not included, in Table 4, these "Outsiders" are to the right of, because above, the positions of both the Bailey-Ford *and* the Darby-Masters factions.)

Table 4

RELATIVE POSITIONS OF BENNINGTON'S LEADERSHIP FACTIONS ON VARIOUS INDICES SUMMARIZING TWO OR MORE NATIONAL AND INTERNATIONAL ISSUES

	Isolates	Thorndyke	Bailey-Ford	Darby-Masters	Outsiders
Index:					
1. Freedom Speech-Press:					
Low (0-2)	----%	6%	12%	20%	50%
Medium (3-4)	55	31	41	60	17
High (5-6)	44	62	47	20	34
2. Isolationism:					
High (2-3)	22%	----%	35%	60%	67%
Medium (1)	----	31	23	20	----
Low (0)	78	69	41	20	33
N	**9**	**16**	**17**	**10**	**6**

1. **Index of Attitudes Regarding Restrictions of Freedom of the Press and of Speech.** This summarizes responses to three questions, asking respondent whether he thought the following should be allowed: (1) Socialist Party to publish newspaper in peacetime, (2) newspapers criticize "our form of government," and (3) Communist Party member to speak on radio, all with regard to "this country." Scoring was 0 for "no," 1 for "yes, qualified," and 2 for "yes" answers.

2. **Index of Isolationism.** This summarizes responses to three questions on recent American foreign policy, as follows: (1) evaluation of the amount of foreign aid sent abroad, (2) evaluation of extent of American involvement "with problems in other parts of the world," and (3) whether the United States should "agree in advance" to defend a West European country in the event it were attacked by Russia. "Too much," "too much involvement," and "no" answers, respectively, are the "isolationist" answers that were scored.

For the six single issues which formed the basis of Table 3, indices of likeness were computed for both the general-other (horizontal) strata and for the three largest (vertical) factions of Bennington's leadership. For the horizontal (general-other) strata, no index figure fell below 75, while two-thirds of them were at the level of an index figure of 90 or more — indicating that the general and the other leaders responded very similarly to these state and national issues. On the other hand, for the vertical structuring of Bennington's leadership (represented by these three central factions), the index figures fell as low as 45 and more than 60 per cent of them fell *below* the 80 mark.

Comparative indices of likeness do not prove the existence of factional groups; but such comparisons do support the prior interview data to the effect that factions did exist *and behave differently* within the politics of Bennington. And the data of this sub-section indicate that these factions were stable, in the sense that they were maintained over a broad range of political issues, and that they were durable in their relative positions.

Additional data on factions were revealed in examination of a limited number of contests for local political office during this period; for leaders within the *same* central faction did not oppose factional colleagues for public office. Rather contests occurred across, to the outside of, or entirely beyond, the lines of the three central factions.

iii. Factional Basis III: Social Characteristics. The existence of these leadership factions is, in the third instance, supported by analysis of their differing social characteristics (Table 5).

It would be incorrect to assert that life has passed these leaders by; but the initial over-all impression gained from Table 5 is that the major dislocations impinging upon most modern American's lives — war, depression, emigration — are tides that have never swept up the average Bennington leader. Indeed, these leaders have been relatively insulated from even the more privatized disruptions of modern life such as divorce, job changes, working within a bureaucratic organization, or living in a metropolitan community.

It may seem that Yankeetown's leaders have advanced by standing still while all about them was motion; but even with this context of stability and insulation, there are differences among the various leadership factions.

Members of the Thorndyke faction, for example, are generally young parents, college-educated, well-to-do in income, engaged in non-self-employed business, commercial, and professional work. Their ages are such that the depression of the 1930's did become a part of their personal life experiences (possibly serving as the origin of their relatively pro-New Deal attitudes). On the other hand, this same age factor meant that the two World Wars did not much intrude upon their personal freedom.

The centrist faction headed by Bailey and Ford seems precisely that: its members tend toward a median age, median degree of nativity, median level of annual income. Its high percentage of lawyers means that the faction tends toward the highest amount of formal education and the greatest degree of self-employment of all factions. The Bailey-Ford faction includes the greatest *number* of social mobiles, perhaps reflecting the fact that aspirations for increased social status can be satisfied by a power position based upon the politics of "moderation" as well as by increased income. Depression and war experiences were minor for members of this faction, while they are approaching an age status in which the problems attendant upon having young children are decreasing rapidly.

The "right-wing" Darby-Masters faction is perhaps the most interesting of all because, in a sense, the uneventful life experiences of its members have left them in a marginal rather than a dominant position in Bennington politics. Its members are older, more Protestant, more nativist, and with deeper roots in the community. They have also had much less formal education than the members of any other faction, and their lower job statuses and lower incomes reflect this apparent relative deprivation. It is unknown whether economic life experience never offered a "main chance" to these men or whether they failed somehow when it occurred; in any event, their position in Bennington's social structure, presumably like that of their fathers, remains relatively stationary (100 per cent) and low.

Table 5

SELECTED SOCIAL CHARACTERISTICS BY LEADERSHIP FACTION

	Isolates	Thorndyke	Bailey-Ford	Darby-Masters	Outsiders
Age:					
51 or older	78%	31%	41%	60%	83%
36 to 50	----	50	41	40	----
35 or younger	22	19	18	----	17
Birthplace:					
Bennington area	22%	44%	53%	60%	83%
Other in state	11	----	12	20	----
Non-metro. NEng.	22	37	18	----	----
Boston-NYC	11	6	6	----	----
Other U.S.	33	----	6	----	17
Non-U.S.	----	12	6	20	----
Religion:					
Protestant	100%	56%	59%	70%	33%
Catholic	----	37	23	30	67
Education:					
Post-graduate	11%	12%	41%	----%	----%
College grad. or some	66	50	12	10	50
High Sch. grad. or some	11	31	35	60	33
Grammar grad. or some	11	6	12	30	17
Occupation:					
Wage worker	----%	6%	----%	30%	17%
White-collar	22	19	35	30	17
Bus.-prof.	22	56	47	30	33
Exec.-manag.	11	6	12	10	----
Farm	11	6	----	----	----
Retired	33	6	6	----	33
Type of employ.:					
Self-employed (incl. ret.)	22%	37%	53%	50%	33%
Familial depression experience (self or father*):	33%	31%	12%	----%	40%
Father-son social mobility:					
Stationary	89%	87%	75%	100%	50%
Upward	11	12	25	----	50
Current annual income:					
Over $8,000	11%	37%	18%	10%	33%
$6,000-8,000	33	19	30	20	----
$4,000-6,000	11	31	23	40	33
Less than $4,000	22	12	23	20	17
Refused	22	----	6	10	17
Veteran status:					
None	56%	69%	59%	70%	33%
N	**9**	**16**	**17**	**10**	**6**

*Question asked if respondent or father (if respondent lived at home) was out of regular work for three months or longer at any point during the depression.

As distinct from these three central factions, the Isolates (who nominated individuals not identified with the three central factions) share many characteristics: high age, high percentage of war experience and of familial depression experience, self-employment, income, marital and parental statuses.

These two aggregates of Bennington's leaders differ mainly in characteristics of religion, nativity, and education. The Outsiders are primarily Catholics, sons of non-self-employed wage-working fathers (67 per cent). Their mobility rate (upward) is high. The only faction that received less formal education than they is the Darby-Masters faction—with whose members the Outsiders share most political positions (cf. Tables 3 and 4). In local politics as in national politics, these Outsiders seem to act like a swarm of angry bees, mad at the unwanted invasions of their peaceful hive by the rest of the world.

The Isolates, on the other hand, apparently enjoyed a less parochial and more secure family background. They came primarily from out of the state (but within the United States). They are Protestants by birth. Their fathers were primarily white-collar workers, executives, or farmers — and self-employed. Just as their parents provided them with a dominant religious identification, they also were able to provide almost all of them with at least some college education. While the Isolates themselves are characterized by the least degree of self-employment, the jobs they hold or held are of relatively high status (i.e., upper white-collar or higher). The political opinions these Isolates expressed seem to reflect their different life experiences.

Concerning processes of recruitment to these factions, we infer that the qualifications for admission of a new member to an existing faction (such as one of the central three) are negative and relate to the first two observed bases of factionalism: that is, first, that the occupation of the new member not conflict and, second, that his general political orientation on most state, national, and international issues not conflict with those of prior members. (One suspects that, in time of economic recession, these rules of admission would be more strictly applied than in the early 1950's.)[22]

To describe Bennington's power structure, a choice of imagery from the natural sciences has been avoided since the words that are available all imply a greater degree of structuring than actually exists in this community. Despite the tendencies noted previously, all that can be said is that there are several central and durable combinations of men within the leadership; that these tend to maintain constant positions relative to one another on both local and non-local political issues; that these combinations have had different "central tendencies" in their social backgrounds; and that individual members of the factions move in and out — "switch" rather than "defect" — on given issues without apparent penalty. At the extremes of this power structure are the Isolates and Outsiders, also maintaining their positions.

But these factions *are* loosely bound, as the cohesion indices of Table 2 demonstrate. It is not known, for example, how the ten leaders in the Darby-Masters faction originally voted in 1950 when Harding — a regular Republican — first won the gubernatorial chair. (See Table 3). It is known that Darby himself was commonly designated as Harding's "strongest supporter" in the area. Between 1950 and 1952, Governor Harding and Thomas Darby split bitterly (in a misunderstanding about patronage). In 1952, Darby announced for Olds, a state senator, also a Republican but identified with the "Preston Group," the remnants of a coalition of liberal Republicans and Democrats who had been briefly victorious in Vermont (1946 to 1950). Darby publicly worked for Olds and claims to have voted for him. Darby alone in this faction makes this claim: the others will seem to have been strongly pro-Harding in 1952.

In the UHS issue when Jonathan Masters had shifted from leading opposition (to the district's creation and the first new school vote) to active defense of the district (against the dissolution move), the leader shifted but the alleged factional followers did not. Thus the last question: the extent to which those nominated as Bennington's leaders in fact had power over one another and non-leaders alike.

D. *Leadership and Power.* In Bennington, three sorts of external evidence were available by which the researcher might seek to validate claims to power inferred from ranking influence attributions. (1) data on nominations and elections to public and private office; (2) records of public votes on issues; and (3) data on non-vote decisions.

i. *Elections to Public and Private Office.* The identification and ranking of leaders on both the general and the (other) politics lists were earlier compared. In all, seven general leaders of the total twenty-seven — each of whom had a rank of 12.5 or larger — were *not* named on the list of forty-three politics leaders. Further, when the general-*and*-politics leaders' ranks were internally compared and contrasted with the rankings on the total politics list, the relative positions of the general leadership lists seemed most nearly "correct" as measured in terms of the objective order of actual election results.

To illustrate, at the 1955 town meeting Hubert Ford (factional leader with rank 2 as a general leader and running as incumbent with Republican re-indorsement for Moderator) defeated Martin Thorndyke (a different factional leader with rank 3 as general leader and running as Democratic candidate). The vote was 1,041 to 1,030. (This, of course, is as perfect a validation of his data as the researcher can hope for.)

In all, there were ten relevant contested nominations and/or elections for public office in the period 1952–1955. In nine of these, a general leader defeated a lesser ranked general leader or another leader; or a politics leader defeated another lesser ranked politics leader. In the exceptional instance, involving the *two* party primaries as well as the general election for town representative in 1952, a general leader with rank 9 defeated a general leader with rank 4.5 in all three races for this office.[23]

Only one relevant private election contest occured in the period of study. One individual received sufficient nominations to rank him 3 as a poltics leader, but his rank as general leader was only 10.5. Respondents differed widely in their appraisal of him in Bennington Village politics, especially because some insisted he had organized the Fellowship of Eagles as a personal force, fortuitously scheduling their "chicken socials" for the night of the village caucus, thus marching his followers over *en masse.* Perhaps he had had such power; early in the period of study, however, he ran again for post of trustee of the F.O.E. and was defeated by a margin of roughly two-to-one in a total of 327 votes cast. His position as a lesser ranked general leader thus seems most appropriate.

ii. Public Votes on Issues. Correlations of policy preferences of an individual with actual outcomes in the issue(s) are probably poor measures of power because systems of partial power encourage participants to make excessive demands to gain what they are willing to settle for. Yet votes on issues provide some measure of the strength of different factions within the leadership and of the leadership more generally.

Statistics on the UHS and Consolidation issues had indicated that, for *involved* leadership, a majority of participating general leaders lost in both instances; contrariwise, a majority of other leaders won in both instances, defeating the new school vote. In addition, if those identified as leaders in these two major local issues are located by their factional memberships and analyzed according to the positions they took, then Table 6 (showing the percentage of each faction on the winning side) indicates that: (1) fewer than the total membership in any faction participated in the issues; (2) those who did participate were disunified; and (3) the three central factions were each defeated once on these issues.

This impression of partial power, of open conflict and of defeats for the general leaders and the central factions of leaders on the *most* important issues, is strengthened by Table 7. So far as leadership factions are concerned, an additional significance of Table 7 is the documentation — to paraphrase Orwell — that most leadership factions (and "groups") take the *same* position, only some take it more than others.[24] The last point of note is the position of the Thorndyke faction in the 1952 gubernatorial and presidential votes (Table 7, Items 5 and 6), for these most closely approximate the actual votes on these same two candidacies in the township. That is, in a one-party state such as Vermont, the Thorndyke faction — despite the labels of "Republican" and "Independent" borne by many of its members — is the local leadership nucleus of the Democratic Party.

Tables 6 and 7 cast an image of leaders going in where non-leaders frequently refuse to be led. Thus the last question for consideration: in what sense or senses do Bennington's leaders have power?

iii. Non-Vote Decisions. In 1954, an extensive drive was launched to build a major, three-story addition to Putnam Memorial Hospital which serves the Bennington area. The fund drive committee of fifteen included five general leaders. The first-ranked general leader (Bailey) served as chairman of

Table 6

PERCENTAGE OF EACH LEADERSHIP FACTION PARTICIPATING ON THE WINNING SIDE OF TWO MAJOR ISSUES

		Isolates	Thorndyke	Bailey-Ford	Darby-Masters	Outsiders
Issue:						
Consolidation		67%	67%	56%	33%	100%
Participating	N	3	9	7	3	4
(Total in faction)	(N)	(9)	(16)	(17)	(10)	(6)
Union High Sch.		60%	....%	20%	80%	....%
Participating	N	5	6	5	5	----
(Total in faction)	(N)	(9)	(16)	(17)	(10)	(6)

Table 7

VOTES ON CANDIDATES AND ISSUES IN 1952–1954 PERIOD, BY LEADERSHIP "GROUPS" AND FACTIONS IN BENNINGTON

Issue or Candidate	Actual Vote	Non-Leader Sample	LEADER-SHIP GROUPS: Gen.	Other	LEADERSHIP FACTIONS: Iso.	Th.	B-F	D-M	Outs.
1. Winning selectman (D)	53%	58%	70%	89%	71%	75%	73%	70%	80%
2. Hire mgr. —against	52	43	47	35	28	33	47	30	60
3. Consolid. study—for	70	76	100	71	86	100	80	70	40
4. Flood res. —for	59	72	89	69	71	87	87	60	60
5. State gov. Harding (R)	33	----	55	62	67	25	71	80	50
Olds (R)*	9	----	13	9	11	12	12	10	----
Connelly (D)	58	----	23	23	11	44	12	10	33
AO			9	6	11	18	6	----	17
6. 1952 Pres. Eisenhower (R)	67	74	77	82	78	56	100	80	50
N		713	22	36	9	16	17	10	6

*Write-in vote, 1952 general election.

the building fund campaign, as a member of the committee on corporation subscriptions, and as *ex officio* member of the committee on business subscriptions — both of the latter in line with his own business activities in the community and his acknowledged position as *the* corporate lawyer in Bennington. The second ranked general leader (Ford) was then president of the board of the hospital and served as chairman of the community relations committee. The third ranked (Thorndyke) served as chairman of the building committee. In early 1955, the fund drive was over-subscribed in its goal of $750,000.

This non-vote decision indicates again that Bennington's factional leaders could co-operate as well as compete. Furthermore, those leaders who desired or who could be induced to participate were fully cohesive. And the decision they successfully executed involved both a substantial expenditure and a significant change in ways of doing things in the community. In the terminology employed in this study, the fund-raising individuals who participated in this decision are leaders, are power-holders.

But power identified must then be specified — "over whom" and "with respect to what?" A hospital, like a political campaign, is rarely built with the mites of innumerable widows. Bennington's fund-raising leaders themselves owned or managed resources, or had access to those similarly controlling resources necessary to this decision. In this sense, they had power over themselves and their friends and co-owners to make such a "charity" decision. A very small proportion of the total community is involved in the making of such a decision. If the hospital addition were to be financed, on the other hand, through an increased levy of the local estate tax upon a far more inclusive group of participants, available evidence indicates that the "decision" would not have been made — that the leaders' power would not have been transferable at this time. For the tax rate had already risen high enough for an effective majority in Bennington.

iv. Limitations on Power. Summarizing the preceding sub-sections, the positive evidence available — on elections, policy-issue votes, and non-vote decisions — indicates: (1) that the relative rank-positions of Bennington's leaders are "correct," in that the relative amounts of power established by cumulating nominations are verifiable and verified by external evidence; (2) but also that the power-distance between these leaders and the less mighty is frequently quite short; and (3) that the power of the same leader varies both over time and between or among policy areas.

In particular, and if one focuses on the gross power differences between leaders and non-leaders on the more frequently occurring policy issues which (unlike the hospital decision) require some kind of referendum, then the conclusion of this study is that these leaders have power in two senses:

1. They can hinder (but not prevent) the bringing up of issues they consider "false" by their control of the community's newspaper and radio station, by their "availability" for serving as panelists on the many forums which take place in Bennington, and by the fact that they are the source from which moderators are chosen for any such public discussions. (These same factors equally enhance their ability positively to bring their own perceptions of issues and solutions to the attention of the public.) Thus in 1949, the leaders finally agreed to the repeated demand by dissident working-men of the community for a public discussion of the "issue" of Bennington's "economic retardation" but they agreed only on condition that the neutral Thomas Darby serve as moderator and that "personalities" (mainly the name of Joseph Bailey, see below) would be kept out of discussion.

2. And, equally interstitially, they can control the manner in which minor issues are resolved. For example, following the 1946 Federal Airport Act, Bennington built an airport with federal and state aid. The airport is a *"Fortune-*esque selling point" to the executives of FiNast, Dobekmun (of Cleveland), and other national corporations. The voters, enthusiastic at first, gradually realized that an airport, once built, must be maintained. It was expensive, perhaps even a luxury by Bennington's standards. At the business portion of the ,1954 town meeting, criticism was expressed that $132,000 had been expended already and ". . . we got stuck." Those in favor of the airport project, including especially Moderator Ford, were next in favor of having the town lease sites for hangars "for a term of not over fifteen years at a rent of one cent per square foot per year." In an atmosphere of growing criticism, therefore, it was of importance to Ford and his supporters that this article, as distinct from two other leasing proposals, be put up for the voice vote of the 200 or less voters who, under the watchful eye of the moderator, would be present at the business meeting; rather than the vote of the nearly 2,200 who normally vote on the printed ballot of the annual town meeting. This article for hangar-leases was approved by voice vote. (But the action generated its own reaction. At the 1955 town meeting, a *ballot* article requesting a $2,500 appropriation for further maintenance of the airport was defeated by 1,243 to 747; and a companion ballot article [included by citizen's petition] was approved by a vote of 1,240 to 684: ". . . the Selectmen [shall] spend no further money on the Bennington Municipal Airport unless the amount is specifically stated and approved by a majority ballot

vote. . . .") That is, when a minor issue comes to be perceived as major, the leaders lose this control.

There remains a question of negative evidence. Two critics[25] have suggested that the major scientific test for demonstrating the existence of power or leadership requires a negative demonstration, i.e., that the same policy results would *not* have obtained if the alleged power-holders did not exist, took no action, or took different action.

It is difficult to conceive of a field study achieving the degree of precision demanded. The fact that policy situations are unique, that replication is impossible, and that the control techniques of modern physical science do not obtain does not, however, mean that power does not exist; it means that in its present state the "science of politics" can only imprecisely demonstrate the existence of its subject-matter.

Questions arising out of the Kaufman-Jones critique were posed Leadership Interview respondents and the answers may be summarized as follows:

1. If those designated as leaders involved in particular issues did not exist, the same disputes would have occurred and new leaders would have evolved to speak for conflicting interests in Bennington. "Consolidation" did not exist as a goal within the mind of Hubert Ford alone, even if he did not exist, there would still have been residents living in the clusters of new homes developed on the edge of Bennington Village but not receiving the fire, water, and police services had by their relatives and friends; there still would have existed minor functionaries in town and village office whose earning capacities and prestige would be threatened by the "economies and efficiencies" of Consolidation.
2. If those designated as leaders involved in particular issues took no action, they would not have been leaders, i.e., their constituencies were still exerting preformed demands, and individuals were designated as leaders because they were acting, bcause they were informally representing group demands. Again, some Catholics wanted to achieve their goal of establishing a central Catholic High School in Bennington; some public school advocates wanted to replace the area high school, still others wanted to replace the far-older grade school building; and there remained two other, tax-conscious groups who wanted no further change in the basic tax rate or who wanted future changes to reflect different non-school services to the community.
3. If those designated as leaders involved in particular issues took different action, they would have to gain *new* constituencies to remain as leaders. When Masters shifted to defend the Union High School District against dissolution, he no longer was a hero for the tax-conscious and "senior citizens" and poorly educated in Bennington, but he did become an object of interest and support for those who had fought for the public high school all along.

The Kaufman-Jones question was posed to Leadership Interview respondents in two additional forms. First, they were asked, "Were there any others in Bennington who might have put this across?" The question was turned to a discussion of executives and managers of the nationally-owned plants in the community (none of whom had been identified as leaders). Respondents offered evidence for concluding that these managers and executives were excluded from leadership by loyalty to their national bureaucracies, the indefiniteness of their stay in Bennington, their companies' "good public relations" orientation and by community distrust of those who are newcomers, educated, and well-paid.[26] Similar conclusions (for different reasons) were reached concerning local labor leaders and the faculty and personnel of Bennington

College. There was no evidence for believing in the existence of a *potential but untapped* (or disinterested) source of leadership in Bennington. Alternatively, respondents were asked if there existed a list of people they might give the interviewer and say, "If you could interest these people you could put it — say UHS — over?" Scott, the newspaper editor, answered:

> If I could pick from anybody in town and say that they were convinced, or see that they were convinced that it was good, and say could they sell it? I think so — I think they could; however, *I don't think they'd ever all agree — it'd be too many different ideas.* [Emphasis added] Jonathan Masters is certainly one . . . and yet I can't quite imagine Jonathan agreeing with Tim Ely or myself or any number — Bayley, Seaton — any number of people. . . .

Another leader — banker, real estate developer, Democratic town chairman during the 1930's, former postmaster — and age eighty:

> Nothing's the way it used to be, seems all flattened out. . . . There's some leaders . . . but they're like ripples, there's no strong push to it. [The village president is] good and he works hard, but he don't have no organization. Schools the same, they're all so kinda flattened out that they don't have any one group that can push anything forward; it's kinda split, well, three or four ways.

This may be merely nostalgia for a simple, happier past; but this respondent suggested two apt images — "ripples" and "all flattened out" — for describing the present-day leaders and the fore-shortened power structure of Bennington. Others made similar comments; almost all seem to believe in the operation of a Gresham's law of leadership in the past two generations.

It may be that the leadership aggregate did constitute a ruling group earlier in this century. A smaller community, with more homogeneous population and doing far less governmentally, could have meant unifactionalism within the leadership aggregate. And one can designate changes — such as the increase in feminine participation in politics, or the changes in the local economy already remarked upon — which have added new or eliminated old sources of local leadership. But one can also identify changes which have occurred and which present the appearance, but not necessarily the substance, of a disintegrated leadership structure. Martin Thorndyke, for instance, commented upon the fact that up until the mid-1930's Bennington's public boards invariably met in *executive* session. Since that time, first, the newspaper and, more recently, the radio station have sought to cover all regular and special public meetings; board members are asked to provide weekly columns on "School Board Activities"; and so on. It is at least evident that a much larger portion of the community now shares information about local issues and the personalities contending in them.

In the period of study, the leadership of Bennington had "achieved" a low degree of integration. There is evidence that those with most power had least desire for such integration. For example, Tel Pelham, State's Attorney and a junior member of the Ford-Bailey firm, quoted Ford indirectly: ". . . there's still an atmosphere around here [the law offices], I know, of, well, 'We don't want to get accused of getting into too much at once,' you know, we don't want to be into too many offices . . ."

Even assuming motivation for integrated control of policy-making, there is evidence of limitation in achieving such a goal. Specifically, a ruling group would have presumably to include Ford's partner, Bailey, who was first-ranked general leader; yet respondents agreed that Joseph Bailey could no longer win election in Bennington,[27] that non-leaders distrusted him, that his personality (including ultra-conservative political opinions, documented in his response to the General Interview) precluded effective co-operation with others. Less idiosyncratically, there remain the limitations imposed by the durable causes of factionalism, as Madison long ago noted, and by the non-leader electorate, for the data point to the conclusions (1) that a capacity for winning elections is positively associated with power-holding and (2) that the norms of an effective majority oppose efforts to rationalize and centralize policy-making. (The Consolidation, the union school distrist, and the manager issues documented previously, all posed this among other issues.) Lastly, given the firm association between formal education and political participation, and also given the changing distribution of formal education since 1945, one might reasonably anticipate that in Bennington as in the society at large the numbers of, and the overt disagreements among, those designated as leaders will both grow.[28]

The Bennington Study, within its recognized limitations, indicated that no single power structure existed in the community. The data suggest that "a community" is in fact to be characterized by a multiplicity of power structures to be empirically determined among different decisional areas. For example, the monolithic, flat-surfaced pyramid, with the empirical features: a small number of power-holders, acting in pre-determined concert, and with wealth as the dominant power-base, this seems appropriate to Bennington's hospital decision but not to the other, non-charity, public policies examined. For in the latter cases the data indicate consistent central factions which compete to control necessary public offices and/or to produce desired policy outcomes, depending on the issue involved. Finally, lacking a formal governmental mechanism for co-ordination (which does exist in larger communities), we may infer from the data on office-holding that there was intent — somewhat self-limited and frequently unsuccessful — to achieve informal co-ordination through overlapping personnel and through controlled focusing of Public attention. But in the last analysis co-ordination was achieved by the non-leaders.

NOTES TO CHAPTER III

1. This study is based on materials contained in the author's *Yankeetown: A Study of Community Decision-Making Processes,* unpublished doctoral dissertation, Yale University, 1957. While "Yankeetown" has been identified as Bennington, Vermont, the fictitious identification of Bennington's residents, however, has been maintained for real and obvious reasons.

For financial assistance, the author is indebted to Yale University for a Sterling Research Fellowship and to The Bennington Communication Study, under the auspices of Columbia University. For their particular assistance in this study, the author would like to acknowledge a large debt to Professors Robert A. Dahl of Yale University, Robert D. Leigh of Columbia University, Director of The Communications Study, and Martin A. Trow, then Field Director of the study.

2. In this research, "leaders," "power-holders," "decision-makers," and "influentials" have been considered synonymously as referring to individuals able to control the actions of one or more other individuals.

3. Two pending elections — one to a Ward Trusteeship of Bennington Village and the other to Selectman of the Town — were followed. School elections were excluded because it was early determined that they were almost invariably *pro forma* ratifications of the covert recruitment by remaining board members of an "acceptable" replacement for a retiring member.

4. In the Leadership Interview, a "leader" was designated as "one who would be important in any attempt to pass or defeat a policy involving a *substantial* expenditure or a *significant* change from past ways of doing things in Bennington." (Italicized words were orally stressed.)

5. This part of the research was undertaken jointly with the Bennington Communications Study whose primary concern was the interpersonal flow of communications within the area. For this research a primary sample of 713 adult males (termed "nonleaders" hereafter in the text) was employed.

6. The Leadership Interviews were employed as a technique for nominating leaders as well as a means for gathering data on the subject of leadership. In addition, the forty-two Leadership Interview respondents included twenty-nine of those sixty-nine finally selected as the total leadership aggregate. The General Interview, administered to 713 non-leaders and to fifty-eight of the sixty-nine leaders, was employed to gather a wide range of sociological and psychological data.

7. While we cannot know with certainty, it is believed that these eleven missed interviews do not conceal the core of a ruling group, for more than half of them were not identified as leaders in either the Consolidation or the Union High School issue. Also, *if* it is reasonable to assume that a ruling group would be drawn from the *more* rather than the *less* powerful leaders in a community, and *if* the number of nominations an individual receives as leader is a measure of his power, then there is further negative evidence. For these eleven were uniformly not in the highest third rank positions according to numbers of nominations; rather they were distributed about equally in the middle and lowest thirds.

8. In the period of study, the school districts within the town were sharing approximately 57 per cent of the more than $700,000 annually collected through all *local* taxation.

9. Here, as at several points following, we select individual leaders for illustrative or comparative comment. These selections are identified by the rank-position of the individual. Rank positions were determined quantitatively (for each name on each of the four initial lists of leaders) in terms of the total number of different nominations received from two or more of the forty-two respondents participating in the Leadership Interview. Such data are necessary for attempting to answer the question: does the methodology correctly locate individuals by their relative positions within the leadership aggregate?

10. In addition to the above reasons for tentatively hypothesizing that the core of a ruling group would be found within the general leader aggregate, there was also negative evidence. That is, the question arose whether it would not be more reasonable to assume that the core of any cohesive leadership group in Bennington would be found among those individuals nominated as political leaders?

Partial comparison of the two lists would lead to an affirmative answer, in that of the top ten ranked politics leaders, nine were also separately nominated as general leaders.

However, Leadership Interview respondents tended to draw an explicit distinction between (a) general-*and*-politics leaders and, (b) *non*-general politics leaders. The latter, for example, include what has been termed, the elective civil service in Bennington's municipal government. These, plus some others, were politics leaders in their ability to get themselves elected and re-elected, perhaps even to throw electoral weight in support of certain other individuals; but respondents were almost unanimous in their judgment that these non-general politics leaders tended not to take stands on local policy issues. The nature of their offices or of their constituencies made it either irrelevant or dangerous to expose themselves by taking stands on issues other than those clearly seen as a threat to, or an enhancement of, their particular "personal" office. The Consolidation issue, with its "rationalizing" proposal for reducing the number of municipal offices, was perceived as a threat by a number of such elective bureaucrats. They took active positions in opposition to Consolidation. And they were identified as such by the Leadership Interview respondents. But such an issue is apparently relatively rare in Bennington politics; and so the respondents were in agreement that those they nominated as non-general politics leaders tended to confine their activities to the area of nominations and elections. This may be seen in the following table, which separately treats those twenty individuals nominated among *both* the twenty-seven general leaders and the forty-three politics leaders.

Consolidation and UHS Policy Issues	Nominated as General and Politics Leaders	Nominated Non-General Politics Leader Only
Named as leader in both	20%	---%
Named as leader in UHS or Consolidation only	45	30
Named as leader in neither	35	70
Number	**20**	**23**

11. See H. D. Lasswell and A. Kaplan, *Power and Society,* New Haven: Yale University Press, 1950, chapter 9, "Structures."

12. On the importance of research into such "blockage," see L. G. Seligman, "The Study of Political Leadership," *American Political Science Review,* 44 (1950), 904-915.

13. Cf. D. R. Matthews, "United States Senators and the Class Structure," *Public Opinion Quarterly,* 18 (1954), 5-22, and *The Social Backgrounds of Political Decision-Makers,* Garden City: Doubleday, 1954.

14. The nearest evidences to deliberate *attempts* to control were (1) the conscious canvassing and co-optation by remaining school board members of a new, acceptable candidate to fill a vacancy, and (2) the encouragement of candidacies of younger members by older members of Bennington law firms.

15. See S. Rice, *Quantitative Methods in Politics,* New York: Knopf, 1928, and J. Turner, *Party and Constituency: Pressures on Congress,* Baltimore: Johns Hopkins Press, 1951. The basic formula for determining the cohesion on a single vote-decision of the members of Party X is:

$$2 \left(\frac{\text{majority X}}{\text{all X voting}} \right) - 1$$

Thus, assuming that Party X had 100 members who voted 60 for and 40 against on Issue I, the index of cohesion of Party X would be 2 (60/100) — I or .20, indicating a low degree of cohesion on a scale which ranges from zero to unity.

The formula for the index of likeness, which Rice devised to determine ". . . the difference between two groups in the degree of support given to a motion," (*op. cit.,* pp. 209-211) is simply:

$$100 - (\% \text{ Group A "for"} - \% \text{ Group B "for"})$$

Index figures in the range of 80 or more (such as reported above in the text indicate a high degree of similar behavior (i.e., percentage differences of 20 or less points).

16. These had been voted on at the 1954 town meeting and were: (1) votes for Selectman; (2) vote on article authorizing employment of a town manager; (3) vote on article authorizing continued study of, and completion of, proposed draft legislation enabling consolidation of town and village governments; and (4) vote on article authorizing allocation of $10,000 to the town's flood reserve fund.

17. "Winners" were liberally defined, in that this classification also includes two of the six leaders who were involved in both issues *and* who won once and lost once. (Of the other four, involved in both issues, one won twice, two lost twice, and one was uncommitted [but involved] twice.)

18. Table 2 also indicates that the closest approximations to the cohesion-test of the existence of a ruling group employed in the text were the average indices of the "winners" and of the "seven involved politics" leaders. The "winners" initial synthetic unanimity degenerated considerably in the two additional sets of issues, but, on the more important (state-national) issues, their voting rate averaged between 75 and 80 per cent unified. So they were examined by means of the third and last test of the existence of a ruling group, the number of victories on issues. On these additional four minor local issues and two state-national issues, the "winners" were successful on pre-

cisely the same number of issues as were both the "uninvolved" and the "loser" leaders. By a synthetic test, there was no evidence of a ruling group.

The "seven involved politics" leaders were also further examined because they are characterized by voting rates of at least three-to-one on all three sets of issues.

Employing this victory-power test defined above, these leaders did *not* win more frequently or more on the more important issues than did the thirteen general leaders with whom they are contrasted. In addition, there was no evidence that these seven interacted as a group.

For example, five of these seven were among the forty-two Leadership Interview respondents; they did not identify themselves as a group. This may reflect a desire for secrecy — but no one of the remaining thirty-seven respondents (among whom, on this presumption, must have been one or more who felt disadvantaged by their secret powerful existence) identified any of them as interacting. On the General Interview data provided by these seven, they did not identify themselves as interacting as either friends, neighbors, or co-workers. They did not nominate one another as "local leader" (except for one unreciprocated choice). Again this might reflect a desire for concealment, but no one of these seven was nominated by any one of the fifty-one others in the total leadership sample.

19. On the important issues, those who were leaders expressed publicly a high degree of disagreement as to the feasibility and desirability of the proposed policy or candidate. Where leaders are unwilling or unable *privately* to compose their differences on public issues, then their announced stands and political activities constitute bids for the support of non-leaders in choosing from among competing alternatives. While we may infer biasing of what in Bennington are perceived as "issues" and "alternatives," within these limits, an overt competition for non-leader support exists.

20. See for example W. H. Form and S. Nosow, *Community in Disaster*, New York: Harpers, 1958. Cf. also J. S. Coleman, *Community Conflict*, Glencoe: The Free Press, 1957.

21. Neither leader nor non-leader samples meet the definition of randomness, therefore statistical tests of significance have been omitted for the reasons presented in S. M. Lipset, M. Trow, and J. Coleman, *Union Democracy*, Glencoe: The Free Press, 1956. (In particular, see Appendix I, "Methodological Note B, Statistical Problems.") If these were random samples, this consistent relation between the Thorndyke and Bailey-Ford factions is a result which would happen by chance less than once in a thousand times.

22. Given these two factors, it may well be that full co-optation of the new member depends finally upon personality characteristics which were beyond the range of study in Bennington.

23. This contest, between a Thorndyke member and a lesser-ranked general-leader member of the Bailey-Ford faction, was also exceptional in that it apparently was a projection into politics of a prior familial-commercial feud and in that each candidate "reported" in the Leadership Interviews that his opponent had spent in excess of $1,500 (for an office carrying a salary of $1,000) — but that he, of course, had spent "considerably less."

In addition to this defeat, this general leader with rank 4.5 also "lost," in an indirect contest for selectman in 1954, to a combination of two general leaders (with ranks 10.5 and 24.5) and of two other leaders. In this, he had backed an unsuccessful candidate who had agreed with him that one of the opposing general leaders involved should lose her job as "selectman's agent" (appointive) if the candidate were to win. By the end of 1954, however, this rank 4.5 general leader had won election and re-election as selectman and had also won election as state senator.

24. The major local exception was on the ballot article proposing the hiring of a town manager. The issue is somewhat complex. After World War II, a "two-manager" system had been adopted in Bennington. By the early 1950's, the leaders found that the successor they had selected (to the original manager) was "impossible to work with." Consequently, the general leaders in each of the three central factions publicly opposed this incumbent ("but not the system"). In 1952 they won a vote to oust him from the town-half of his job; and in 1954 they won in Bennington Village — the manager article was defeated at the regular meeting and even more decisively (seven and one-half to one) at a special village meeting to "reconsider." In Leadership Interviews, these leaders still maintained faith in the system. It may be conjectured that a

majority of actual voters failed to see this subtle distinction between the flesh-and-blood manager and the abstract manager system.

25. See H. Kaufman and V. Jones, "The Mystery of Power," *Public Administration Review,* 14 (1954), 204–212.

26. Cf. R. O. Schulze and L. U. Blumberg, "The Determination of Local Power Elites," *American Journal of Sociology,* 43 (1957), 290–296.

27. Bailey had not run for local office since the mid-1930's. In the 1940's, Bailey, a Catholic, divorced his first wife; married his present wife, in the Baptist Rectory; and later removed his residence from Bennington to a house located in an isolated valley on the outskirts of a hill town adjoining Bennington.

28. Given the tendency toward equalization of educational opportunity, personality, especially motivation, should become a more central focus of leadership studies. See H. D. Lasswell, "The Selective Effect of Personality on Political Participation," in R. Christie and M. Jahoda (eds), *Studies in the Scope and Method of "The Authoritarian Personality,"* Glencoe: The Free Press, 1954, 197–225.

Resistance to Unification
in a Metropolitan Community

BY *AMOS H. HAWLEY*

AND *BASIL G. ZIMMER*

THE RISE AND DEVELOPMENT of the metropolitan community is one of the major social trends of the twentieth century.[1] The accumulated data bear out and surpass the forecast of N.S.B. Gras concerning the replacement of the town based economy by a metropolitan economy in the western world.[2] Bogue's allocation of the entire territory and population of the United States to metropolitan areas probably is no exaggeration of the prevailing situation.[3] Virtually every collective activity in which people engage today is encompassed in the organization of a metropolitan center.

Students of metropolitanism work with two conceptions of the metropolitan community. One is cast in theoretical terms, the other is a rough operational formulation of the former. Theoretically, the metropolitan community embraces the total population, together with the area it occupies, which carries on its daily life through a common system of relationships administered from a given central city. In view of the dynamics of modern life, a unit defined in this way has no stable boundary. The boundary shifts and changes with gains and losses of transportation advantages as between neighboring central cities and with alterations of the competitive balance. Nor does the boundary often fall on the lines which divide the political units used for the reporting of official statistics. Hence, for purpose of comparative analysis and description a more manageable principle of delineation is needed, even though it may mean sacrifice of accuracy. The concept of the standard metropolitan area has been developed in the U.S. Bureau of the Census as an operational definition of the metropolitan community.[4] It denotes an aggregate of at least 1,000,000 including a central city of 50,000 or more population, and the county containing the central city, together with all contiguous counties which are economically and socially integrated with the central city.[5] The standard metropolitan area admittedly is an approximation of the metropolitan community. But its serviceability outweighs many of its descriptive defects. Even on this modest basis, the 168 standard metropolitan areas recognized in the 1950 census contained over three-fifths of the total U.S. population, though only 4.3 per cent of the land area.

The pre-eminence of the metropolitan community in the settlement pattern and organization of American society notwithstanding, it is still a somewhat disconnected and incomplete social unit. Change, in this as in so many other instances involving complex social units, has moved forward unevenly in what has seemed to be a serial or wave-like manner. For analytical purposes, it is convenient to treat change as having certain identifiable components or phases. Thus, we shall deal with metropolitan development in terms of a number of phases which may or may not occur in any necessary temporal order.

The phases may be listed in the following order: (1) the growth of a large central city on the basis of inter-regional exchanges; (2) the improvement and extension of local transportation and communication routes into the hinterland; (3) the reorientation of the hinterland population toward a closer interdependence with the central city; (4) the rapid accumulation of urban population and urban land uses in the hinterland; (5) the adaptation of social and administrative systems to the territorially expanded community.

The growth of a large city is a necessary condition for the subsequent development of a metropolitan community. For it is only a large city that can provide the array of services and opportunities required to focus attention upon a particular place. Conversely, the large city has, or is capable of developing, the instrumentalities for organizing and integrating the diverse activities scattered over a wide area. But a city attains large size primarily on the basis of a substantial export function vis-à-vis other regions. Its growth, therefore, is based on those local advantages which foster its participation in the inter-regional economy rather than on its function as a local service center. At the outset, then, the city which later becomes a metropolitan center grows more or less independently of events in the many minor civil divisions scattered about it.

But as a city grows larger it accumulates facilities for the attraction and mediation of trade and other activities in the surrounding area. It soon becomes necessary to extend and improve local roads and communication lines sufficiently to give full play to the central city's service facilities. As direct lines of access are pushed into the hinterland, the partial isolation of village and farm populations is destroyed. Freed from exclusive dependence on slow and roundabout movement over interregional routes for their contacts with the outside world, they can turn directly to a local metropolis for their daily requirements. Within the enlarged universe of daily interchange, the large city becomes a convenient point for the centralization of many functions formerly scattered widely over the area.

The developments which make possible the attachment of the occupants of an enlarged hinterland to a central city also reduce the necessity for a dense concentration of the population and industry in the central city. Accordingly, in response to the enlarged range of locational choice, urban residents and urban activities spread over the adjacent areas, first along the thoroughfares but subsequently into the interstitial zones. While the growth of urban occupancy of lands outside the central city's boundaries may begin as a centrifugal movement from the city, that growth is soon supplemented by accretion from without. Thus, what was once a relatively compact urban community contained within the municipal boundaries of a single city gives way to a diffuse community distributed over numerous locally governed areas.

The last phase in the maturation of the metropolitan community is the integration of the whole in a social and an administrative, as well as an economic, unity. This phase may be expected as an inevitable consequence of the preceding developments. Yet, although it has been taking form bit by bit here and there and always in a piecemeal fashion, it is the one uncompleted phase remaining even in the most highly developed metropolitan communities. To the extent that the several phases are separated in time, frictions develop. For the onset of one phase seems to imply the next, and if the next phase is not promptly forthcoming the effect of the preceding events is to produce imbalance, disorder, and confusion. These consequences have emerged in most acute form in connection with the delay of the last phase. The distribution of the members of an organization, i.e., the metropolitan community, over a number of semi-autonomous political or administrative units impedes, when it does not prevent, joint action in dealing with the day-to-day requirements of collective life. Moreover, it invites inequities and infringements of various kinds. Residents of one administrative area, for example, may use the facilities of another adjacent one without contributing to their maintenance, or they may so manage their affairs as to create a health hazard or other nuisances for the occupants of the adjacent area. Every administrative area is exposed to such difficulties, though the risks and the costs usually fall most heavily on the ones that have the greatest investment in public facilities and services. For this reason, the central city is especially vulnerable to the effects of dense populations residing on the periphery of its jurisdiction. On the other hand, satellite residents contribute to the wealth of the central city, but do not share in the tax revenues from industry and commerce. Consequently, locally raised revenues for services must come largely from residential properties. When industry expands in the hinterland, the tax wealth is lost to the central city but the growing population in the satelite areas places an increasingly heavy burden on the central city services, thus adding to the costs of government in the latter area.

We may view the metropolitan community that has yet to complete the final phase of its development as involved in a situation of diffused and unorganized power. Let us look upon the metropolitan community as a social system. Conceptually a social system is an organization adapted to the performance of a set of functions. Organization is the means of mobilizing and co-ordinating the power required to execute one or more functions. In large social systems, the principal parts are sub-systems each of which is also an organization of power for the conduct of a more or less specialized function. But the sub-system derives its power from two sources: from its own organization and from the parent system in which it is supported. A community is in effect a sub-system set within the larger systems represented by the state and the nation. It is, of course, an organization which engages in certain functions and presumably it has the power required for the purpose. It has the power, that is, to operate systematically in the production and distribution of goods and services of all kinds. But it also possesses a degree of administrative autonomy within a prescribed territory by virtue of power delegated to it by the state government.

Now it should be apparent that the emergence of the metropolitan community imposes an organization upon a constellation of territorial units (cities, villages, townships, school districts) each of which derives certain powers directly from an outside or non-local source, i.e., the state. The one basis of power is not, therefore, co-ordinate with the other. So long as that disparity obtains, the metropolitan community cannot operate in a coherent or effective manner.

Metropolitan communities throughout the nation are confronted with this situation of divided and incompletely organized power. Although the problems resulting from the lack of integration are most serious in the large communities, they are encountered in some degree in virtually all sizes of metropolitan communities. Efforts to accomplish the political or administrative unifications have met with almost uniform failure. A deep pessimism that full integration will ever be achieved has settled upon most responsible observers of metropolitan phenomena.[6] Consequently, attention has shifted to the devising of partial and expedient resolutions of the anomaly.

The problem, then is: What are the roots of the resistance to the establishment of a single municipal government over the entire metropolitan community? What factors make for the persistence of an obsolescent governmental structure? It is unlikely that there is a simple answer to the questions. The explanation of any aspect or circumstance in a social system as complex as the modern metropolitan community must certainly involve manifold "causes." The best that can be done in the present state of knowledge is to advance a number of propositions as a means of isolating the possible "causes." Some combination of the several propositions may constitute the explanation of the failure of governmental unification to take place.

First, assuming that the metropolitan community has actually developed a unity in all respects except for its governmental organization, it may be that the frictions and unmet needs resulting from administrative disunity have not advanced far enough to have made action looking to a solution seem necessary. If this proposition is not supported in fact, there is the possibility that ameliorative action is prevented by a lack of consensus among residents as to the proper course action should take. That division of opinion may arise from social class cleavages. Or it may result from unwillingness on the part of substantial numbers of residents to pay the increased taxes improved service would require. It is also possible that there is a deep suspicion of the competence and the responsibility of centralized government. Finally, the knowledge of government and of what to expect from it may be so deficient that residents are really unable to act intelligently in the resolution of their problem.

These propositions will be examined with data pertaining to the metropolitan area of Flint, Michigan. Since a study of an individual metropolitan area is hardly adequate as a basis for generalizations concerning all such areas, no satisfactory test of the hypothesis can be realized. An analysis of their application to a specific case, however, will illuminate the situation in Flint and should be suggestive of guidelines for later research involving the population of metropolitan areas.

The following discussion draws freely on the accumulated works of Research Fellows and the teaching staff who have been participants over the past twelve years in the Metropolitan Community Seminar of the University of Michigan. The latter part of the discussion deals intensively with the contemporary situation. As will become evident, data for this part of the report have been obtained from a series of field surveys based on probability samples of residents in the area. Unfortunately, the boundary of the area is not constant throughout the report. It has been adapted to the requirements of various research undertakings.

Metropolitan Emergence

The manufacture of vehicles has been the main economic base of the city of Flint since the 1880's. On the strength of its national leadership in the production of carriages, Flint by 1900 had attained a population size of 13,103. Its industrial organization, skilled labor force, accumulated capital, and transportation access to the principal markets facilitated the transition to automobile production in the years immediately following 1900. The Buick Motor Company was founded in Flint, in 1906, and two years later the General Motors Corporation was organized there. Flint's population rose to 38,550 during the first decade of the century, to 91,599 by the end of the second decade, and to 156,492 by 1930. The period of dramatic population increase ended in 1930. Thereafter growth was erratic and relatively slow. We shall return to the matter of population increase in a later connection. The first event of major consequence so far as metropolitan development is concerned was the rapid growth of the city.

Just as Flint's growth was based on the rise of the automobile industry, the automobile in turn revolutionized the pattern of local life in and around Flint. Whereas at the turn of the century Flint, as a prosperous small city, existed more or less independently of its hinterland, the motor vehicle converted it into the functional center of an expanding metropolitan community. That effect was not immediate, however. Adapted at first primarily to intracity use, the automobile had to await the development and surfacing of rural roads before its potentialities as an agent for change could be realized.

The impact of efficient highway transportation on outlying settlements is illustrated by the case of Linden, a village situated on the extreme southern edge of Genesee County in which Flint is located.[7] A farm service and shipping center in 1900, Linden was linked to Pontiac and Detroit by the railroad. It had infrequent exchange with Flint, which was but 17 crow-flight miles to the north. A round trip to Flint by passenger train, via Holly or Durand at which a change of trains was necessary, required a full day. Freight shipments from Flint seldom consumed less than two days. Accordingly, only one business establishment of some forty or more in Linden drew its supplies from Flint wholesalers. The village served as a link between the national economy and the farms scattered over an area within a team-haul distance of the village. Hence the tempo of local life varied with the weekly and seasonal rhythms of farm activities.

With the coming of the improved roads and the motor vehicle, Linden was brought within less than an hour's travel time of Flint. As a result the village underwent a profound reorientation and transformation of its economy. Farmers were no longer dependent on the produce marketing agencies in

Linden. They could deliver farm products with their own vehicles to buyers in Flint and on the same trip shop for their consumer needs in a much larger retail market than a village could offer. Linden declined as a farm trade center. As this was taking place the residents of the village were also responding to the new accessibility of Flint. Daily newspapers published in the larger city began to circulate in Linden. Retail merchants turned to Flint for their wholesale purchases. Even more important, Linden workers were absorbed into the Flint labor force. In 1900 employment in Flint on the part of Linden residents was impossible without a change of residence. But in 1930 twenty-nine workers, 14 per cent of the gainfully employed, commuted daily to Flint by motor vehicle. That proportion increased to 46 per cent by 1950.

Thus Linden was drawn into and made a part of an enlarged community having Flint as its service and administrative center. In the process, the village has become a suburban residence for the families of workers employed in the industries of the metropolitan center. The experience of Linden was repeated, with local variations in the time of beginning and the rate of transition, in virtually all of the village centers scattered over the country.

The consequences of the perfection of the motor vehicle, on the one hand, and the improvement of roads, on the other hand, are nowhere so clearly manifested as in the differential rates of population growth in the Flint standard metropolitan area. An inspection of Table 1 reveals that in the decade 1900–10 the population of the city of Flint increased by almost 200 per cent. Apparently that growth occurred at the expense of the remainder of Genesee County, for in all distance zones surrounding Flint there were net

Table 1

PER CENT CHANGE OF POPULATION IN THE FLINT AND
IN COMPARABLE STANDARD METROPOLITAN AREAS, BY
DISTANCE ZONES AND BY DECADES, 1900–1950

Type of Place	FLINT STANDARD METROPOLITAN AREA				
	1940–50	1930–40	1920–30	1910–20	1900–10
Total Area	18.9	7.7	68.4	94.7	54.4
Central City	7.7	−3.2	70.8	137.6	194.2
Satellite Area	32.2	28.2	41.7	17.2	−6.3
0- 5 Miles	55.0	57.7	112.8	131.9	−8.4
5-10 Miles	43.2	40.2	74.3	47.9	−7.9
10-15 Miles	22.7	26.0	34.6	0.0	−13.1
15-20 Miles	37.7	23.1	19.7	5.2	−5.9
	COMPARABLE STANDARD METROPOLITAN AREAS				
Total	17.5	4.6	25.2	30.4	24.5
Central Cities	7.6	0.8	31.5	43.8	38.0
Satellite Areas	29.4	9.3	19.0	19.5	15.0
0- 5 Miles	43.3	12.7	25.1	38.5	25.6
5-10 Miles	38.8	14.7	27.0	21.4	15.6
10-15 Miles	19.3	5.4	19.5	16.1	14.0
15-20 Miles	18.0	6.5	3.0	11.0	10.3

population losses during that decade. In the next ten years, 1910–20, the growth of Flint's population subsided to 137 per cent, a rate which was almost matched by the rapid upsurge of population in the area within five miles of the central city. Population losses in the remainder of the county ended with 1910, though little or no growth occurred beyond 10 miles from Flint until after the passage of another decade. In 1920–30 Flint's growth rate fell below that of both the 0–5 mile and 5–10 mile zones. Substantial increases also occurred in areas beyond 10 miles from the city's center. Since 1930, population growth has been concentrated in the satellite area, i.e., the part of Genesee County lying outside of Flint.

A comparison of population growth trends in Flint and environs with those of all metropolitan areas whose central cities were comparable in size and in percentage of manufacturing employment, shown in the lower panel of Table 1, suggests that what happened in the Flint area, from 1900 to 1940, was but an extreme manifestation of what in fact has been a general tendency. Central cities at first grew rapidly and then more and more slowly. Satellite area population, on the other hand, has grown at rates which, relative to those of central cties, have increased rapidly from decade to decade. In the last decade, however, the pattern of growth rates in the Flint area shows a close resemblance to the average pattern for similar metropolitan areas.

The changing distribution of population in the locality resulting from the different growth rates is set forth in Table 2. Flint's proportion of the total increased from one-third to three-quarters from 1900 to 1930. In the meantime the proportion in the fringe, following an early decline, increased slowly and the fraction contained in the remainder of the county declined drastically. But after 1930, the trend was reversed. The central city's share of the total contracted, while the proportions in the outlying areas increased.

Table 2

PER CENT DISTRIBUTION OF POPULATION IN GENESEE
COUNTY, BY TYPE OF PLACE FOR CENSUS YEARS,
1900–1950

Census Year	Flint	Fringe Area[a]	Remainder of County	Total
1900	31.4	12.0	56.6	100.0
1910	59.7	7.2	33.1	100.0
1920	73.0	9.0	18.0	100.0
1930	74.0	11.0	15.0	100.0
1940	66.5	16.2	17.3	100.0
1950	60.2	21.2	18.6	100.0

a Includes Flint, Burton, Genesee, and Mt. Morris Townships, and the city of Mt. Morris.

If the date at which population growth rates in the outlying area equal or exceed the rate of the central city marks the inception of metropolitan status, then it appears that Flint and its surrounding area emerged as a metropolitan community around 1930. More than likely that event occurred in the latter part of the preceding decade. The centrifugal growth of population became a prominent feature of the developing settlement pattern approximately ten years after the road surfacing program was launched.

Manufacturing industry has also undergone a relative redistribution roughly similar to that observed in population. The great growth of industry in Flint, as measured by the number of plants, the number of workers employed, and the value added by manufacture, took place in the first two decades of the present century. Comparatively slight changes occurred during the next twenty years. But industrial expansion in Flint accelerated once more after 1939. During the early phase of industrial growth in Flint, manufacturing declined in the remainder of the county in all respects but the value added by manufacture. The latter increased by over 200 per cent between 1899 and 1919. The number of manufacturing workers in the outlying area increased after 1919, as did the number of establishments after 1929. Extraordinary increases followed 1939. These trends are shown in Table 3.

Comparisons of trends based on per cent changes, such as those in Table 3, may conceal important differences, however. In fact, manufacturing establishments in Flint are many times larger than those located in the county. The average numbers of workers per establishment were 356 and 15, respectively in 1947. The corresponding figures for average value added per establishment were 2,249 millions of dollars and 76 millions of dollars. Thus the expansion of industry in the county has involved, with one or two notable exceptions, a multiplication of small plants. Nevertheless, the trend toward deconcentration of industry will doubtlessly continue. For the greater abundance of space, the scattering of population, and the ease of transportation and communication constitute an attractive invitation to locate industry in the county. Evidence of this for more recent years is to be found in the distribution of General Motors workers in the area. These workers account for more than 90 per cent of the industrial employment. In 1950, 92 per cent worked in the city of Flint; however, by 1955, this had decreased to 75 per cent, and in 1957, only 67 per cent of the General Motors workers held jobs in the city. Conversely, the proportion of General Motors workers holding jobs outside of the central city increased from 8 per cent to 33 per cent during the seven year period.

The growth of both population and of industry in the hinterlands of Flint are indicative of a large-scale invasion of rural lands by urban uses. More

Table 3

PER CENT CHANGE OF MANUFACTURING INDUSTRY,
1899–1947

Census Year	Establishments		Wage Workers		Value Added	
	Flint	Remainder	Flint	Remainder	Flint	Remainder
1899	—	—	—	—	—	—
1909	65.0	—	261.6	—	418.0	—
1919	2.9	−50.0[a]	247.1	−11.4[a]	914.6	202.9[a]
1929	1.0	−36.3	28.8	13.9	37.2	51.0
1939	.9	7.1	3.3	12.8	−6.2	10.6
1947	20.1	176.7	42.6	237.3	140.3	301.3
1954	22.9	50.6	9.7	934.9	—[b]	—[b]

[a] Change from 1899 to 1919.
[b] Value added not reported and cannot be estimated.

than one-fourth of the 400,000 acres of farm land reported in the Census of 1900 had been converted to urban uses by 1950. The process began slowly in the first decade of the century, gradually accelerated in the next decade, and reached a crescendo in 1920–30, when some 75,000 acres passed from farm to urban uses. A large part of that was annexed to the city of Flint, but much of it was removed from farm use for suburban residential development. In the depression years of the 1930's, the trend was reversed and 1200 new farms were created. Virtually all of the new farms, however, were farms only by courtesy of census definition, for their average size was less than 13 acres. Apparently many urban workers living outside of the central city planted their small acreages in garden crops to supplement curtailed wages and salaries. In any event, the possession of farm lands by urban activities was resumed after 1940. And by 1950 farm acreage had reached a new low figure of 293,000, despite the use by the Bureau of the Census of a more liberal definition of a farm.

The projection of Flint's influence over the surrounding area brought all of Genesee County and parts of the counties adjoining it on the east, north, and west within Flint's trade area. Figure 1 shows the boundary of the area within which Flint department store sales, women's apparel store sales, and

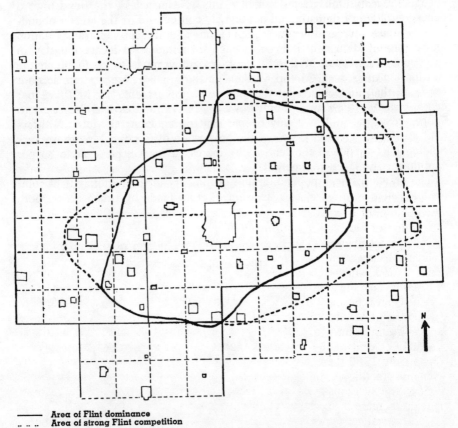

——— Area of Flint dominance
.. .. .. Area of strong Flint competition

Figure 1. Service Area of Flint, Michigan

newspaper circulation predominate over those of competing centers, that is, Detroit, Grand Rapids, Lansing, Saginaw, and Port Huron.[8] The area is that in which the resident population daily turns to Flint for its principal retail services, its recreation and entertainment, and much of its employment. Approximately the same area of influence as that shown in Figure 1 was obtained in an analysis of 1953 traffic flow data.[9] This involved plotting traffic gradients along trunkline thoroughfares and linking their low points with straight lines.[10]

The growth of dependence on Flint of the population scattered over the remainder of the county is also manifested in the change of the place in which children are born. As late as 1930, 72 per cent of all registered births to satellite area residents were delivered in homes and nearby places, the remaining 28 per cent presumably occurring in hospitals in Flint. The proportion of all births to satellite residents which were delivered in Flint increased rapidly during the next two decades. And in 1950, slightly over 92 per cent of all expectant mothers whose homes were in the satellite area elected to have their babies delivered in Flint.

What are the consequences of the expansion of the community for its central core? An analysis of vehicular traffic flow on an average week-day in 1950 reveals a fairly regular decline in the frequency of trips to the central business district originating in successive distance zones.[11]

There are several other indications that the general trend toward a more open type of settlement is taking its toll of the central business district of Flint. Between 1948 and 1954, the number of retail stores in the central business district declined 6 per cent (30 stores), while in the remainder of the city, the number increased 13 per cent (165 stores).[12] During the same period, the gross amounts of retail sales increased 36 per cent in the central business district and 110 per cent in the remainder of the city. Although these changes occurred in virtually all categories of retailing, they were most pronounced in those types which require large amounts of space, such as building supplies, automobiles, motion picture theaters, and gasoline sales. The change, incidentally, seems to have occurred primarily from failures or other terminations of business activity in the central business district and the creation of new establishments in the outer area rather than through the relocation of old retail establishments.[13] The outward drift of retailing, however, has not reached beyond the city's boundaries to any great degree. Retail establishments in the remainder of the county declined 6 per cent in the same period, while sales increased 70 per cent. The latter figure may presage a greater movement in the near future.

The central business district has also lost some of its value as a location for the offices of certain types of professional workers. Physicians and surgeons are a case in point. In 1940, about 31 per cent of the general practitioners and 74 per cent of the specialists maintained offices in the central business district; by 1950 these proportions had declined to 12 and 64, respectively. General practitioners appear to have scattered more widely than have specialists and surgeons. This shift, incidentally, has occurred in spite of a significant increase in specialization of medical practice in Flint.

Centrifugal movements such as those described may underlie the shift of property values that seems to have been taking place. Assessed valuation of property in the central business district appears to have followed an erratic course since 1930; the net effect of this has been to produce a decline. On the other hand, the remainder of the city, after recovering from reduced assessments during the depression years, has gained assessed valuation rapidly.[14] Some of the difference in the two trends may be attributable to assessment procedures which favor the tax position of the central business district. A general reassessment of central business district property, in 1956, lends plausibility to that inference. In any event, the outer parts of the city have been gaining an increasing share of the total tax burden.

Despite the significant enlargement of the scope of the Flint community to metropolitan proportions that has occurred since 1900, only minor changes in the territorial distribution of local government power have been effected. A series of annexations of township lands to Flint, between 1901 and 1919, increased the size of the central city from 6.3 square miles to 16.7 square miles. The last and most substantial annexation was accomplished in 1920, increasing the city's scope to 29.4 square miles. Except for the losses through annexation in the central city, the townships in Genesee County have remained unchanged since 1900. The greatest change has occurred in the boundaries of school districts. Numerous consolidations reduced the number of school districts in the county from 137, in 1920, to 36, at present. All of the consolidations, however, have taken place outside of the four townships immediately adjacent to the central city. The sixteen school districts within those four townships today were present in essentially the same form in 1900. Other minor changes have appeared as two small special service districts for water supply purposes. This chaotic political and administrative situation persists with a vigor that is hardly affected by the expansion of the community.

In recapitulation, it seems that metropolitan development in the Flint area has followed the proposed sequence fairly closely. Rapid population growth began in the middle of the first decade of the present century and continued to about 1930. The improvement and extension of local transportation routes was inaugurated some ten years after the onset of rapid central city growth and was brought to its present state in 1934. The orientation of activities in the outlying area to Flint began with, and followed upon, the improvements of roads, moved ahead rapidly during the 1930's, and has continued down to the present. Although population growth in the outer area accelerated in the 1910–20 decade, not until the 1930–40 decade did population increase in the whole of the Standard Metropolitan Area outside of the central city exceed that within the central city. The diffusion of industry from the central city began between 1929 and 1939, but moved ahead most rapidly after 1947. There is no doubt that the population and activities in the city of Flint and in the surrounding area to a distance of some 15 or 20 miles have become integrated in a single functional entity. But the political sub-division of the territory involved has remained virtually as it was in 1900. The last stage in the sequence, political and administrative unification, has not taken place. It is the failure of this last stage to develop that we wish to emphasize. Before doing so, however, let us examine the growth of the outlying area as a residential site and the character of its appeal to residents.

To this point we have dealt with the metropolitan community in its broad aspects. The discussion to follow will focus on the densely settled area immediately adjacent to the central city, the so-called fringe area. In this zone, which includes virtually all of the territory in the four townships adjoining the city of Flint, the effects of metropolitan development are most pronounced and therefore most acutely felt. The fringe area, because of its compactness and ready accessibility, offers a convenient opportunity to observe many of the concomitants of metropolitanism. Presumably, what is found there will obtain in diminishing degree with increasing distances from the central city.

Residential Movements

The differential rates of population growth described in the preceding section indicate that, in the early decades of the present century, Flint grew at the expense of its outlying area while in later decades the reverse was true. Unfortunately, no data are available on population exchange between central city and outlying area for the entire period from 1900 to 1950. But it is possible to analyze the sources of population change for the years from 1930 to 1950.

As it may be noted in Table 4, Flint experienced a net loss of over 4,900 people during the decade of the 1930's. That loss resulted from a net loss through migration of 28,486 people and an excess of births over deaths amounting to 23,537. As many as half of those who left the central city may have moved but a short distance to the outlying area, for that part of the metropolitan area gained 14,730 through migration. In the 1940 to 1950 decade Flint again shows a substantial migration deficit, though natural increase was more than sufficient to compensate for the loss. At the same time migrants brought an addition of 15,559 people to the outlying area. Unfortunately, there is no way of knowing where the people who left Flint actually went or from where the migrants came who contributed to the growth of the outlying area.

Three other sources of information are at hand which throw more direct light on local population shifts. These are a special tabulation of the 1935–40 migration data collected by the Census Bureau and two sample surveys by the Social Science Research Project of the University of Michigan, one conducted in 1948 and the other in 1955[15]

The population movements described in Table 5 display a pronounced

Table 4

POPULATION CHANGE BY TYPE OF CHANGE, 1930–1950

Place and Decade	Total Increase	Excess of Births over Deaths	Net Migration
Flint			
1930-40	−4,949	23.537	−28,486
1940-50	11,600	24,678	−13,078
Remainder of Genesee County			
1930-40	21,252	6,522	14,730
1940-50	31,419	15,860	15,559

Table 5

PER CENT OF RESIDENTS OF FLINT AND SATELLITE AREA, BY MIGRANT STATUS, AS REPORTED IN THREE SEPARATE SURVEYS

Migrant Status	Total	Central City	Satellite Area
	Census 1935–40[a]		
Total Per Cent	100.00	100.0	100.0
Local Migrant[b]	7.9	.9	27.9
Non-migrant[b]	92.1	99.1	72.1
	Sample Survey, 1948[c]		
Total Per Cent	100.00	100.0	100.0
Local Migrant	15.0	8.8	42.3
Non-migrant	85.0	91.2	57.7
	Sample Survey, 1955[d]		
Total Per Cent	100.00	100.0	100.0
Local Migrant	31.4	19.8	77.4
Non-migrant	68.6	80.2	22.6

[a] Amos H. Hawley, op. cit., includes all of Genesee County.
[b] Local migrant is a resident who changed his place of residence from central city to satellite area or from satellite area to central city. A non-migrant is a resident who has not made such a change.
[c] Betty Tableman, **Intra-Community Migration in the Flint Metropolitan District,** Social Science Research Project Reporte, 1948. Includes Metropolitan District of 1940.
[d] Includes Urbanized Area, 1950 Census definition.

centrifugal pattern. In the 1935–40 data, over one-fourth of the satellite area residents had moved from the central city, while less than 1 per cent of the population in the latter place had lived elsewhere in Genesee County, five years earlier.[16] In the 1948 survey, the number whose last move was outward from the central city amounted to more than two-fifths of the fringe area residents.[17] The larger number is partly due to the use of a more restricted definition of fringe area. This however, does not account for the substantially larger percentage of central city residents who had formerly lived outside it. And in the 1955 survey, which dealt with a slightly smaller area than the 1948 survey, three-fourths of the fringe area residents had moved there from the central city and about one-fifth of the central city residents had moved from the immediately adjacent area.[18] Despite the lack of complete comparability among these findings it seems very probable that the local movements during the past two decades have contributed heavily to the rapid accumulation of population in the fringe.[19]

A change of residence from one section of the metropolitan area to the other seems to be the result of a decision based on familiarity with the whole area. For over 90 per cent of the household heads who moved into the central city and over 80 per cent of those who moved out from the central city were either born in Genesee County or had lived there at least ten years (Table 6).

To the extent that the central city and the satellite area are different kinds of places it is reasonable to expect that residence changes would reveal that difference in the types of people involved. As a rule, the populations residing in the satellite zones of the metropolitan areas are younger, more highly educated, more frequently employed in white collar occupations, and have larger numbers as members of complete families than the population of the central cities. It cannot be determined from published census data, however, whether the differences in characteristics are due to selectivity of local movements or to some other kind of selection. Fortunately, we have other information for the Flint area which enables us to examine the effects of local residence change on population composition.

Table 6

PER CENT DISTRIBUTION OF HOUSEHOLD HEADS BY
YEARS OF RESIDENCE IN COUNTY AND PLACE OF
PREVIOUS RESIDENCE, 1955 SAMPLE SURVEY

	CENTRAL CITY			SATELLITE AREA		
Years Lived in Genesee County	All Residents	Former Residents of Satellite Area	Other Residents	All Residents	Former Residents of Central City	Other Residents
Total	100.0	100.0	100.0	100.0	100.0	100.0
2 years or less	8.5	1.5	10.3	6.0	2.5	18.6
2-5 years	4.8	3.0	5.3	6.3	6.2	7.1
5-10 years	7.9	3.0	9.3	12.6	10.3	20.0
10 years or more	60.9	71.6	58.4	52.1	58.8	28.6
Born in county	17.3	19.4	16.4	22.7	21.8	25.7
No answer	.6	1.5	.3	.3	.4	—

In the residence changes across central city boundaries which took place from 1935 to 1940, the fringe area gained disproportionate numbers of persons 25 to 45 years of age, who were married and had children, were engaged in skilled and semi-skilled manual occupations, and had 1 to 4 years of high school education. The central city incurred losses in all categories of its population. But the losses were smallest among persons aged 15 to 25 and 45 years of age and over, unmarried and female, in white collar occupations and with 1 to 4 years of college education.[20] Thus it appears that the 1935–40 resident relocations were working significant changes in the populations of both the central city and the fringe area.

The evidence of selectivity found in the 1955 sample survey parallel those found in the 1935–40 census data in a number of respects. As may be noted in Table 7, household heads residing in the fringe area are younger than those who live in the central city. But those who have moved into the central city are more highly concentrated in ages under 45 years than are central city residents who have not formerly lived in the fringe area. Conversely, household heads who left the central city for settlement in the fringe were more numerous in the ages of 45 years and over than were fringe residents who had not so moved. The general effect of the peculiar selectivity operating in the two streams of movement appears to be that of reducing the differences in ages and occupations of household heads as between the central city and the fringe area.

Table 7

PER CENT DISTRIBUTION OF HOUSEHOLD HEADS BY CHARACTERISTICS AND BY PLACE OF RESIDENCE AND PLACE OF PREVIOUS RESIDENCE

| | CITY OF FLINT | | | SATELLITE AREA | | |
Characteristics of Head of Household	All Residents	Lived in Satellite Area	Other Residents	All Residents	Lived in Central City	Other Residents
Age	100.0	100.0	100.0	100.0	100.0	100.0
Under 45 yrs.	49.9	55.2	48.1	55.0	52.6	62.9
45 yrs. and over	50.1	44.8	51.9	45.5	46.9	37.1
No answer				.5	.5	
Education	100.0	100.0	100.0	100.0	100.0	100.0
8 yrs. or less	30.8	26.9	32.0	34.2	34.6	32.8
9-12 yrs.	51.6	59.7	49.5	59.0	59.2	58.6
13 yrs. or more	16.4	11.9	17.4	5.8	5.8	5.7
No answer	1.2	1.5	1.1	1.0	.4	2.9
Occupation	100.0	100.0	100.0	100.0	100.0	100.0
Manual	58.7	62.7	58.4	70.9	70.4	64.3
White Collar	26.7	23.9	27.0	22.0	21.0	25.7
Other and no answer	14.6	13.4	14.6	7.1	8.6	10.0
Size of Household	100.0	100.0	100.0	100.0	100.0	100.0
2 persons or less	30.3	34.4	30.2	24.9	25.9	21.4
3-4 persons	50.4	44.7	50.6	46.6	47.3	43.4
5 persons and over	19.3	20.7	19.2	28.4	26.8	34.2
Composition of Household	100.0	100.0	100.0	100.0	100.0	100.0
Children under 17 yrs. of age	50.1	53.7	48.0	62.3	59.7	71.4
Children all 17 yrs. and over	11.3	7.5	12.5	11.5	13.2	5.7
Without children	30.0	29.9	30.9	23.3	24.7	18.6
Single persons	8.5	8.9	8.5	2.9	2.5	4.3

Residents of Flint, according to Table 7, are more highly educated than are residents in the fringe area, that is, the central city has a larger proportion of its household heads with 13 or more years of school completed and a smaller proportion with less than 9 years of education than has the outlying zone. This finding is consistent with differences reported in the 1950 census. Movement into Flint from the fringe zone appears to involve disproportionate numbers of household heads with 9 to 12 years of education. No evidence of educational selectivity is apparent in the outward movement from the central city. Relocations of residents in both directions involve manual workers primarily, though to a larger extent in the movement from central city to fringe.

The households of central city residents tend to be smaller than those of fringe residents. In the relocations of residences the central city has gained 1 and 2 person households primarily, while fringe area gains have been concentrated principally in 3 to 4 person households. But a larger proportion of the households that have moved into Flint have children under 17 years of age than characterizes the remainder of Flint's households. Conversely, the households that have moved to the fringe have included a smaller proportion with school-aged children than is found in other fringe households. Larger than expected proportions of households, the children in which are 17 years of age and older, and of childless households, appear in the movement from central city to fringe area. This finding appears to differ from the evidence in the 1948 survey that the outlying area exerted a special attraction on families which had existed as such for 6 to 18 years.[21] On the other hand, the situation in 1948 may have been only a stage in a trend toward an increasing age of families drawn to the fringe zone.

Another kind of evidence pertaining to the relative attractiveness of the central city and the fringe for residents is the reasons given for the relocation of residence. Reasons are subject, however, to several kinds of error, notably error due to failure of memory and error due to stating one when actually two or more reasons may have led to a residence change. Be that as it may, Table 8 states and compares the frequencies with which various reasons were given in 1948 and 1955. It will be observed that in both years more than half of the household heads who had moved their families to the fringe area reported their reasons as either the attractiveness of land and housing or the greater space and privacy obtainable. But in the intervening seven years, greater space and privacy became almost three times as important as it was in 1948. Unsolicited comments on taxes were seldom offered. Only 4 per cent of the 1955 respondents mentioned lower taxes as a reason for moving to the fringe. In the 1948 survey 24 per cent responding to a special question on taxes admitted that the prospect of securing lower taxes was an important secondary reason for leaving the central city.[22] The 1955 data revealed no significant differences in reasons offered by different age groups. Household heads with ten years or more of education were considerably less influenced by real or assumed tax differences and much more eager to escape the noise, dirt and safety hazards of the central city than were heads with less than 10 years of education. Greater space and privacy had the strongest appeal for households with school-age children, while the physical attractiveness of land and housing and lower taxes were most important for the household heads whose children were over 17 years of age.

Of the reasons given for moving to the central city from the fringe area dissatisfaction with fringe housing ranked high in both 1948 and 1955. Inconvenience of location was more than twice as important in 1948 than in 1955. Interestingly enough, fewer than 10 per cent in each year claimed to have left the fringe area because of unsatisfactory public service. An additional 7 per cent gave unsatisfactory public transportation as a reason in 1955, however. The inaccessability and poor quality of services were most influential on household heads under 45 years of age, with 10 years or more of education and with school-age children; in other words, the type of people most inclined to desert the fringe for the central city.

Still another way of observing the comparative attractiveness of the central city and the fringe is through the advantages and disadvantages of living in each place as judged by residents of the alternate place. To residents of the central city the most attractive feature of the fringe area is the greater space and privacy to be had there, as may be seen in Table 9. No difference in that respect exists as between former residents of the fringe and other central

Table 8

PER CENT DISTRIBUTION OF REASONS GIVEN FOR
RESIDENTIAL CHANGES IN THE 1948 AND
1955 SAMPLE SURVEYS

Reasons Given by Head of Household	MOVEMENT OUT OF CENTRAL CITY 1955 Survey	1948 Survey
Total	100.0	100.0
Land and housing attractive	22.4	42.0
Greater space and privacy	30.3	13.0
City noisy, dirty and unsafe	7.1	10.1
Lower taxes	4.1	-----
To be with friends and relatives	4.9	-----
Other	28.7	34.9
No answer	2.5	-----
	MOVEMENT INTO CENTRAL CITY	
Total	100.0	100.0
Housing unsatisfactory	23.5	32.3
Public services unsatisfactory	8.8	9.7
Public transporation unsatisfactory	7.4	-----
Location inconvenient	14.7	32.7
Work related reasons	11.8	12.8
Other	30.9	12.9
No answer	2.9	-----

Table 9

PER CENT DISTRIBUTION OF ADVANTAGES AND
DISADVANTAGES OF LIVING IN FRINGE AREA AS REPORTED
BY CENTRAL CITY RESIDENTS, 1955 SAMPLE SURVEY

Advantages and Disadvantages	Total	Former Residents of Fringe Area	Other Residents
Advantages	100.0	100.0	100.0
Quiet, cleanliness and safety	19.3	26.5	17.5
Greater space and privacy	34.0	32.4	34.3
Lower 'taxes	3.7	2.9	3.9
Room for animals and garden	5.5	5.9	5.4
No advantages	20.9	17.6	21.8
Other and no answer	16.6	14.7	17.1
Disadvantages	100.0	100.0	100.0
Inadequate public utilities	11.5	19.1	9.6
Inadequate fire and police protection	4.3	4.4	4.3
Poor roads	4.9	5.9	4.6
Inadequate public transporation	25.0	19.1	26.4
Inaccessible and inconvenient	33.0	33.8	32.9
No disadvantages	8.0	4.4	8.9
Other and no answer	13.3	13.3	13.3

city residents. Those who have once lived in the out-lying zone, however, see
its quietness, its cleanliness, and its safety as much more important advantages than does the remainder of the central city population. It is also to be
noted, though the percentages are small, that central city residents are most

impressed by the lower taxes levied in the fringe area. And, finally, fewer of the previous residents of the fringe area report no "advantages" for their area of former residence. In short, household heads who moved from the fringe are not unaware of the advantages they sacrificed in changing their place of residence.

Central city residents view the inaccessibility and inconvenience of living in the fringe as its biggest disadvantage. Those who have experienced living conditions in the fringe zone emphasize its inadequate public utilities much more frequently than do other central city residents. Many more of the latter group, on the other hand, regard the lack of adequate public transportation in the fringe area as its main disadvantage than of those who have lived there. By and large former residents of the satellite area are most critical of the out-lying area.

Turning to the appraisals that fringe area residents make of the central city, shown in Table 10, one-fifth agree that the chief advantage is the central city's public uitilities, that is, sewer, water, street lighting, etc. One-fifth of those who once lived in the central city — twice as many as those who have not — cite the transportation system as the important advantage of the city. A relatively small percentage of that group are impressed with the convenience of living in the central city. But over one-fourth can think of no advantage of the central city over the satellite area.

The principal disadvantages of the central city in the estimation of fringe area residents are the insufficient space and privacy it affords and its noise, dirt, and traffic hazards. Two-thirds of all responses are concentrated on these two features of central city living conditions. Household heads who formerly lived in Flint stress these conditions more frequently than do those who have never lived in the central city. The only other disadvantage mentioned, the higher cost of living, drew less than 10 per cent of the replies.

The inquiry into advantages and disadvantages pertained to the fringe area and to the central city in general. Both of the two segments of the metropolitan area, however, are heterogenous in physical composition, in population, and in other respects. Hence, opinions that apply to one or the other as a whole may not apply to the particular neighborhoods of residence. Accordingly, further questions were asked concerning things liked and disliked about the immediate neighborhood, the results of which are presented in Table 11.

The frequency with which neighbors are mentioned as the feature liked most about the neighborhood in both central city and fringe is noteworthy. Of interest, too, is the fact that residents of each place, who formerly lived in the alternate place, refer to neighbors less often than do other residents. While neighbors are the element of the neighborhood liked by the largest number of fringe area residents, the most frequently mentioned attraction of the neighborhood in the central city is its accessibility. Relatively small proportions of fringe area residents, particularly of those who formerly lived in the central city, consider the accessibility of their neighborhoods to be one of the appealing aspects. Fringe residents appear to give greater weight to cleanliness and safety. This characteristic is appreciated especially by former residents of the central city, as is also the space and privacy found in fringe neighborhoods. There are few members of any of the classes of residents who find nothing of their liking in their home localities.

The striking outcome of the inquiry into dislikes of the neighborhood is the large proportions of former residents of the fringe area who are dissatisfied with the public utilities available in their central city neighborhoods. Whether their expectations of central city service were too great, or that most such responses originated in neighborhoods which were, in fact, inadequately serviced with public utilities, cannot be determined from the data at hand. The same group, it will be recalled from Table 9, felt that one of the main disadvantages of the fringe area was the inadequate provision of public services there.

Table 10

PER CENT DISTRIBUTION OF ADVANTAGES AND DISADVANTAGES OF LIVING IN CENTRAL CITY AS REPORTED BY SATELLITE AREA RESIDENTS, 1955 SAMPLE SURVEY

Advantages and Disadvantages	Total	Other Residents	Former Residents of Central City
Advantages	**100.0**	**100.0**	**100.0**
Good public transportation	18.0	20.3	10.0
Good public utilities	20.3	20.7	18.6
Accessible and convenient	14.8	13.7	18.6
No advantages	28.0	28.7	25.7
Other and no answer	18.9	16.6	27.1
Disadvantages	**100.0**	**100.0**	**100.0**
Noisy, dirty, unsafe	21.2	21.9	18.6
Lack of space and privacy	45.3	46.5	41.4
Higher cost of living	9.6	9.9	8.6
No disadvantages	9.0	10.4	4.3
Other and no answer	14.8	11.2	27.1

The Services Subjectively and Objectively Viewed

The criticism of public service disclosed in preceding paragraphs suggest the advisability of a more direct inquiry into the evaluations placed upon specific services by the people using them. This was done with a selected array of the most important services. Household heads were asked to express their degree of satisfaction with each service in the list. The results are set forth in Table 12. It is to be observed that over 90 per cent of the central city respondents were satisfied or very satisfied with most of their services. Education, streets and roads and street lighting received the lowest frequencies of satisfactory appraisals, but even these were 80 per cent or higher.

Fringe residents appeared to be reasonably satisfied with all but a few of the services, though smaller proportions reported themselves to be very satisfied than were found among central city residents. Much larger numbers of dissatisfied residents occurred in the fringe. Dissatisfaction with sewage disposal, streets and roads and street lighting was especially prevalent. Despite the rather favorable evaluations by fringe residents, only 15 per cent

Table 11

PER CENT DISTRIBUTION OF THINGS LIKED AND DISLIKED ABOUT NEIGHBORHOOD OF RESIDENCE BY PLACE OF RESIDENCE AND PLACE OF PREVIOUS RESIDENCE, 1955 SAMPLE SURVEY

Likes and Dislikes	CENTRAL CITY			FRINGE AREA		
	All Residents	Former Residents of Satellite Area	Other Residents	All Residents	Former Residents of Central City	Other Residents
Likes						
Neighbors	25.3	20.6	26.4	34.5	33.8	37.1
	100.0	**100.0**	**100.0**	**100.0**	**100.0**	**100.0**
Neighbors	25.3	20.6	26.4	34.5	33.8	37.1
Education and recreation facilities	3.2	4.4	2.9	2.9	2.9	2.9
Space and privacy	2.3	2.9	2.1	14.5	16.7	7.1
Cleanliness and safety	18.7	17.6	18.9	18.4	20.0	12.9
Accessibility	35.3	38.2	34.6	14.2	11.7	22.9
Other and no answer	13.5	13.4	13.6	14.1	13.3	17.1
No likes	1.7	2.9	1.4	1.3	1.6	
Dislikes	**100.0**	**100.0**	**100.0**	**100.0**	**100.0**	**100.0**
Neighbors	4.2	2.9	4.2	2.5	2.9	1.4
Inadequate public utilities	15.3	29.0	12.0	28.3	28.2	25.7
Lack of space and privacy	6.5	7.2	6.4	3.5	2.9	5.4
Noise, dirt, and unsafety	10.8	7.2	11.6	4.1	4.1	4.1
Traffic and parking problems	8.2	10.1	7.8	5.3	6.1	2.7
Other and no answer	13.3	5.8	15.2	14.7	13.5	18.9
No dislikes	41.7	37.7	42.7	41.0	42.1	41.8

Table 12

PER CENT DISTRIBUTION OF HOUSEHOLD HEADS BY LEVEL OF SATISFACTION WITH PUBLIC SERVICES, BY TYPE OF SERVICE

Service	CENTRAL CITY					FRINGE				
	Very Satisfied	Satisfied	Dissatisfied	No Opinion	Total	Very Satisfied	Satisfied	Dissatisfied	No Opinion	Total
Education	39	41	5	15	100	35	45	9	11	100
Police	46	47	5	2	100	28	54	16	2	100
Fire	57	38	2	3	100	30	54	11	5	100
Water	58	38	3	1	100	56	30	11	3	100
Sewage	51	41	5	3	100	30	31	33	6	100
Refuse	57	39	3	1	100	40	43	11	5	100
Streets, Roads	34	47	18	1	100	17	44	37	2	100
Street lighting	44	44	11	1	100	12	29	49	10	100

reported that no improvement was needed. The corresponding percentage for central city residents was 50.

The services provided in the fringe appeared in a much less favorable light when evaluated comparatively with the central city services as a standard. As may be observed in Table 13, only water and education were judged to be better in the fringe than in the central city by more than 10 per cent of the residents. In all other instances central city services were judged superior by large proportions of residents in the fringe. Even so the proportion who considered garbage disposal, education, and police and fire protection to be of equal quality in both places are so large as to suggest ignorance of what the central city provides. Before commenting further on the evaluations of service, let us briefly describe the actual state of available services.

Table 13

PER CENT DISTRIBUTION OF HOUSEHOLD HEADS RESIDING
IN FRINGE BY COMPARATIVE EVALUATION
OF FRINGE SERVICES

Services	Better in Fringe Than in Central City	About the Same in the two Areas	Better in Central City Than in Fringe	No Answer	Total
	EVALUATIONS				
Water	39.7	32.2	25.9	2.2	100.0
Education	26.9	54.0	14.0	5.0	100.0
Police	10.2	47.5	39.5	2.8	100.0
Streets (local)	9.4	30.0	58.1	2.5	100.0
Fire	7.5	48.4	41.6	2.4	100.0
Garbage disposal	6.8	73.6	17.9	1.7	100.0
Sewage disposal	3.9	25.4	69.5	1.2	100.0
Street lighting	1.5	11.1	86.2	1.2	100.0

Although the number of school districts in Genesee County declined through consolidations from 137, in 1920, to 36, in 1955, the number of districts in the fringe zone remained virtually unchanged. Despite their antiquated geographic limits, most school districts in that zone strive to provide full kindergarten through twelfth grade programs. Their capacities for financing educational programs vary considerably, however, since taxable wealth as well as the school-age population is unevenly distributed among the sixteen districts of the fringe. The per capita taxable valuation on property, the average of which is but half that in Flint, ranges from less than $3,000 per school child to over $20,000 per school child. Only two of the districts compare favorably with Flint in this respect. Both of these contain large industrial establishments.

Barring the two exceptions, school districts in the fringe obtain from local property taxes less than 20 per cent of the costs of school operation. Several districts obtain less than 10 per cent. The amounts secured from outside sources, mainly from state aid, are not sufficient, however, to permit levels of operation comparable to that prevailing in the central city. Per capita

operating expenditures, again excluding the two wealthy districts, are 27
to 40 per cent below operating expenditures in Flint. Differentials in physical
plant are even more marked since, with the exception of small federal grants,
the local district must bear the total costs. Thus, it is in respect to buildings
and facilities that local resources become of prime importance.

As a consequence of the modest fiscal basis on which fringe school districts
operate, they compare unfavorably with Flint on most objective evidence of
quality of programs offered. For example, while 16 per cent of the elementary
teachers in Flint are without a Bachelor's degree, over 51 per cent of fringe
elementary teachers lack such a degree. This ranges as high as 78 per cent
in one district. At the high-school level over half of the teachers in Flint have
pursued post-graduate education at least to the point of obtaining a Master's
degree, but in the fringe less than one-quarter have done so. Annual salaries
are lower in all fringe districts than in Flint and in most the difference is
$1,000 or more. Nevertheless, fringe teachers are responsible for approxi-
mately 20 per cent more pupils in their class-rooms than are Flint teachers.
A substantial proportion of the crowded class-rooms are located in poorly
heated, improperly lighted buildings unequipped with suitable fire protection.
Moreover, relatively few special services are provided for fringe children.

Although the educational services offered in the fringe are made to appear
inferior when compared to those provided in the central city, public education is nevertheless the most adequately financed and highly developed of all
services available to fringe residents.

Police protection in the fringe is provided by four full-time policemen and
a small number of part-time policemen. Most of these are elected township
constables. Others are employed without references to particular qualifications. The direct outlay for police protection in no place exceeds one dollar
per capita, whereas in Flint the amount expended is $7.50 per capita. As a
consequence, police protection is not only uneven from place to place but
through the daily cycle as well.

Only the city of Flint has an organized full-time fire department. All fire
departments in the fringe rely wholly or in part on volunteer firemen. The
ten fire stations in the fringe are manned by nine full-time firemen, eight of
whom are in one township, and about 140 volunteers. Fire station operating
costs vary from one-tenth to one twenty-fifth of the cost in Flint. Deficiencies
in equipment and experienced men are mitigated to some extent, however, by
a mutual aid pact among all of the governmental units in the county. By the
terms of this pact every fire fighting company will render assistance to any
other when called upon.

The inequalities in fire protection manifest themselves in high costs. Insurance rates in most of the fringe are 28 and 30 cents per one hundred
dollars of protection as compared to 16 cents in the central city. The higher
costs of insurance more than make up for the taxes levied in the central city
to equip and operate fire companies. Total costs to the home owner on a
$12,500 home, including both taxes and insurance, were, in 1955, in the
central city $28.05 and in the fringe $37.50, a difference of about 34 per cent.

The entire fringe area obtains its water from ground sources. Two-thirds
of the population are dependent on private wells, while the remainder are
served by a common public supply. The private well with a pump represents

an outlay for the householder of some $200 in excess of that involved in attaching to a public water system. Capital outlays for water equipment are expected to rise steadily, for the progressive lowering of the water-table will require deeper wells and larger pumps. An acute water shortage looms in the near future. A more immediate hazard flows from the many septic tanks in the area. The prevalance of heavy clay soils results in surface drainage of much of the effluent and subsequent seepage into wells.

Refuse and garbage disposal is provided in two of the four fringe townships by contract between the township government and private firms. In the remaining two townships the matter is left to individual discretion. Cost differentials aside, the problem affecting all parts of the area is that of disposal. The expected exhaustion of presently used dumping space within the next two or three years means either that substantial capital outlays for incinerators or other equipment will be required or that the hauling distances and therefore costs will be greatly increased. In the meantime uncontrolled disposal will maintain a health hazard in certain parts of the area.

In general the streets and roads in the fringe area are inferior, especially when considered against the standard presented by the central city. Approximately 20 per cent of the fringe road mileage, in contrast to some 81 per cent of the central city mileage, is hard-surfaced. The problem of maintenance, always serious where unsurfaced roads prevail, has been aggravated by the growth of traffic in recent years. Furthermore, a recent change in legislation has both reduced the allocation of highway funds for county expenditures and imposed a heavier burden on local government within counties for road maintenance and improvement. County funds must now be matched by township funds. The shortage of township funds for road purposes has led to increased resort to special assessment arrangements. But dust control and grading are persistent problems over the entire area. Moreover, the streets and roads in the fringe are very sparsely lighted.

In view of the very primitive level at which most fringe services are provided it is strange that they should have received any favorable evaluation. Evidently fringe residents have rather modest service expectations. Or perhaps their evaluations involve considerations that are different for fringe and central city. In any event, the objective facts amply confirm the subjective evidence, i.e., the evaluations; public services in the fringe are inadequate for urban settlement. Whether the fringe can sustain its attractiveness as a residential site may hinge on its ability to improve the services to households. In the meantime the state of public services in the fringe is of direct concern to the central city. For it has health and welfare implications that are not confined by political boundaries.

Solution to Service Problems

The dissatisfaction with public services expressed by fringe residents may be taken as defining a problem or set of problems. Having contended daily with the frustrations and inconveniences of service deficiencies, many local residents have been brought to the conviction that a higher level of governmental performance than that provided by the townships is needed. They argue that their service requirements differ in no appreciable degree from those of central city occupants and that everything the central city provides for its citizens is necessary also in the fringe. There is, therefore, not only a recognition of a problem, but a readiness to act to obtain a solution. Various procedures for the solution of service problems are available. All involve some form of governmental action or reorganization. Conceivably, the township government could remain as it is and expand its service functions to meet existing needs. There is an inconsistency here, however, for the township government is closely limited in its general taxing powers. This handicap could be eliminated by incorporation of the township as a municipality. Township incorporation is, then, a second way of moving toward a solution of the problem. A third possibility is to enlarge the functions of county government to the point where it could provide the service requirements generated by urban settlement. The county possesses most of the powers required for the purpose. A fourth alternative is that of merging part or all of the fringe with the central city through the process known as annexation. That, in a short space of time, would bring the service level in what is now the fringe to equivalence with the level obtaining in the central city. Still other alternatives might be considered. But attention here is directed only to the four.

After considering the four alternatives, a sample of household heads residing in the fringe indicated their preferences for the procedure to be followed in dealing with service problems as shown in Table 14. More than half expressed as their first choice the desire that service needs be provided by the township government as it is presently constituted.[23] The remainder concentrated on no one alternative. Annexation to the central city appealed to the second largest proportion, though the 18 per cent who announced such a preference represent a small minority. There is reason to believe that had not the survey in which these data were gathered followed closely on the receipt of tax bills in certain sections of the fringe the proportion favoring annexation would have been much lower. No one of the alternatives received majority support as either second or third choice. But annexation was clearly a last choice for a large segment of the population. By contrast, in

Table 14

PER CENT DISTRIBUTION OF PREFERRED SOLUTIONS TO
FRINGE PROBLEMS, BY ORDER OF PREFERENCE

Solution	ORDER OF PREFERENCE			
	First	Second	Third	Fourth
Total	100.0	100.0	100.0	100.0
Township remain as it is	54.0	16.5	14.0	11.4
Township become a city	8.0	28.1	39.2	14.8
County	16.5	42.1	23.0	10.7
Annex to Flint	18.4	6.1	13.1	53.4
Don't know and no answer	3.1	7.2	10.7	9.7

response to the same question, nearly half of the central city respondents selected annexation as the preferred solution to fringe area problems.

Since annexation offers the clearest path to governmental unification in the area, an attempt was made to explore the climate of opinion in the fringe more fully. This was done through the series of questions listed on the stub of Table 15. It will be observed that household heads reported as their beliefs that no more than a sixth of fringe residents favored annexation. But that estimate seems to disclose an inability to correctly assess public opinion, as the large proportion of "don't know" answers (14.4 per cent) suggests. Almost one-fourth of the residents indicated their own attitudes to be favorable, while three-fourths declared opposition to annexation. A very similar distribution of responses was obtained from the question: Would you vote for annexation in the near future? Many, however, believe that annexation will occur in the near future (46 per cent), even though they themselves are opposed to it. And of those who believe annexation will not occur soon more than half (52 per cent) believe it will ultimately take place. Evidently,

Table 15

OPINIONS OF FRINGE RESIDENTS ON ANNEXATION OF THE FRINGE TO THE CITY OF FLINT

OPINIONS ON ANNEXATION

Questions on Annexation	Favor, or Yes	Oppose, or no	Don't Know, No Answer	Total
How do people in the fringe feel about annexation?	16.6	69.0	14.4	100.0
Do you favor or oppose annexation?	22.3	73.8	3.9	100.0
Do you think this area will annex in the near future?	46.0	49.4	4.6	100.0
Do you think the area will ever annex? (Applies only to those not answering "yes" to the above.)	52.0	31.4	16.6	100.0
Would you vote for annexation in the near future?	23.5	72.6	3.8	100.0
Would you ever vote for annexation? (Applies only to those not answering "yes" to the above.)	29.7	63.3	7.0	100.0

respondents felt that support would come from sources other than themselves, for large majorities stated they would not vote for annexation in the near or distant future. Whether these curious findings reflect a grudging recognition of certain facts or simply indecisiveness must be left to speculations. There is also the possibility that residents in the fringe are unaware of how annexation is actually accomplished.

Support for annexation is found primarily among household heads who are under 35 years of age and who have families which include children of school age. These people earn modest incomes and occupy inexpensive homes, though they are well educated and engaged in the more prestigeful white-collar occupations. It is just this type of person who is most critical of the available services. In one sense the supporters of annexation are relatively inarticulate, for eight of every nine of them belong to no civic or other formal organization other than the church.

The staunchest opponents of annexation are over 35 years of age and have small families depleted by the marriage and departure of children. Most of them, too, are employed as semi-skilled workers, domestic servants or laborers, and their incomes are below 75 dollars per week. Few have had more than a grade school education. This is a profile, of course, of only the extremes in opinions regarding annexation.

Fiscal Support for Public Services. It might be surmised that the differences in the annual expenditures for services as between the two areas are so great that very large increments in the fringe would be required to bring the expenditures to a uniform level. Consequently such differences might constitute a barrier to governmental unification. An investigation of this matter involves numerous complexities, however. We shall try to avoid as many of these as possible at the risk of over-simplification.

An inspection of the per capita costs of government in all its activities, except for special assessment projects, and without regard to the sources of the services or the sources of revenues, indicates that government in the central city is actually less costly than government in the fringe. The per capita amounts in 1956–57 were as follows:

Flint City	$150.46
City Funds	57.02
School Funds	78.25
County Taxes[a]	15.18
Fringe Townships	154.05
Township Funds	34.66
School Funds	107.26
County Funds	12.12

[a] Refers only to the county taxes levied in the two areas.

The levels of service in the two areas differ markedly; nonetheless the per capita costs of government in the fringe exceed the costs in the central city. The larger expenditures from the school funds in the fringe more than outweigh the lower amounts charged to the township and couny funds. The higher per capita costs of government in the fringe is likely due in part to less efficiency in the operations of government, but more particularly it can be attributed to differences in the composition of the populations in the two areas. In the fringe a much larger proportion of the population is of school age or younger. It is noted, however, that these figures do not represent direct out-of-pocket expenditures by local residents. A good part of the total originates as rebates from State funds. A very important item in these monies is the sales tax reallocation to local governments. In this, as in other respects, the distribution is unequal. Whereas about three-fifths of the sales tax yielded by the county is paid by central city residents, of the amount returned to the County only one-half goes to Flint. The other 50 per cent is distributed to the townships and school districts outside of Flint. Thus, virtually all of the funds spent for operations in the townships are obtained from state tax rebates. Of the remaining township expenditures two-thirds comes from the state road fund. Of the funds spent on school operation half originates from local taxation in the central city as compared with only one-fourth provided from local taxation in the fringe. It is clear that city residents subsidize the governments of the townships.

Although the fringe resident has a very real advantage in the matter of direct expenditures for the maintenance of government, he is receiving an inferior quality of service and, as has already been observed, he is not satisfied with it. Furthermore, he has some charges to pay which the central city resident does not have. In some sections of the fringe, refuse disposal costs $6.00 to $12.00 more than in Flint; fire insurance rates on a home valued at $12,000 run $15.00 to $17.50 higher in the fringe; and the interest charges on the capital outlay required for water and sewage disposal average about $16.00 more in the fringe. Even so, the city resident annually pays out more for his services than does the resident in the fringe. Unfortunately, there is no way of adjusting cost differences for quality differences in order to obtain a true comparison of city and fringe residence conditions.

Attitudes Towards Increased Taxes

The low dollar cost of service in the fringe notwithstanding, the fringe occupants are willing to accept higher taxes in order to secure better services.[24] As may be seen in Table 16, the willingness to pay higher taxes varies directly with the value of house occupied and the taxes paid in the central city and inversely in the fringe. This is what might be expected where one is well served with utilities and the other is not. These data may be somewhat better understood when it is realized that three-fourths of the fringe homes are in the low value classes and that over 80 per cent of the fringe household heads paid property taxes of less than $100 during the past year. The relation of type of surfaced streets on which homes are located and the response to the tax question is of more than passing interest. In general, willingness to pay higher taxes is associated with service dissatisfaction. But 60 per cent or more of those who are reasonably well satisfied with fringe services reported a willingness to pay increased taxes.

The categories in the first column of Table 16 are too broad to represent social and economic distinctions adequately. That is accomplished more satisfactorily in certain sections of Table 17. There it is to be observed that attitudes favorable to tax increases in the fringe are most frequent in the higher occupational and educational levels and in the middle-income group. But receptiveness to higher taxes cannot be regarded as just a function of social class position, assuming that that is fairly represented by education, occupation, and income considered separately. For a majority in all but the "not working" category indicated a favorable attitude. In fact, fringe heads in every social background category are much more favorably disposed toward higher taxes than are their counterparts in the central city.

The distributions of attitudes favorable to higher taxes with reference to age and head of family composition are suggestive of why indicators of social class positions do not disclose a greater differentiation in the population. We refer to the importance of the family as a creator of demands for services. Doubtlessly the manifold needs of the family are what focus the most critical light on the service deficiencies in the fringe area. And the fringe, it should be remembered, is settled preponderantly by family units.

In the light of the evidence, it hardly seems likely that governmental unification is resisted on the basis of the increased costs to individual taxpayers

Table 16

PER CENT DISTRIBUTION OF ATTITUDES TOWARD TAX
INCREASE, BY HOME AND TAX RELATED CHARACTER-
ISTICS, BY PLACE OF RESIDENCE

Property Related Characteristics	CITY			FRINGE		
	Tax Increase Favor-able	Unfavor-able	Total Per Cent	Tax Increase Favor-able	Unfavor-able	Total Per Cent
REPORTED MARKET VALUE OF HOME						
Under $10,000	37.8	62.2	100.0	76.0	24.0	100.0
$10,000-$15,000	37.5	62.5	100.0	73.3	26.7	100.0
$15,000 and over	44.4	55.6	100.0	72.0	28.0	100.0
ASSESSED VALUE OF HOME						
Low	38.1	61.9	100.0	74.3	25.7	100.0
Medium	38.6	61.4	100.0	72.4	27.3	100.0
High	42.6	57.4	100.0	64.7	35.3	100.0
PROPERTY TAX PAID						
Under $75	42.9	57.1	100.0	73.2	26.8	100.0
$75-$150	34.3	65.7	100.0	71.4	28.6	100.0
$150 and over	45.7	54.3	100.0	62.5	37.5	100.0
TYPE OF STREET SURFACING						
Hard surface	38.6	61.4	100.0	63.1	36.9	100.0
Gravel	33.3	66.7	100.0	70.2	29.8	100.0
Dirt	56.3	43.8	100.0	85.7	14.3	100.0
SIZE OF LOT						
Under 60 ft.	38.4	61.6	100.0	81.7	18.3	100.0
60 to 74 ft.	45.5	54.5	100.0	70.5	29.5	100.0
75 ft. and over	53.3	46.7	100.0	67.9	32.1	100.0

which might follow the event. There is, however, at least one reservation
that must be attached to this conclusion. That arises from the uncertainty
as to what willingness to pay higher taxes means. For no information is
available on how much increase would be tolerable. But the presence of
different standards is revealed by the fact that 79 per cent of the fringe household heads reported a willingness to pay higher taxes to the township while
only 62 per cent announced a willingness to pay increased taxes to the
central city.

Judgments of Governmental Effectiveness

Having failed to find an explanation of the resistance to governmental unification in tax consideration, we must look elsewhere. A possible basis for
the reluctance to join the central city may exist in suspicions and doubts regarding the integrity, the responsiveness to citizen's needs, or other optimal
qualities of large city government. Most fringe residents, in fact, felt that the
size of government affects the efficiency of its operation. Of course, it is not

improbable that such a view is simply conventional: were the issues to be presented in a different light more discriminating judgments might be elicited. For example, comparative evaluations of township and central city governments with reference to a number of specific attributes might circumvent the categorial commonplaces which are exchanged in casual conversation. This approach was employed and the results are set forth in Table 18. It should be remembered in reading this table that three-fourths of the fringe residents formerly lived in the central city. They have had some experience, in other words, on which to base comparative judgments.

On most attributes the township governments received a larger number of favorable appraisals than did the central city government. But in no instance does the distribution of comparative judgments indicate unqualified support of township government. Although 47 per cent felt that township government was economically least burdensome, almost as many (45 per cent) asserted that either there was no difference between the two areas in this respect or that the central city government was least burdensome. On all other attributes the favorable appraisals of township government are clearly in the minority. But the central city government was viewed even less favorably on most of the items. The large proportions who could make no dis-

Table 17

PER CENT DISTRIBUTION OF ATTITUDES TOWARD TAX INCREASE BY CHARACTERISTICS OF HEAD OF HOUSEHOLD, BY PLACE OF RESIDENCE

| Selected Characteristics | CITY | | | FRINGE | | |
| | Tax Increase | | Total Per Cent | Tax Increase | | Total Per Cent |
	Favorable	Unfavorable		Favorable	Unfavorable	
AGE OF HEAD						
Under 35 years	42.9	57.1	100.0	77.0	23.0	100.0
35-44 years	63.0	36.9	100.0	77.3	22.7	100.0
45-65	35.7	64.3	100.0	65.3	34.6	100.0
65 years and over	12.5	87.5	100.0	58.3	41.7	100.0
OCCUPATION						
Prof. clerical	48.6	51.4	100.0	82.8	17.2	100.0
Skilled Operatives	40.3	59.7	100.0	70.7	29.3	100.0
Other	37.5	62.5	100.0	52.6	47.4	100.0
Not Working	18.9	81.1	100.0	43.8	56.3	100.0
EDUCATION						
Grade School	28.8	71.3	100.0	68.5	31.5	100.0
High School	37.9	62.0	100.0	70.7	29.3	100.0
College	63.6	36.4	100.0	90.0	10.0	100.0
TAKE HOME PAY						
Under $75	34.5	65.5	100.0	51.9	48.1	100.0
$75-$99	48.1	51.9	100.0	76.8	23.2	100.0
$100 and over	46.7	53.2	100.0	73.2	26.8	100.0
FAMILY COMPOSITION						
Children over 17 yrs.	52.0	48.0	100.0	78.0	22.0	100.0
Children under 17 yrs.	45.0	55.0	100.0	73.0	27.0	100.0
Without Children	30.0	70.0	100.0	62.0	38.0	100.0
Single Person	12.0	88.0	100.0	50.0	50.0	100.0

tinction between townships and central city governments are worthy of note, especially in the matter of competence of officials. This finding would be instructive, if we could assume that it represented well-reasoned judgments. Unfortunately, such an assumption would be very dubious. The "about the same" response probably was given by many unobservant and apathetic citizens. This interpretation finds some support in an analysis of citizens' knowledge of government.

Table 18

PER CENT DISTRIBUTION OF COMPARATIVE EVALUATIONS OF TOWNSHIP AND CENTRAL CITY GOVERNMENTS BY FRINGE RESIDENTS

COMPARATIVE EVALUATION

Attributes of Government	More in Twp.	About Same in Both Areas	More in Central City	No Opinion or No Answer	Total
Relative lack of economic burden- someness of government	47.2	30.3	15.5	7.0	100.0
Extent individual is free of government controls	40.0	40.2	9.9	9.9	100.0
Relative value of talking to officials	39.2	34.1	15.7	10.0	100.0
Extent government is free of influence from special interest	37.5	37.8	13.3	11.4	100.0
Extent officials are aware of problems in neighborhoods	34.9	44.8	14.0	6.3	100.0
Extent officials are concerned with the individual	33.4	43.8	14.3	7.4	100.0
Extent people have a say in running government	31.5	48.7	13.6	6.3	100.0
Relative interest of officials in neighborhood	24.7	40.7	25.7	9.0	100.0
Relative competence of government officials	12.6	64.6	13.8	9.0	100.0

Table 19

PER CENT DISTRIBUTION OF HOUSEHOLD HEADS BY NUMBER OF ELECTIVE OFFICES AND ELECTED OFFICIALS OF TOWNSHIP GOVERNMENT IDENTIFIED

IDENTIFICATION

Number Mentioned	Elective Offices in Township	Name of Officials Holding Office
Total	100.0	100.0
None	40.0	35.1
1 or 2	23.7	40.7
3 or 4	25.9	16.9
5 or more	7.7	3.6
No Answer	2.7	1.6

Knowledge of Local Government. In an attempt to measure knowledge of government, fringe residents were queried about the number of offices in the townships to which they elect officials and the names of persons presently occupying those offices. The responses to these questions are shown in Table 19. It is noted that two-fifths of the residents were unable to name a single official position and only about one-third could name more than two offices. That two-thirds of the household heads could name no more than two offices to which they elected persons indicates limited familiarity with local governmental structure. Such a lack of knowledge is strong supportive evidence against the popular interpretation that residents are "close" to their government in the township areas. Further support of this is found in the responses to the question regarding persons presently occupying elective offices. Even when the 40 per cent who were unable to identify an office are excluded, one-third of the remaining household heads were unable to name any of the elective officials and three-fourths of the respondents were able to name no more than two persons presently holding an elective office.

As a further measure of knowledge of government as well as participation in local government, questions were asked about knowledge of the meeting place of various governmental bodies and attendance at meetings of the bodies during the past two years. Responses to these questions are shown in Table 20.

As noted earlier the fringe area is divided into many small school districts, yet it is observed that only half of the residents knew where the school board meets, and only slightly more than one in ten had attended a meeting of this body during the past two years. An even smaller proportion were familiar with

Table 20

PER CENT OF HOUSEHOLD HEADS WHO KNOW PLACE OF MEETING AND WHO ATTENDED MEETING OF SELECTED GROUPS

Type of Group	KNOWLEDGE OF MEETING PLACE				ATTENDANCE AT MEETINGS			
	Know	Not Know	No Answer	Total	Have Attended	Have Not Attended	No Answer	Total
School Board	49.4	49.4	1.2	100.0	11.6	86.9	1.5	100.0
Township Board	45.3	53.8	1.0	100.0	14.5	84.3	1.2	100.0
Zoning Board	29.5	70.0	1.5	100.0	8.0	90.3	1.7	100.0
Board of Supervisors	22.5	75.5	2.2	100.0	3.4	95.4	1.2	100.0

the meeting place of the township board, but attendance at meetings was higher. Less than one-fourth were aware of the meeting place of the County Board of Supervisors and only 3 per cent had ever attended a meeting of that body.[25]

Attendance at meetings is related to length of residence at present address. But, the proportion who have attended a meeting does not exceed 25 per cent in any length of residence category and that proportion is attracted only by the township board. It is also noteworthy that more of the respondents who evaluated the township government most favorably knew the elected offices of their governments than did those who were less favorable in their evaluations. On the other hand, those who felt the township governments compared unfavorably with the central city attended meetings of local government bodies more frequently. Perhaps meeting attendance is largely for purposes of protest on the part of otherwise disinterested persons. Protest, and certainly unsatisfied protest, would be associated with a deprecatory view of township government.

Although the governmental units in the fringe area are small, the evidence of knowledge about local government and participation in government is far from impressive. Central city residents demonstrate more knowledge and more participation in local government.

Still further comparative evidence between the two areas is to be found in the proportion registered to vote and in the proportion who reported that they have voted in at least one of the last two local elections. In both areas approximately four-fifths of the household heads claim that they are registered voters. However, a larger proportion of the central city residents reported that they voted in local elections than was found among fringe residents.

The available data on knowledge about local governments are admittedly crude. Nevertheless they raise a reasonable doubt concerning the ability of fringe residents to think constructively about solutions to service problems.[26] This has been suggested, too, by some of the inconsistencies among expressed opinions. Ignorance may be but part of the answer. There may also be a lack of local leadership from which to obtain definitions and clarification of issues. If such leadership were present, however, it might encounter difficulty in gaining access to the population. For, less than one-fourth belong to any formal organization other than a labor union or a church. The corresponding proportion in the central city is in excess of two-fifths. Thus, it seems that fringe residents are relatively inarticulate as well as inaccessible to leadership. This is especially true of the supporters of annexation: six of every seven of them belong to no organization. But it is also the non-members who, on the one hand, have the most unfavorable opinions of township government, and, on the other hand, know least about township government. Were it not that the total number of organizational members is so small, the non-members would appear to be a disaffected category of residents. The fact is, many other non-members share the opinions held by members. Organizational membership seems merely to be a symptom of the preference for the status quo.

Preferred Solution Related to Evaluation of Needs. Part of the resistance of fringe residents to governmental unification as indicated earlier may be due to their inability to assess correctly local needs and attributes of local government. Thus, this leads us to a more direct inquiry into the relationship between evaluations and attitudes concerning governmental reorganization. Before doing so however, it is noted that objective observers are generally critical of the rural type township government in densely settled fringe areas. There is general agreement among them that such areas have the same problems and needs as central city areas. Consequently there is a need for more government. In respect to the latter, they view annexation as an effective means whereby fringe area service problems could be economically solved.

We have already observed that fringe residents generally lack knowledge of local government on which to base mature judgments. Pursuing this further, we find that fringe residents, who view the needs of their area as would an objective observer, are much more likely to favor governmental reorganization. These data are shown in Table 21. The residents who do not see a need for more government, in large proportions (72.1 per cent), prefer to continue under the existing township. Only 6 per cent prefer annexation. Support for annexation comes largely from residents who express a need for more government. Resistance to annexation is strongest among residents who feel that no more government is needed. These data further suggest that resistance to governmental reorganization is due to lack of knowledge of the needs of the area.

In Table 22 we again find that support for annexation comes largely from residents who assess local needs realistically. Residents who express a need for more government are four times as likely to support annexation as those who report that more government is not needed. Resistance to annexation is staunchest among those who feel that there is no need for more government. Among the latter more than 92 per cent are opposed to annexation

Table 21

PREFERRED SOLUTION TO FRINGE PROBLEMS BY NEED FOR MORE GOVERNMENT

PREFERRED SOLUTION[a]

NEED FOR GOVERNMENT	Township as is	Township Become City	County	Annex	No Answer	Total Per Cent
More Government Needed	44.6	9.1	18.2	26.8	1.3	100.0
More Government Not Needed	72.1	5.5	15.6	6.1	.7	100.0

[a] First choice only.

in that they would not vote for it if placed on the ballot at the present time. By contrast one-third of the residents who want more government would vote in support of annexation.

In Table 23, it is noted that the supporters of annexation are much more critical of township officials than are residents who oppose such an approach. Three times as many of those who support annexation report that township officials are less aware of neighborhood problems than is found among the opponents of annexation. Similarly, those critical of the relative competence of township officials are four times as large among the supporters of annexation. The inability to distinguish the relative competence of township officials is particularly marked among the opponents of annexation, but we note the large proportion of fringe area residents who express no real difference between the officials of the two areas.

Although the fringe residents are clearly opposed to annexation as a solu-

Table 22

VOTE FOR ANNEXATION BY NEED FOR MORE GOVERNMENT

ANNEXATION VOTE

NEED FOR GOVERNMENT	Yes	No	Total Per Cent
More Government Needed	33.3	66.7	100.0
More Government Not Needed	8.3	91.7	100.0

Table 23

COMPARATIVE EVALUATIONS OF ATTRIBUTES BY VOTE FOR ANNEXATION

EVALUATION OF ATTRIBUTES

Vote for Annexation	More in Township	About Same in Both Areas	Less in Township	No Opinion No Answer	Total Per Cent
		Official Awareness of Problems			
Yes	21.6	44.3	27.8	6.2	100.0
No	40.7	44.3	9.7	5.3	100.0
		Relative Competence of Officials			
Yes	6.2	57.7	32.0	4.1	100.0
No	15.0	67.3	8.3	9.3	100.0

Table 24

VOTE FOR ANNEXATION BY ADVANTAGES AND DISADVANTAGES OF ANNEXATION

VOTE FOR ANNEXATION

Advantages and Disadvantages of Annexation	Would Vote Now or Later	Would Never Vote For	No Opinion No Answer	Total Per Cent
Total	46.2	48.4	5.3	100.0
Advantages				
Better Services and Facilities	63.7	33.8	2.5	100.0
Other	46.4	48.8	4.9	100.0
Don't Know Any	26.5	67.4	6.1	100.0
No Answer	16.7	61.1	22.2	100.0
Disadvantages				
Higher Taxes	42.1	55.9	2.0	100.0
Other	35.7	57.1	7.1	100.0
Don't Know Any	77.6	14.9	7.5	100.0
No Answer	31.0	41.4	27.6	100.0

tion to their problems, among many, this is only a temporary resistance. When the data presented in Table 24 are compared with the data shown in Table 15, it is found that nearly one-fourth of the fringe population would not vote for annexation at the present time but would do so later. Unfortunately the meaning of later is non-specific. These data show that less than half of the fringe population report that they would never support an annexation vote.

The expected advantages and disadvantages of annexation are found to be important influences on how residents would vote on such an issue. Thus, among residents who report better services and facilities as an advantage of annexation, nearly two-thirds would vote favorably either now or later. This pertains to nearly half of the fringe respondents. However, among the approximate one-third who report that there wouldn't be any advantages gained by annexation, more than two-thirds would never vote for it. The large proportion in the no opinion and no answer category again is worthy of note.

In respect to the expressed disadvantages of annexation, the high proportion of favorable votes in the higher taxes category is of particular interest. Although three-fifths of the fringe residents report that higher taxes would be a disadvantage of annexation, more than two-fifths of this group would vote favorably, now or later. This is a higher proportion than among those who list other disadvantages. This lends further support for our earlier interpretation that resistance to governmental unification is not based on fear of increased costs to individual tax payers which might follow. Support for annexation is particularly marked among the small minority who report that there wouldn't be any disadvantages. Here too, we find support for reorganization among those residents whose evaluations are comparable to those of an objective observer. Conversely, resistance is most pronounced among those who are incapable of making such judgments. It is noted, however, that the latter group contains a large proportion of the total residents, whose combined voting strength at the polls would outweigh the supporters of annexation in the fringe area.

Conclusion

The development of the Flint metropolitan community clearly has drawn the area immediately adjacent to the central city, to say nothing of more outlying areas, into such intimate relations with the central city that for all practical purposes they constitute a single unit. That unity would be complete had governmental unification followed in the normal course of events. Since it did not, the immediately adjacent or fringe area has languished in an underdeveloped condition. It is deficient in virtually all of the services required for reasonably efficient and sanitary urban living. This, despite the accumulation there of a relatively dense residential population most of which resided formerly in the central city and is therefore urban in origin as well as in the character of its settlement. Not is this judgment of the fringe merely that of an outside spectator equipped with standards alien to the locality. The residents are themselves aware of, and highly critical of, the service inadequacies in their neighborhoods. They, moreover, indicate a readiness to act toward a solution of the problem. They recognize a need for the enlargement of governmental functions, and they are prepared to pay higher taxes.

The readiness to act, however, does not contemplate the merging of the fringe with the central city. More than three-fourths of the sample interviewed were opposed to such a proposal, preferring to rely on an alternative path to the solution of the service problem. Most wished to proceed through the township government in its present form. This involves something of a contradiction; for it is not possible both to retain the township government as it is and to expand greatly the number and scope of its activities. But apart from that, continued reliance upon the township gives no assurance of an efficient solution. Many of the service problems over-reach township boundaries. Hence, serious efforts to deal with them would result in a melange of inter-governmental arrangements.

On the surface, it would appear that the most rational and simple manner of resolving service inadequacies is to consolidate the fringe and the central city under a single municipal government. This could be done by annexation. Why then, is this means not adopted, or rather, why is it actively resisted? The question gathers force from the comparative evaluations of township government. These indicated considerably less than enthusiastic support for the township, contrary to the expressed preference for the development of needed services by townships. On the other hand, the knowledge of local government possessed by fringe residents, as revealed by certain gross indicators, seems extremely meager. It raises a question of their competence either for deciding upon a solution for service inadequacies or for making comparative appraisals of local governments. In this may lie a large part of the explanation of the large number who judge township and central city governments as about the same.

We are brought to the conclusion, at least tentatively, therefore, that the resistance to governmental unification rests largely in ignorance of government and what to expect of it. Support for annexation, it will be recalled, was concentrated among the most highly educated respondents and those whose perception of local needs and evaluation of attributes of government closely resembled those of objective observers. The conflicting opinions expressed by the bulk of the population raise doubts as to whether the connotations of annexation are generally understood. One can hardly avoid the suspicion that annexation has become an invidious term. It appears to call forth an unreasoned response, a response which defeats the objectives of the persons concerned. Whether this is a correct surmise or not, it seems clear that further work on the problem dealt with here should give careful attention to the kind and amount of knowledge about local government possessed by the population in question. This should include an exploration of the folklore gathered about semitechnical terms and the legal and administrative processes they denote.

In the meantime fringe residents hold the balance of power in any effort at governmental unification, though they constitute but a third of the total population involved. Barring the development of a legal means for circumventing their autonomy, the only promise of success would appear to rest in a process of education in the meaning and processes of government.

NOTES TO CHAPTER IV

1. R. D. McKenzie, *The Metropolitan Community,* New York: McGraw-Hill, 1933; Donald J. Bogue, *The Structure of The Metropolitan Community: A Study of Dominance and Subdominance,* Ann Arbor: University of Michigan, 1949; Amos H. Hawley, *The Changing Shape of Metropolitan America,* Glencoe, Ill.: The Free Press, 1955.

2. N. S. B. Gras, *An Introduction to Economic History,* New York: Harper and Bros., 1922.

3. Donald J. Bogue, *op. cit.*

4. Henry S. Shryock, Jr., "The Natural History of Metropolitan Areas," *The American Journal of Sociology,* 43 (1957), 163-70.

5. *Census of Population: 1950.* Vol. II: *Characteristics of Population,* Washington, D.C.: U. S. Government Printing Office, 1952, XIV-XV.

6. See "A Symposium on Metropolitan Regionalism: Developing Governmental Concepts," *University of Pennsylvania Law Review,* 105, 1957.

7. Samuel A. Pratt, "Metropolitan Community Developments and Economic Change," *American Sociological Review,* 22 (1957), 434–440.

8. Marion E. Dunlap, *The Urban and Metropolitan Status of The City of Flint,* Social Science Research Project Reports, University of Michigan, 1948.

9. Robert B. Reynolds, "Central Places of Flint Metropolitan Community." Unpublished Social Science Research Report, University of Michigan, June 1954.

10. A further measure of the growth of Flint's importance as a focal point is observable in the changes in the ratio of workers in the major industrial installations in the central city to resident population of satellite urban places at differing distances between 1936 and 1950. During this period there was a 38 per cent increase in the ratio of industrial workers to resident population in the city. However, in the area five to fourteen miles distant from Flint the ratio increased by over 125 per cent, whereas in the next distance zone there was more than a four-fold increase. That Flint's influence was rapidly extending in the hinterland is evident by the particularly large increases which occurred in the more distant locations. These data, it should be noted, pertain to village and urban satellite places. Doubtless a similar pattern obtains in the unincorporated areas as well. See, Leo F. Schore, "The Separation of Home and Work in Flint, Michigan," Social Science Research Project, University of Michigan, June, 1954.

11. Harry P. Sharp, "The Non-Residential Population of The Central Business District of Flint, Michigan," Social Science Research Project, University of Michigan, June, 1954.

12. *Central Business Statistics, Flint, Michigan,* 1954 Census of Business, Bulletin CBD-10, U. S. Department of Commerce, Bureau of The Census, Washington, 1956.

13. Kalliope Mohring, "Mobility of Retail Establishments in Flint," Unpublished Social Science Research Project, University of Michigan, 1955.

14. Deil S. Wright, "Changes in The Assessed Valuations of Real Property in The Central Business District of Flint, Michigan, 1930-1951," Social Science Research Project, University of Michigan, December, 1953.

15. Amos H. Hawley, *Interstate Migration in Michigan, 1935–40,* Michigan Governmental Studies, No. 25, Bureau of Government, Institute of Public Administration, University of Michigan, 1953. The Metropolitan District, 1940, included the city of Flint, Burton, Genesee, and Mt. Morris Townships. The urbanized area of 1950, included the city of Flint and all adjacent areas with a density of approximately 2000 per square mile. The 1935–40 data are in the form of answers to a question asked in the census of 1940: Where did this person live on April 1, 1935? All persons who reported an address in a different county in 1935 than the one occupied in 1940 are defined as migrants. Persons who moved to their 1940 address before or after 1935, or who had never moved, are identified as non-migrants. Each of the sample surveys included approximately 1 per cent of the household heads residing in a defined area. Beyond that similarity lie important differences. The migration questions in the 1948 survey pertained to the last move only, whereas the migration data obtained in the 1955 survey are in the form of previous places of residence without regard to the number of intervening moves. Furthermore, the area covered by the earlier survey was the metropolitan district of 1940, while the later survey was a little more inclusive than the urbanized area as defined in the 1950 census. The difference between these two areal definitions is not great, however.

16. Amos H. Hawley, *op. cit.*

17. Betty Tableman, "Intra-Community Migration in The Flint Metropolitan District," Social Science Research Project, University of Michigan, June, 1948.

18. A survey conducted in 1956–57, involving a somewhat smaller area revealed that 80 per cent of the fringe residents had previously lived in the central city.

19. Amos H. Hawley, *op. cit.*

20. Amos H. Hawley, *op. cit.,* 70-98.

21. Betty Tableman, *op. cit.,* 19.

22. Betty Tableman, *op. cit.,* 38.

23. Basil G. Zimmer and Amos H. Hawley, "Approaches to the Solution of Fringe Problems: Preferences of Residents in The Flint Metropolitan Area," *Public Administration Review,* 16 (Autumn, 1956).

24. Basil G. Zimmer and Amos H. Hawley, "Home Owners and Attitudes Toward Higher Taxes," *Journal of The American Institute of Planners,* Spring, 1956; and "Property Taxes and Solutions To Fringe Problems: Attitudes of Residents of the Flint Metropolitan Area," *Land Economics,* 32 (November, 1956).

25. As compared with the knowledge of the meeting place of the township board on the part of the fringe residents, it was found that in the city of Flint a much higher proportion knew where the city commission held its meetings and a larger proportion had attended a meeting of this body. City residents were also more familiar with the meeting place of the county board of supervisors and equaled the fringe residents in the proportion who attended a meeting of this group. City residents, however, had a larger proportion who did not know the meeting place of the school board and attendance at such meetings were also lower in the fringe.

26. Morris Janowitz, Deil Wright, and William Delaney, in their study of *Public Administration and The Public—Perspectives Toward Government in a Metropolitan Community,* Michigan Governmental Studies, No. 36. Institute of Public Administration, University of Michigan, 1958, also found a relatively low level of knowledge prevailing in a random sample, even in respect to a matter that bears directly on individual welfare — the social security system.

Dilemmas of Action Research
on the "Metropolitan Problem"

BY *SCOTT GREER*

DURING THE YEAR 1956-57, it was calculated that over 100 studies of "the metropolitan problem" were in progress, planned, or recently completed. They ranged from the efforts of citizens' committees without staff or resources, to well staffed projects carrying out "crash programs" of action research on the policy problems of urban areas.

One of the most ambitious of these was the Metropolitan St. Louis Survey. The Survey began the study of the St. Louis Metropolitan Area's problems in June, 1956. With a senior staff of political scientists, sociologists, and economists, a budget of almost one-third of a million dollars, and a peak work force of some 150 persons, the Survey was a major investment in social science as a tool for the study and reformulation of policy.

The purpose of this paper is to examine the "natural history" of the Metropolitan St. Louis Survey, the results, and the way in which the former predetermines, or does not predetermine, the latter. In doing so, it will be necessary to discuss: (1) the origins of the Survey in public events and in the ideology which interprets those events, (2) the translation of ideology into research goals in the light of the demands of social action, (3) certain salient findings, (4) the implications of these latter for the ideology from which the Survey was launched, and (5) the dilemmas of action research in the social sciences.

This paper is thus an effort to relate the demands of ideology, action, and the scientific enterprise as they interacted within the framework of one specific research project. Like any discussion of the social sciences which commences with their origins in the problems of the day, this may be read as damning criticism: it indicates that the roots of the social sciences are, today, in the world of common sense definition of problems. This is not, however, peculiar to the study of urban society: problem orientations are nearly universal in the fields and disciplines which make up the social sciences. The positive value of the Survey stands forth more clearly against the background from which it develops. Such enterprises, harboring difficult intellectual, moral, and operational problems, may yet yield a substantial theoretical pay-off from even a little controlled research, for they operate at the growing edge of both knowledge and public policy.

I. The St. Louis Survey in Historical Perspective

The Movement to Save the Cities. The Survey was, from its inception, a combination of applied and basic research. The first stated purpose of the Research Plan was "to prepare . . . alternative proposals for action designed to remedy some or all of the major ills arising out of the present pattern of government in St. Louis City and St. Louis County, and to provide ways and means to meet major metropolitan needs, present and future."

Such a formulation rests upon certain basic assumptions, which were stated as follows: "the governmental pattern . . . gravely impairs efficiency and dilutes responsibility . . . impedes the orderly and healthy development of the expanding community . . . (while) many major needs of the people . . . which government is expected to meet are not being uniformly met and cannot be met adequately by uncoordinated, piecemeal local action."

These statements have a plausibility that results from their tendency to summarize whatever dissatisfactions one may have with an urban social complex. However, it is important to ask "Who has defined the 'major ills,' and what were their criteria?" The Survey movement is not a new one; the "metropolitan" adjective has been prefixed to an old noun. To understand the metropolitan surveys of the present it is necessary to recall the history of the "social movement" of which they are a part.

Cities, as dense agglomerations of population, are subject to ubiquitous and fertile problems, historically cumulative. We have, in urban areas, highly differential populations living in close proximity. Considering only the interdependence resulting from proximity, the following functional necessities result: (a) the location and movement of people and goods within the area must be ordered; (b) waste must be effectively disposed of; and (c) public safety and a degree of order must be maintained. These are minimal necessities: they are classic sources of urban problems.

Such necessities are functions of formal government in modern society, and approaches to them as problems are usually by way of the structure and functioning of urban government. This government, however, viewed as an institution of the culture and a segment of the society, is not fixed but is continually forming. Its structure, power, and access to resources are in a state of continual flux.

The rapid increase in the scale of modern western society has been reflected in the disproportionate increase of the urban portion of the population. Cities have increased in number, in absolute size, and in relative share of the population, and this has occurred much faster than appropriate changes in the legal definitions and powers of the "City." Consequently, a continual discrepancy results between the responsibility and power in the hands of the urban government.

The size and internal differentiation of the City's *electorate* increased even more rapidly than its population. When the political integration of this population is considered, together with the increase in functions resulting from continuous and rapid change, the sources of many public issues are laid bare. The legitimacy of power and the structure of government are inherited from the past; the field of function is continually changing as it emerges from the present.

Two kinds of problems were continually identified by the nineteenth-century publicists of the educated classes: "corruption" and "crime." Both reflected the differential administration of law and the suborning of the polity to the welfare of civic officials. Such causal breakdowns reflected both the inadequacy of the legal controls over the incumbents and the inadequacy of the older civic machinery as a supplier of essential services to the mushrooming cities. The resulting costs to important segments of the business class were immediate and tangible: the merchant is a classic source of loot for the banditti. There was, then, a social base in public indignation and in the interests of economically powerful persons for reform movements, intended to remove shame from the cities.

It is not necessary to recount the various battles and campaigns of this war. Suffice it to say that, with the aid of massive changes in the population (including the acculturation of ethnics, the increase in education and income, and the consequent decline of differentiation on these bases) the municipal government of urban America was made to approach considerably closer the norms acceptable to the economic interests and the moral preferences of the population.[1]

The ideology of the reform movement rested upon assumptions congenial to the business interests who were a main resource of reform campaigns. Adrian identifies two such assumptions, "(1) that the political party and politicians in general were not to be trusted and (2) that the principle of 'efficient business management' could and should be applied to the city government."[2] Minimizing conflicts of interest among the citizens, the ideology had the effect of masking those political processes allowing the resolution of real conflicts within a framework of legitimacy. Those accepting the ideology were committed to concern with the city, not as a pluralistic universe of interests and power, but as a corporation whose chief problems were those of "public administration." Overemphasis upon the analogy between business enterprise and municipality distracted attention from the great discrepancy between control systems in the two forms of organization and, at an extreme, even elided the fact that somewhere, somehow, basic policy must be made before there can be any administration. In this manner the social response to a plethora of conflicts was a definition of civic politics as a problem in "management."

The movement to save the cities emphasized rationality and accountability in management, economy and efficiency in operation, and the disinterested, non-political commitment proper to the bureaucrat: urban government in this definition approaches very closely to Max Weber's ideal type of bureaucracy. In the academic discipline of Political Science, a bureaucracy arose for the purpose of training bureaucrats for such structures, at the same time that its own ideology directed a further bureaucrazation of government. The subject area of local and, particularly, municipal government became a near monopoly for the students of public administration; research was ordinarily applied to the problems as defined by administrators, and the literature of the field took this orientation. Applied political scientists took as their badge of expertise, their training in public administration.[3]

The movement to remove the shame from the cities had its origins in the 1870's and had lost much of its original force by the 1950's. However, after World War II, a new target arose called "The Metropolitan Problem." The City, as a population complex, now tended to lie across numerous municipal, county, state, and even national boundaries; and to the old discrepancies between the responsibility of government and the power of government were added those due to spatial limitations in the scope of governmental control. Postulating interdependence between the elements of a real, or social City, the political fragmentation was defined as a set of limits upon the city's capacity to provide the minimal essentials in the way of governmental services. "The metropolitan problem" became a summarizing term for a series of problems, including "inadequate governmental structure," "service and regulatory defects," "financial inequalities and weaknesses," and "deficiencies in citizen controls."[4]

The increasing proportion of the population living in such metropolitan areas provided a dramatic argument for the urgency of study and action; if the United States is in the process of becoming a nation largely metropolitan in residence, then it is in the public interest to examine the implications of this change for governmental structure. At the same time the older move to improve the cities was carried over in the approach to metropolitanization. The definition of the subject as *"The* Metropolitan *Problem"* indicates the presence of value assumptions at the outset of the enterprise; and research projects in this field have usually been intellectually oriented toward the *improvement* of the cities through changes in governmental structure.

Within the framework of this intellectual tradition, the Metropolitan St. Louis Survey was conceived and launched.

The Immediate Origins of the Survey. In 1876, the City of St. Louis withdrew from St. Louis County and became at once a city and a county, one of the most radical structural changes that had occurred in an American city up to the time. In the process, the boundaries of the City were enlarged to include 61 square miles (as against 18 square miles), an area which seemed adequate to the most imaginative boosters of the day. However, the unprecedented growth in world urbanization during the nineteenth and twentieth centuries was reflected in St. Louis and, by 1910, very substantial satellite settlements began to appear in the adjacent county (also known as St. Louis County, and hereafter to be called "the County"). The socio-economic complex of the metropolitan area spread rapidly outwards, until today the urban area includes parts of five counties, three in Missouri and two in Illinois; only 45 per cent of the population is to be found in the City of St. Louis. The proportion continues to decline, as the outlying areas absorb all of the population difference reflected in growth.[5]

The effects of consolidating municipal and county governments in the City of St. Louis were, ironically, to prevent further expansion of the City boundaries; thus they have been the same since 1876. In 1926 and in 1930, serious efforts were made to readjust the boundaries of City and County through popular referenda; both failed. The rapidly increasing population of the County, however, was not averse to municipal government as such; between

1945 and 1950 a total of 44 new municipalities were incorporated, ranging in size from a population of 57 to several thousand. This was largely due to fear of annexation by existing cities.

While the boom in suburban living and governing was indicative of growth in the City-County area, the City of St. Louis had ceased growing in population and was, in many areas, suffering structural decay. The population came to include a disproportionate share of the Negro residents and the poorer residents of the metropolitan area. The neighborhoods of highest social rank became almost wholly concentrated in St. Louis County, while the blighted areas were chiefly in St. Louis City. The political map of the City-County area which emerged was one containing 149 units of government: one large governmental unit at the municipal level (the City of St. Louis), two at the county level (the City of St. Louis and St. Louis County), ninety-six small municipalities, twenty-nine small school districts (and a large one for the City), numerous fire protection districts, and only one over-all government — a newly created metropolitan sewage disposal district. This maze of local governments lacked a structure having the power to legislate for the City-County area as a whole.

The immediate climate of opinion which fostered the Survey rested upon this history — a past unity, a dissolution of the social city into a multitude of political fragments, and sporadic efforts at reintegration. At the same time, there was a growing belief in the middle 1950's that St. Louis might be in the process of "rising from the dead." One concrete symbol was at hand in the impressive public housing developments rising on the sites of ancient slums. Another was the election of a reform mayor (a professional engineer who had ended air pollution while serving as Smoke Commissioner). His ability to secure the support of a small group of economically powerful citizens in "Civic Progress Incorporated" (again, a "non-partisan" group) and the success of a large capital bond issue in a referendum which this group sponsored, furthered the belief that leadership was available for a new era. Another augury of change was the success of a referendum on a Metropolitan Sewer District in 1954; with its establishment the District became the first governmental unit to include both central city and the urbanized part of the County since the separation of City and County in 1876.

The metropolitan daily newspapers were actively promoting belief in the need for a change and one ran a series called "Progress or Decay" in which it was stated that the metropolitan area stood at the "crossroads of decision." National magazines of prestige carried major articles featuring the activities of Civic Progress, contrasting photographs of Negro slums with those of handsome public housing developments, and comparing the St. Louis "renaissance" with the rebirth of the Golden Triangle in Pittsburgh.

In this atmosphere a Citizens' Committee for City-County Coordination was organized with the avowed purpose of using a constitutional clause which permitted City and County to readjust their governmental relations. Like most such movements, this one reflected the interests of certain population segments and organizations, the ambitions of specific politicians, and the general excitement of a crusade. According to the Missouri Constitution, it was necessary only to file a small number of signatures from City and County to set in motion machinery which would lead to the drafting of a new constitution for the area. During 1955 and 1956, the signatures were gathered and considerable publicity, favorable and unfavorable, was showered upon the nascent movement.

The Missouri Constitution makes possible four changes in the relations between the City and the County; these are: (1) merger of the two in one City, (2) re-entry of the City of St. Louis into St. Louis County, (3) annexation of part of the County by the City, and (4) establishment of a new metropolitan district, similar to the Sewer District. The general lines of battle soon became defined in the press and in speeches by political leaders as "merger" versus "leave us alone." Merger seemed to be much more popular in the city, and *laissez faire* in the suburbs, judging by the public statements of influential residents.

The general situation was confused by imputations of private motives and bad faith, as usual, and the arguments pro and con suffered from a lack of documentation. As the situation progressed, certain civic-minded scholars began to feel that a question of considerable importance for local government in the area might be settled through default, confusion, and ignorance. In order to decrease the latter two conditions and to allow for a reorganization of the action campaign, these individuals drafted a proposal for a study of the situation by a team of objective social scientists. St. Louis University and Washington University, with the support of community leaders, submitted the proposal to the Ford Foundation whose support they won. This support was supplemented by a grant from the McDonnell Aircraft Charitable Trust.

The purposes of the project were first stated as follows:

1. To prepare, for consideration by a Board of Freeholders, alternative proposals for action designed to remedy some or all of the major ills arising out of the present pattern of government in St. Louis City and St. Louis County, and to provide ways and means to meet major metropolitan needs, present and future.

2. To provide, for consideration by citizens in other metropolitan centers:

   a. an evaluation of techniques used to gather information on typical metropolitan problems; and

   b. an analysis of attributes of residents in a metropolitan area, including their complaints and frustrations pertaining to governmental services and costs, and their reactions to suggested proposals for change; and

   c. an analysis of referendum campaign techniques and an assessment of their effectiveness.

3. To aid in the development of a systematic conceptual framework within which research in the general field of metropolitan government may be more meaningfully conducted.

4. To increase the supply of trained research workers in the general area of local government.

For these purposes, a time period of fifteen months was specified. This specification resulted from the pressure of the Citizens' Committee which indicated it would hold off formal action only this long. If the research results were to be of use in changing the form of government through the action of the Board of Freeholders, they had to be produced in this time period. The Metropolitan St. Louis Survey probably had the largest budget and most ambitious agenda for the shortest period of operating time ever allowed a study of metropolitan government.

II· Basic Assumptions of the Survey

As the Survey began work, its responsible administrators took every opportunity of saying publicly, "We have an open mind, and no preconceived notions as to what is best for the St. Louis Area." This statement, a response to the previous public image of the movement as one for merger of all local government into "one big city," was really an effort to define the Survey as essentially diagnostic and prescriptive. To understand the definition of the problem and the method of examination and prescription, we must remember that the Metropolitan St. Louis Survey emerged from both the ideology and lore concerning the improvement of cities and a specific action program to improve the St. Louis City-County area.

The goals were diffuse and contradictory, as is visible in the above quotation; however, that of constitution building quickly became dominant. The emphasis upon change led to concern with predicting the effects of planned change. The tradition of improving the cities led to the substantive goals of efficiency and order. In brief, the aim was to change the governmental pattern of the City-County area in these ways through drafting an outline of a new constitution which would be accepted by the voters in referenda.

The emphasis upon change had these general consequences: (1) it turned attention from the question, "How does government really function under the present circumstances?" toward the question of "How would it function under other circumstances?" (2) it emphasized the political consequences of any decision, since change could be effected only through persuasion. However, the change envisaged was notably *constitutional* change; it amounted to using the Missouri State Constitution's provisions to write a new charter and create a new government. This emphasis upon the provisions of the constitution led to the slighting of change which could not take place under that legal instrument (for example, it eliminated serious consideration of the half million residents of the metropolitan area in Illinois).

It also led to great emphasis upon public opinion, for the changes according to the Constitution could only be effected through a majority vote in two separate referenda (one in the City, one in the County). One positive consequence was a great concern to gauge the popularity of various changes; a negative consequence was the absence of major research investment in the study of the "power elite" of the metropolitan area. The concern with public opinion did encourage great sensitivity to the various citizens' groups and civic leaders who commented publicly on the Survey's purposes, reports, and recommendations.

Believing that governmental problems result from inefficient organization which allows irresponsibility and inaction in elected officials, the Survey concentrated upon formal governmental structure. Within this area, much attention was given the provision of services to the population. Fire protection, sewage disposal, police protection, and similar services were the "output" of government, with taxes the "input." The problem was defined as maximizing output for a given input. The Survey was also concerned that governmental output throughout the area reach an optimal level. (This level was very difficult to define clearly, for reasons to be considered later.)

The ideology caused an emphasis upon the organizing of an adequate human machine; it leaned heavily upon the maxims developed for public administration. There was interest in the notion that control should be integrated under one authority to avoid duplication of services and conflicts in jurisdiction. There was also concern for the most economical size of unit and the economies of scale as applied to government. In this complex of goals, focus upon the administrator as provider of garbage disposal services or public order, rather than as representative of interest groups, is a logical outcome. Some traditional directives for achieving these goals are civil service, non-partisanship accounting and recording systems, and administration by "managers" rather than "leaders."

Another aspect of the ideology, however, emphasizes the responsiveness of government to the citizens, and the equity of the service-providing system with respect to costs and benefits. Here, received dogma is much more confused and the directives are frequently obscure and contradictory. *The bureaucrat should be accessible to the citizen, but the only known machinery making this possible for citizens at large, the political party, violates the image of the bureaucratic municipal government.* It is also frequently assumed that the smaller unit of government provides such accessibility, as compared with citizenship in a vast metropolitan governmental unit, but small cities cannot profit by the economies of scale postulated in the management approach. Furthermore, the responsibility of government to the people is one of the mechanisms for insuring "equity" in the citizen's cost benefit ratio in exchanges with his government, and equity was another value of basic importance to those who originated and defined the Survey's purposes. Doctrine is complex, and, again, the directives are confused.

It is implied in the Research Plan that persons should not receive governmental services for which they are not paying and should not pay for more services than they receive; at the same time the desirability of a minimal level for the entire area is emphasized. When, however, tax sources are based upon property, it is obvious that great inequality will result in services within a metropolitan area, unless there is equalization of services by governmental decision. However, the redistribution of income by government is an extremely complex issue of political and economic policy.

Finally, the ideology includes the assumption that government has an importance for the social and economic "health" of the metropolitan area beyond the immediate provision of certain basic services to the population. Economic growth and decline were felt to be both causes and consequences of governmental disorder in the St. Louis area; the changing population, composition, and distribution were also seen as related vitally to the problems of government and *vice versa.* With these questions, however, we reach the edge of the ideology; here it was incumbent upon the Survey to create its own frame of reference.

III. Research Strategy

The Metropolitan St. Louis Survey was designed and its "charter" written by political scientists who were relying upon the general approach of their discipline, with its strong emphasis upon public administration. At the same time, however, the Research Plan envisaged a much broader inquiry into the status of government as one part of a total metropolitan economic and social complex. The basic questions were formulated in terms of governmental policy, but the answers were to be sought in many aspects of the metropolis. It is important that the research directives be read with this in mind, and an effort has been made to present them in much the same form as their original statement in the Research Plan of the Survey. Thus, the following outlines reflect the questions that political scientists asked of sociologists, economists, and of themselves.

The three sections will be discussed separately; the Sociology section's work will be discussed last and in greatest detail, since this is the work with which the author was most familiar. However, the very nature of the ideology and the hypotheses it engendered lead to considerable cross-fertilization among the research persons from the three disciplines.

The Government Survey Section. The scholars who concentrated upon the study of local governmental units began work several months before the economics and sociology sections were in operation; their findings, in preliminary form, thus constituted the background for the other sections' work.

The first task was a simple but expensive one; as most of the various units of government do not have to report essential data to any central agency in Missouri, it was necessary to do a field study of more than 100 units of local government. Since the purposes of the Survey emphasized the governments as corporate service-providing agencies, concern was with (1) legal and constitutional structures, (2) fiscal procedures and resources, and (3) service-providing functions and structures. The first concern led to knowledge of the legal power to act and conditions of action in each governmental unit; the second, in general, showed the flow of resources into the system via taxes, borrowing, and licensing; and the third dealt with the amount and quality of services provided the citizens in the government's jurisdiction.

The rules of public administration and the goals of the movement to improve the cities lead to specific hypotheses. The unit of attention was an image of the City-County area as one large complex, and the general question was: "How well is this big structure performing its various functions?" This broke into several questions: (1) what is the minimal level of service being provided to all sections of the urban area, (2) how is this related to the present, fragmented political structure of the area, and (3) what are the inequities resulting? Thus governmental fragmentation was a key area of interest.

It was hypothesized that the *ad hoc* development of governmental units with little rational control would have these consequences: (1) great variation in the legal foundations and the real purposes of governmental units in the metropolitan area, even resulting in governmental legitimacy used chiefly to *prevent* integration, (2) overlap in the units of government providing the same or similar services, resulting in conflicts of authority and duplication of services, (3) great variation in the size of governmental units, resulting in an assignment of services (which must be provided the citizens according to the usual division of labor among local governmental units in America) utterly disproportional to the jurisdictional and fiscal resources of the governing unit.

It was further hypothesized that this congeries of heterogeneous and overlapping governmental units would produce these results: (1) great variation in output, or service levels, among the different units, (2) great variations in the efficiency, or cost benefit ratio, among the units, and (3) a generally low level of some services throughout the area, due to the deleterious effects of poor services in one governmental unit upon the services in other, interdependent units.

These are, in general, dysfunctional results in terms of the "input-output" model of local government. It was also hypothesized that certain inequities would result from the over-all pattern. (1) Persons in some parts of the metropolitan area would be taxed twice for the same services; (2) some persons would receive services for which they did not pay; and (3) there would be no reasonably constant relationship between the cost of government and the benefit from government among the various sub-areas of the metropolitan region. In other words, taxes would vary with idiosyncratic governmental variables unrelated to either the services provided or the type of neighborhood in which one lived or owned property.

Finally, it was hypothesized that size of governmental unit would have no relationship to the vitality of the local political process. Neither the proportion of offices for which there was active competition, nor the proportion of the electorate which voted for local officials, would be significantly related to the size of the unit. This hypothesis amounted to a tentative rejection of the notion that governmental fragmentation helps to "keep government close to the people."

This latter hypothesis has an obvious bearing on the community action programs for which the survey was conceived as a resource. Just as one argument for integrating smaller units into a large government is the putative efficiency of the larger unit, so one argument for the smaller unit of government is its "accessibility" to the citizens. The previous hypotheses are also directly relevant to the action program, in the following manner: (1) the present governmental structure produces inadequacies in service levels, inequities in services and in cost benefit ratio, lack of responsibility of government to citizen and thus of citizen confidence in government; (2) the result is, in general, dissatisfaction with existing government, particularly great in those areas where services are poorest and inequities greatest; (3) this, in turn, produces a widespread willingness to change the governmental pattern of the City-County area.

This complex implied a very rational model of political behavior in local government, one in which the citizen was seen as *primarily* a customer of a service-producing bureaucracy. He is envisaged as competent, concerned, and rational; he sees his government from a bookkeeper's perspective, and reacts much like a political scientist whose training has been in public administration.

These propositions were not initially stated as hypotheses; *their validity was assumed, for they were part of the over-all ideology of the movement to save the cities.* The Government section of the Survey could not test hypotheses (2) and (3) above: this remained for the Sociology section's work. However, a major part of the resources of the governmental section went into the assessments of services required to test hypothesis (1).

These several clusters of hypotheses lead to an intensive comparison of legal structure and history, fiscal resources, operating organization and service levels, and electoral statistics, for the 149 governmental units of the City and County. Some of the results will be noted later.

The Economics Survey Section. There was a degree of overlap between the Government section and the Economics section, for both were concerned with the problem of ascertaining the cost of government and its relationship to the provision of services; public finance is an area common to both Political Science and Economics.

Three major projects were undertaken by the Economics section; one dealt with the interaction between the governmental structure and the economic structure, one with the relationship between size and efficiency in government as a service-providing agency, and one with the analysis of the economic base of the metropolitan area in a time perspective.

In studying the relationships between government and economic activity, it was hypothesized that (1) fragmentation of the governmental structure resulted in differences among the land areas in zoning and in governmental services which (2) channelled population and industrial movements (3) resulting in the waste of many sites, relative to their most productive use, as well as great discrepancies between the location of taxable property and the location and irrational land use. Thus, the governmental structure affects industrial and residential distribution in the area which, in turn, has major consequences for the governmental structure.

The second major project, the "cost of government" study, was intended to assess the cost of given governmental services as related to the size and other characteristics of the service-providing unit. In these efforts, the "input" and "output" of governmental units were related by statistical methods, while other relevant factors (such as population characteristics, density, and so forth) were held constant. The hypothesis was, simply, that there are economies of scale in governmental service agencies, as in other economic enterprises. The exact nature of the relationship was not hypothesized. At the same time that attributes of the various governments were analyzed statistically through multiple regression techniques, a simpler approach was used in which the known requirements of a given level of service for given size units were the bases of estimates which allowed the comparison of large units and smaller units. This technique was applied to a geographical subregion of the County which exhibited a prolific brood of "governments"; the present costs and services were compared with those estimated to hold for one inclusive governmental unit.

The third project, the economic base study and forecast, rested upon an ambitious effort to study the entire metropolitan area as an economic aggregate in relation to an economic environment. The "input-output" model was used, and there were no specific hypotheses. The aims were, however, to analyze the economic base and forecast its growth and change in terms of trends in the national ecenomy, to derive from these forecasts predictions of future population and its distribution together with industry location, and, consequently, future governmental revenue and needs. Closely connected with this study was the examination of factors, chiefly governmental, leading to the location of new industry in the area, expansion of existing industry, or failure of industry to locate. This is, of course, one important focus for the study of government and economic enterprise described above.

The Sociology Section. In the Research Plan, emphasis was placed upon the opinions and definitions held by the citizens of the metropolitan area. Although not stated as formal hypotheses, two important questions were asked: (a) What metropolitan problems are perceived, and how are they defined, by the population in the City and in the County? How do these perceptions and definitions vary among major geographical and socioeconomic segments of the metropolitan population? (b) What are the reactions of the citizens to proposals for change in the governmental structure of the area? A part of this project was the testing of the following hypotheses: (1) many citizens do not know what governmental agency is responsible for specific governmental services; (2) widespread criticism exists, among the citizens, with respect to the adequacy and/or cost of given services.

A second major need was the description and analysis of the metropolitan area's population. It was deemed important to answer these questions: (1) How is the socio-economic differentiation of the population related to governmental differentiation — what kinds of people live in different municipalities, counties, and so forth, in the metropolitan area, and, (2) what kinds of change, in the total population and in its spatial-governmental distribution, are taking place through time?

A third approach was the relation of population characteristics to voting behavior. In this study, particular attention was given the successful referendum for the Metropolitan Sewer District which, in 1954, had gained favorable majorities for the District in both City and County. The purpose of this study was to ascertain, if possible, the types of population aggregates which had supported the move to integrate the sewer districts of the City-County area. (It was hoped that such analysis would indicate the types of population most likely to favor integration of other governmental functions.)

The population of the City-County area was analyzed through the use of data from the 1950 decennial census. The population of each of the census tracts in the area was described in terms of sociological indexes of social rank, segregation, and urbanization (or urbanism).[6] The tract map, with the different social attributes indicated, thus constituted a "social mosaic" of the metropolitan area which could be compared with the political map.

When the social characteristics of City and County and the various subdivisions of each were measured for 1950 and preceding years, it was possible to indicate the changes in the nature and distribution of the population within political boundaries over time. And, when voting records were broken down to provide estimates of the vote within each census tract, the relationship between social characteristics and voting could be ascertained.

The questions dealing with citizen opinion and attitude were approached through a sample survey of the City-County area. A systematic random sample of households was drawn in City and County; one in each hundred dwelling units of the County was selected for the sample, and one in each four hundred units of the City. Altogether, the final sample amounted to 1800 interviews, 515 in the City and 1285 in the County.

The political opinions and reactions to governmental services were considered to be more than basic descriptive data, or even prognostic indicators for the state of health of the metropolitan area's government: they were also considered as *effect* variables, ultimately explicable in terms of sociological theory. Thus it was necessary to relate political behavior and opinions to (1) the over-all differentiation of the population by social class, ethnic background, and style of life, (2) the differentiation of neighborhoods and local communities as social systems, and (3) the differential participation of respondents in different kinds of social systems within the metropolitan environment. One of the most important kinds of social systems is, however, the political system of influence, communication, and overt social action. For these reasons, the interview schedule was much more than a set of opinion questions and standard questions about the socio-economic background of the respondent.

The point of departure was the classic survey question, "What is it really like at the grass roots?" What does local government mean as a social fact to the non-specialists in local government — as a political arena, as a provider of services and collector of taxes, as an image of a total community? What metropolitan problems are "real" at this level? And, closely connected with these questions, the policy question: "What conditions produce the massive resistance to metropolitan integration inevitably encountered by referenda on "merger"? How does a given *ad hoc* structure of government marshal the support among the voters which has repeatedly defeated efforts at metropolitan integration? A related question of importance was, "Who are the 'metropolitanites,' the citizens of the metropolitan area as a whole — or do they exist?" To what degree has functional interdependence of population within the metropolis resulted in anything resembling "community"?

IV. Some Salient Findings on Political Behavior

Three important congeries of ideas became hypotheses which were tested by the sample survey of citizen opinion in conjunction with research into governmental units. The first was the general notion that "widespread criticisms exist among the citizens with respect to the cost and/or adequacy of services." The second concerns the kinds of population and governmental unit most conducive to citizen participation in the governmental process. The final complex has been described earlier as the "rational model" of citizen-government relationships. This, it will be remembered, comprises assumptions that the citizen rationally evaluates governments by the services provided in relation to his needs and the cost of government; that his satisfaction with government results from such evaluation, and that his willingness to accept change is a direct function of his degree of dissatisfaction with present governmental services.

The Extent of Dissatisfaction. The Survey tended to bring over into its operations the rhetoric of the movement to save the cities by improving government. One important part of this rhetoric is the belief that, if governmental structure is *ad hoc* and irrational, the citizens will respond through general dissatisfaction and criticism. Though no quantitative estimates were made, it was believed that a large portion of the residents of the area were dissatisfied with *some* governmental service.

While a large proportion indicated some dissatisfaction (approximately 80 per cent had some suggestion for changes or improvements), there was very little consensus as to the improvements desired and there was no significant criticism of most major services of government. Thus, less than 10 per cent indicated they desired improvements in any of these services: police protection, fire protection, water supply, garbage, trash and sewage disposal, or pollution control. Schools, the subject of continual agitation, were identified as "problem areas" by less than 5 per cent of the subjects in the area. A miniscule proportion indicated a desire for lower taxes.

Certain service areas did elicit suggestions from substantial proportions of the respondents, however. Most important targets of criticism can be grouped around two aspects of urban life, (1) the neighborhood and (2) movement within the metropolitan area. Half of the respondents volunteered suggestions and criticisms concerned with the condition of their residential streets, 21 per cent were concerned with maintaining or improving the "character of the neighborhood" (slum clearance, slum prevention, rezoning, clean-up campaigns, and the like), and 12 per cent wanted improvements in parks and playground facilities. Thirty per cent indicated that they wanted improvement in traffic conditions and parking, and 10 per cent criticized public transportation.

Because the open-ended question indicates something about the "saliency" of a subject for the respondent, results are here given in some detail. However, a check list of structured questions, a "satisfaction inventory," elicited very similar responses. When asked how satisfied they were with each of a dozen major governmental services, the most dissatisfaction was expressed with those indicated above. In addition, a small proportion (15 per cent) indicated dissatisfaction with sewage disposal; these persons were almost all residents of the County. Another 15 per cent were dissatisfied with police protection and they were chiefly residents of the City.

From the complex welter of governmental services, only four elicited negative judgments from as many as 30 per cent of the residents in the metropolitan area. These were traffic, public transportation, the condition of residential streets, and parks and playgrounds.

A basic assumption of the ideology of the movement to improve local government in the metropolis is the belief that taxes are of great importance to the citizens and, as a corollary, that basic inequities in the value of services rendered as related to cost are an important source of dissatisfaction. As noted, almost none of the respondents suggested, in response to the open-ended question, that taxes should be lowered. Furthermore, when giving their reasons for wanting a change of governmental structure, less than 20 per cent indicated that "lower taxes" was an important reason for change. Finally, in response to a direct question on the equity of taxes in relation to services provided, only a minority (approximately 40 per cent) felt they were too high.[7]

In the study of government services provided in the various parts of the metropolitan area, considerable emphasis was placed upon the functionally and financially important services of police protection, fire protection, the schools, and the like. When, however, the citizen's perspective is examined it is evident that, for him, these services are not defined as "problems." There is no indication that any functional breakdown is imminent in local governments. Nor, on the other hand, were the respondents very concerned with what their governments were costing them. Instead, they were very interested indeed in the improvement of two aspects of urban living — facility of movement within the metropolitan area, and the upkeep and livability of their own immediate neighborhood. Government impinges on all citizens as a regulator of movement and upon many as a maintainer of residential streets and provider of parks and playground facilities. These latter services are not, traditionally, defined as the central "problems" of metropolitan government. If problems are to be ascertained by studying popular definitions, however, they are, together with traffic and transit, the major problems of the St. Louis area.

Participation in the Political Process. It was generally assumed that the smaller suburban municipalities had a definite superiority over the central City in making government interesting and accessible to the citizens — of "keeping government closer to the people." The approach of the Sociology section investigated a similar hypothesis. The smaller size of the governmental units and the higher average social rank of the population, together with the "familistic" rather than "urban" way of life in the suburbs, were expected to work in the same direction: in brief, they were expected to result in more voting, more faith in the importance of local elections, and more effective access of the citizen to the local government officials.

The findings were not an unambiguous verification, nor did they support the null hypothesis that size of governmental unit made *no* difference. With respect to participation in the electoral process, a larger proportion of the City population had voted in each type of local election for which comparison was possible. Over 67 per cent of the City respondents had voted for municipal officials, compared with 57 per cent of those eligible in the County, and half the City respondents had voted in School Board elections, compared with 43 per cent in the County. Furthermore, the difference is largely accounted for by the much higher proportion of County residents who either didn't know they could vote or thought they *could not* do so. Thus the hypotheses must be reversed to account for these findings. Residents of suburban municipalities seem *less* competent and *less* involved.

Although County residents were less likely to have voted in local elections, they were much more convinced of the importance of such elections. When asked a question from Campbell's "Sense of Citizen Duty Scale," as follows: "A good many local elections aren't important enough to bother with. Do you agree or disagree?", 82 per cent of the County residents disagreed, but only 68 per cent did so in the City. Assent to the ideological importance of local elections is greater in the suburban populations, though the proportion who have voted is greater in the City.

In order to gain a picture of the citizens relationship with the service-providing agencies of local government, a series of questions was asked which dealt with complaints made. The residents were asked if they had felt like complaining, and if so, whether they had complained, and if so, to *whom* had they complained.

The same percentage had felt like complaining in City and in the County — 38 per cent. A majority of those who had felt like complaining did so in the County (54 per cent) but in the City only a minority did so (32 per cent). (Almost all complaints dealt with immediate necessities of the household — sanitation, utilities, street repairs, and the like.) There is an important difference in the "target" of the complaint. Forty-one per cent of those in the County complained to specific persons, compared with only 25 per cent in the City. And in the County 20 per cent had complained to *elected* officials, as compared with only 5 per cent in the City. The residents of the County municipalities do, in some ways, have greater access to the officialdom of local government. However, City residents are more apt to be members of the electorate for local government than the suburbanites. In short, the attitudes of the County residents are not implemented by their voting behavior.

Any explanation of the City-County differences in voting by distribution of population categories (social rank, urbanization, migration) also falls short, for the City-County differences persist for every major subsegment of the two areas. However, a clue to the difference is available through the study of voting for the County Government officials in the suburban municipalities. The vote for these officials is quite comparable in the total (and in most sub-segments of the population) with that for City officials in St. Louis City. When it is realized that these elections are partisan elections for officials in large-scale government, while the suburban municipalities hold non-partisan elections for officials in very small-scale government, a hypothesis can be formulated which accounts for the difference as a result of political structure.

The fragmentation of suburbia into scores of muncipalities and school districts might be said to have "trivialized" local elections. If the cake is cut into enough pieces, nobdy gets a taste of either power, patronage, or glory. (It is significant that within the suburbs the proportion of offices contested increases consistently with the population of the municipalities.) As a corollary, large scale government is "news" for the metropolitan mass media. Finally, the "non-partisanship" of local government in the suburbs (with the exception of the County government) is probably another way of trivializing the election campaigns.

Voting is not, however, the only measure of citizen response to local government. A much larger proportion of those with complaints about their services had approached the officials of the County municipalities. The very structure of local government in the suburbs, which takes the excitement and significance out of elections by breaking the units very small, also provides an army of elected officials. These officials (something over 600 in St. Louis County) perform a basic governmental function: they are accessible and they listen to the grievances of the population. However, they seem more comparable, in some ways, to union stewards than to the Mayor of St. Louis City.

The Rational Model of Citizen-Government Relationships. The research assumption of the Survey, within the context of its action orientation, implied an interconnected set of notions which we have called the "rational model" of citizen-government relationships. This model assumes that irrational governmental structure and its consequences for services and equity will result in dissatisfaction on the part of the citizens; this, in turn, provides the bases for change, for the citizens who are dissatisfied will accept proposals to improve the situation.

When the first hypothesis, that lack of services results in dissatisfaction with government, is tested, there is no very clear relationship between the two. Dissatisfaction is relatively rare for almost all governmental services, and where there is dissatisfaction it is, frequently, in just those areas where services are very good. Dissatisfaction with public schools is highest in the high rank, familistic areas of St. Louis County which have the best public schools in the metropolitan area.

At the same time, dissatisfaction with taxes in relationship to benefits from government is highest among those parts of the population which pay the lowest local taxes and whose governmental services are, in some interpretations, "subsidized" by the larger taxpayers. Concern with tax equity is more common in the County than in the City — but within each area the high rank neighborhoods with many home-owners are least apt to complain about their local tax bill.

Thus, on the basis of dissatisfaction with present services, there is no support for a broad movement in favor of governmental change. However, ironically, the second link in the chain is weaker than the first. The people of the City-County area, very satisfied with most governmental services, are at the same time overwhelmingly in favor of improving their governments through inter-government cooperation and many approve of some form of integration. Seventy-five per cent are, by any of several indicators, in favor of change as against the *status quo*. Their reasons for believing in change are not clear. However, when those who believed their community should co-operate with others in performing some governmental services were asked "in what way it would benefit their community," 80 per cent gave answers which can be summarized as "more and better services." Only a minority (18 per cent) emphasized tax reduction.

Still the rational structure is questionable indeed, for, when asked what services should be integrated, the only one mentioned by as many as 10 per cent of the respondents was police protection. This was mentioned by some 15 per cent, chiefly in the County. Yet the proportion of County residents who were dissatisfied with police protection was negligible.

In short, the citizens of the area are not dissatisfied with many governmental services. This is reinforced by their *very* favorable judgments of all local governments. No more than 10 per cent thought the relevant government was doing a "poor" job in City, County, or the County Municipalities. At the same time, a large majority is in favor of change, and less than one-fourth prefer to leave the governmental structure as it is. The reasons for this support of reform are, at the present stage of analysis, obscure.

Summary. These findings may appear to be chiefly negative. There is no really widespread criticism of most governmental service nor of the equity of the tax load. There is no more dissatisfaction in the smaller units of government than the larger. Nor, on the other hand, do these smaller units evoke more interest in local elections. There is no broad basis for reform in dissatisfaction rationally derived from the inadequacies of governmental structure as seen by political scientists.

However, deductive logic applied to the implicit empirical assumptions of the ideology of civic reform yields a wide selection of various and contradictory propositions about the nature of local government and the possibilities for change in any given metropolitan area. These findings here reported perform the very useful task of narrowing the range of possibilities.

(Thus, it was on *a priori* grounds as plausible to expect a larger electorate in the suburbs as to expect what emerged from the research, e.g., a larger electorate in the City.) Through such tests the congeries of notions inherited from the movement to save the cities may be sifted and ordered, made internally coherent and more congruent with the nature of things.

By eliminating certain possibilities, the remaining assumptions are made to appear rather strange. Much more interesting questions than those derived from ideology begin to emerge as findings are compared with assumptions, and the latter emerged as discredited (or at least, unsupported) hypotheses. The lack of close relationship between dissatisfaction with present governments and willingness to accept change raises this question: what is the basis of the support for reform in metropolitan areas? Who are those who champion "merger," "one big city," a "metropolitan community?" On the other hand, who are the opposition? What, we must ask, provides the staying power of the "do nothing" suburban municipality? Why should the political process in the City involve a larger proportion of the potential electorate than in the suburb?

Our findings seem to indicate that the basis for governmental change in the St. Louis area does not rest upon the ancient cries of "Wolf" which were inherited from the movement to save the cities. Instead, the indications are that an economy of relative abundance has affected the kinds of demands made upon the local government by its citizens. When more citizens are interested in parks, playgrounds, and swimming pools, than in lowering taxes or improving police protection, one might venture to guess that some level acceptable to most citizens has been reached with traditional governmental services and that the *expansion* of governmental services is the real interest of a substantial proportion. There are, after all, certain goods which only government can supply and these include more than the "functional prerequisites" for the minimal functioning of the city; they include such articles of consumption as those mentioned earlier, as well as pleasant neighborhoods and clean air. It is not really likely that traffic conditions will ever "strangle" the economic life of a metropolitan area; however, our evidence indicates that they may come pretty close to strangling the individual resident in his capacity as a consumer of mobility.

V. Some Dilemmas of Action Research on Metropolitan Problems

The Metropolitan St. Louis Survey was ambitious in its scope; the general aims were as broad as the "metropolitan problem." Financial resources were, for once, apparently adequate. However, as work began it became obvious that intellectual resources were not nearly adequate — not because of the personnel of the study, but because of the poverty of conceptual beginnings and systematic information concerning metropolitan government. Thus the Survey, although an exercise in the application of social science to a policy question, was forced to operate as an intellectual enterprise focused upon *basic* research.

There are certain hiatuses between the process of application and the process of basic research, particularly when they deal with the same empirical problems. As a method of simplifying this discussion, the effects of "action orientation" upon the intellectual enterprise of basic research will be discussed, followed by a discussion of the Survey as an action program.

Problems of Basic Research in an Action Framework. The resources and support for the Survey had been contingent upon an orientation toward improving government in the City-County area. The structure of control and the focus of research reflected this emphasis. Furthermore,* the time schedule (15 months of field research during which two public reports were issued) was determined by the belief that the Survey would represent a kind of staff resource for the entire City-County area in its efforts to improve itself. This time schedule, as it turned out, was inadequate for the action program: the referenda are still far in the future.[8] The short period allowed for data gathering, and the subsequent dispersal of personnel, set a rigid limit on the research operations. There was every pressure for rapid application of known techniques and the translation of familiar concepts into tools for handling the given problems.

The Survey was defined as diagnostic and prescriptive, an operation which was to determine the ills of the metropolitan governmental structure, and the cures for these ills. This involves two assumptions: (1) the value of the analogy to problems of physical health in the "metropolitan problem," and (2) a competence on the part of the Survey staff to take the pulse of the metropolis and prescribe.

These assumptions led to basic ambiguities. What, for example, are the bases upon which minimal "levels" of service — schools, transit, police protection — may be calculated? What is an equitable relationship between taxes and services provided by government? What is an acceptably "vital" political process at the level of the County, the municipality, the school district?

It has been indicated already that, by present standards of gauging public opinion, nothing like a crisis in governmental services existed. Nor was there any danger of organizational collapse; on the contrary, local government and its services are probably being slowly though steadily improved. Thus one basis for a diagnostic criterion, the probability that the structure will not be able to survive unless action is taken, was notably absent. The prognosis for metropolitan *health* must be based upon value assumptions and these cannot be derived from the procedures of empirical science, yet the role of the medicine man forces one to speak as a "scientist" concerning matters of illness and health, salvation and damnation. In the process, it is very easy to lose sight of value judgments made, previous to research, informing research, but neither proved nor disproved by the results.

Because of the Survey's role and the time limits, the extremely important enterprise of disentangling value theory from empirical theory, ordering each, and attempting to relate them as separate kinds of thought which interpenetrate in policy decisions, was given a second place in the work procedure. It was logically prior to any field work which could be done.

At the same time, concentration upon what should be — what kind of government *should* handle what kind of services, what minimal level was required, what equity was desirable — led to a muting of the more basic problem — *What is the existing state of things?* and *How does it work?*

Yet this is also logically prior to the question of bringing about desirable changes however determined.

The Survey was forced to make premature application of social science, some of which was little more than the expert guess of the "experts." The results of basic research, which could have guided some of the policy decisions, were not available, for this research was being carried out coterminously with the drafting of a "plan of government" for the area. The physician was diagnosing heart ailments while attempting to test the proposition that the blood circulates.

Problems of Action in a Research Framework. The Survey was initiated with the hope that reform action would ensue; it will be judged by some on its action outcome. However, the personnel of the Survey were prohibited from taking any effective steps to initiate or guide a community movement. The legitimacy of the Survey as a public operation, and therefore its influence, depended upon the white mask of the scientific practitioner — one who "had an open mind and no preconceived notions." Furthermore, the Survey's status as a project supported by tax-free foundations meant that it could not engage in a local political campaign which would inevitably injure some interests in the community. The "action" program was curiously aim-inhibited.⁹

At the same time, the task of devising a new governmental structure for the metropolitan area meant, if taken seriously, a real attention to the conditions for the legitimizing of that government by referenda. If the plan of government were to be more than another "utopia," it had to take into account the probabilities of popular support in City and County separately.

As an action organization oriented to improving governmental structure, forbidden to organize power in the community, though dependent upon referenda results for success, the Survey tended to mask any basic conflicts of interest, though such conflicts constitute the political process. The non-partisan, integrative mode of thought, inherited from the movement to improve the cities, became an important part of the assumptions about action. At the same time, much attention was given to the figments of popular comment about the City, the County, and possible relationship and conflicts between the two. Many more basic questions, such as, for example, the existence, strength, composition, and integration of a metropolitan power structure, were elided.

Having no reliable information upon the nature of influence in the area as a whole, or in its major governmental sub-divisions, it was not possible to mount a frontal attack upon the question of "whose ox would be gored" in the event of merger, re-entry into the County, and the like.

The net result was to give great weight to findings from the sample survey. The opinions of the 1800 citizens interviewed were allowed to stand for public opinion in the area, and little weighting could be given the organized groups which most assuredly will have a good deal to do with the outcome of any referenda on the issue of City-County integration. Furthermore, the opinion of the citizens was, necessarily, studied in a period when there was no active campaign to change the governments; thus the validity of the sample survey is confined to a period of calm when there is no official act in the offing.

Nevertheless, it is quite probable that reform will emerge from the course of events in St. Louis and that the Metropolitan St. Louis Survey will have some effect on the nature of the changes. Acting as staff to an entire metropolitan community, the Survey did discover a general willingness to consider governmental change. There was widespread dissatisfaction with certain functions as they are performed: one of these, the regulation of traffic within the metropolitan area, can only be improved through a solution which is area-wide in its scope. This particular "problem area" is an object of dissatisfaction to many in all major segments of the population, and more salient among the suburban population than those of the City, the persons of high income than those of low, the "majority Americans" than those of "minority" ethnic status.

On other problems, however, the opinions of the experts in public administration and those of the public do not jibe. There is little concern for inequities in public school facilities and budgets among the population as a whole, though these seem major to the experts. Even more basic, planning and zoning are of little concern to the public. However, there *is* much concern for parks and playgrounds among the residents of the area, although these did not seem to be basic metropolitan problems. In cases of this sort, the dilemma of policy becomes quite pressing. Should the social scientists urge a propaganda campaign to change the public definition of the "problems"? Upon what value premise, and with what right?

The dangers of premature application are great in an area where application has so far outrun basic theory and research.[10] The "metropolitan problem" has an obscure quality because its origins lie in a simple summarizing of the results of metropolitan growth. It is really many problems, defined in an *ad hoc* manner. This "problem solving" approach deserves some attention, for it dominates thinking in many quarters.

Developed as a logical extension from the expert's role as a diagnoser and prescriber for the ills of the metropolitan body politic, this approach leaves the most interesting nine-tenths of the iceberg, the concept of "health," under water. Values are implicit and "problems" are identified on a particularistic basis wherever implicit values are depreciated or contravened. Various levels of value are not related: the problem of responsibility of government to citizen is one problem; that of minimal service level is another. Thus, choices tend to be, essentially, rational with respect to a very limited area defined as problematic, but the effects of the solutions may be extremely dysfunctional for other values and, therefore, irrational as public policy.

Thus, the "problem solving" approach to local government eliminates policy, for it assumes a fixed policy which is never made explicit. In democratic society, however, substantive policy is never fixed; it is contingent upon a given balance of power, representing a given dominance of values. One cannot discuss the metropolitan problem until he has a framework in terms of which these *ad hoc* problems become aspects of policy. But in policy making, it is quite clear, "to choose is to reject." With very few exceptions, public policy making is always a readjustment of equity.

If this sketch of the problem-solving approach to the metropolis has any truth to life, then some of the needs of theory with respect to metropolitan governmental processes begin to emerge. Values must be made explicit, and their relation to the power and influence structure of the metropolis must be spelled out. They must be generalized at a level which will allow some economy of thought and, perhaps, theoretical elegance. It should then be possible to compare them in a common frame — to allow the interests of many to enter a common arena. In such an arena, choices can be made in terms of a common calculus, one which will emphasize the cost of a given benefit as *loss* of others. The "problem solver" will face *his* problems — somebody's ox is always being gored.

NOTES TO CHAPTER V

1. For this discussion I have relied principally upon Charles R. Adrian, *Governing Urban America*, New York: McGraw-Hill Book Company, 1955, particularly Chapters 3 and 4.

2. *Ibid.*, 62. These assumptions were probably general in the urban society of the time, but they were far from being universal. It is necessary only to extrapolate a socialist position or a conflict-oriented syndicalist position in order to note the ideology's consonance with the thinking of Main Street.

3. For a spirited discussion of this development, see Lawrence J. R. Herson, "The Lost World of Municipal Government," in *The American Political Science Review*, 51 (June, 1957), 330–345.

4. *The States and the Metropolitan Problem*, prepared under the directorship of John C. Bollens, Council of State Governments, Chicago: 1956, 17-22.

5. This paper will deal only with the City-County Area which, however, includes the great majority of the Missouri portion of the metropolitan area. The Illinois side was not a subject of the Survey.

6. The Shevky-Bell typology of urban areas was used as the method of analyzing populations. Cf. Esref Shevky and Wendell Bell, *Social Area Analysis*, Stanford, California: Stanford University Press, 1955.

7. This item was adapted from one used by Morris Janowitz in studying perspectives toward the public bureaucracy in general. The results of the St. Louis study are practically identical with those reported by Janowitz for Detroit (the latter found that 41 per cent believed taxes to be too high); cf. Morris Janowitz, Deil Wright, and William Delany, *Public Administration and the Public—Perspectives Toward Government in a Metropolitan Community*, Michigan Governmental Studies No. 36, University of Michigan, Ann Arbor, 1958.

8. Ironically, the referendum for a new charter in the City of St. Louis occurred just at the end of the period of field work; this referendum could not be studied within the time period of the Survey, though such study would have yielded important findings. The new Charter was defeated by a very large margin.

9. Professor Thomas Eliot, a member of the Board of Control of the Survey, has discussed these difficulties in some detail in "Dilemmas of Metropolitan Research," *The Midwest Journal of Political Science*, 2 (February, 1958), 26–39.

10. Norton Long, "The Local Community as an Ecology of Games," *American Journal of Sociology*, 64 (1958), 251–261.

An Electoral Contest
in a Norwegian Province

BY *HENRY VALEN*

AND *DANIEL KATZ*

Objectives and Design of the Stavanger Area Study

ONE OF THE OBJECTIVES of the Norwegian study in Stavanger and the surrounding area in southwest Norway was an empirical exploration of the relationship between the various political parties and the social and economic groupings of the society. The study made such exploration possible because it was based upon systematic interviewing with a representative number of political leaders from five of the six Norwegian parties as well as interviews with a cross section of the voters in this area. Interviews were conducted directly before the Storting election of 1957 with 1,017 voters and 149 party leaders. The leadership interviewing included one province, four communes, and twenty-one election districts. The data permit a description of party structure and party functioning and an analysis of the impact of party activity upon the electorate.[1]

The study was designed primarily to measure the effect of one type of factor, operative at the community level, upon political behavior and attitude — namely, the local party organization. Thus the independent variable in the investigation was the character and activity of the local units of the five Norwegian political parties in the four communes in the Stavanger area. The smallest unit is the election district, but not all parties have formally designated leaders at this level in every commune. In all, twenty-one election districts were included in the sample and interviews were conducted with party representatives working at this level wherever parties had such representatives; in all, some 55 local leaders were interviewed. The dependent variables had to do with the perceptions, attitudes, and behavior of the electorate. This design permits the systematic relating of characteristics of local party organization to responses of the electorate. Since the study was conducted within the two communities of Stavanger and its semi-rural southern environs, the usual information about community background is available.[2]

Our concern in this paper is with a consideration (1) of the character of the Norwegian party system, (2) of the nature of the structure of Norwegian parties as they function at the community level, (3) of the factors related to voting preference, and (4) of the relations of parties to the social organizations in the community. The emphasis upon relationship to social structure is based upon the assumption that a political party is both the expression of common citizenship interests of its members in local and national affairs, and the reflection of more specific interests of sub-groups within the national structure. The political tie or bond between the citizen and his party may be dominantly political and direct in nature or it may be mediated by existing social structure. The increasing interest in political sociology and in pressure groups focuses upon this second type of relationship and more empirical investigation is desirable.

The Stavanger Area. A Short Description

The city of Stavanger is the capital of the southwestern Norwegian province of Rogaland. The provincial administration is located here; all political parties and all kinds of organizations have their provincial headquarters in the city. According to tradition, the city was founded around the year 1100 A.D. as a religious center for southwestern Norway. It also became a political and trade center for this part of the country, and it still has this character.

Stavanger is the fourth largest Norwegian city with a population of 52,700 inhabitants (in 1955). The area around Stavanger, which is called Jaaren, is relatively densely populated. It had in 1955 about 120,000 inhabitants, which is more than half of the population for the whole province. In Stavanger the population has been relatively stable; from 1930-55 it increased only 13 per cent. In Jaaren the population increased in the same period by about 36 per cent. There has been a tendency for Stavanger people to settle in the surrounding communes.

Stavanger is an old industrial city. In 1950 (the last census available) 47.5 per cent of the men in the active population were working in industry and construction. This proportion has been fairly stable over the last thirty years. The most important industries are canning, metal, and shipbuilding. After industry, trade and shipping are the most important economic activities.

The area around Stavanger is one of the best farming districts in the country. Over the last twenty to thirty years the area has, however, been characterized by an extraordinarily strong growth in industrial production. In fact, the area is in a period of rapid transition from an agricultural to an industrial community.

For our study we selected Stavanger and three communes a few miles south of Stavanger: the two neighboring rural communes of Hoyland and Time, and the small town of Sandnes. These communes are connected by roads and railways, and both economically and culturally they may be considered as constituting a community. At the same time they cannot be regarded as suburbs of Stavanger. The selected communes are strongly characterized by recent industrialization. Iron and metal industries, textile industries, and food production are the most important industrial activities in this community. Finally, it should be mentioned that the Stavanger area is a stronghold for the lay religious and temperance movement. One of the big religious lay organizations has its national headquarters in Stavanger. It may be added that the temperance movement in Norway originated in Stavanger.

Party Structure and Function

A. *Historical Perspective.* Organized political parties in Norway date back to 1884 when the Liberal party and the Conservative party were formed. The establishment of formal political organizations followed immediately upon the introduction of the parliamentary system in that year. The country then was still in a union with Sweden — a union which began in 1814 and ended in 1905. Until 1884, the country had been ruled by a class of civil servants, many of whom became the leaders of the Conservative Party. For some thirty years Norwegian politics was dominated by the Liberals and Conservatives who alternated in the control of the government. The Labor party, which was formed in 1887, was originally supported by only a small proportion of the voters. As it developed its strength it drew members from the fishermen and small farmers as well as from the urban workers.

When the two-party system ended around 1920, the parliamentary situation became unstable. In the election of 1915, the Labor party obtained about one-third of the votes, and in 1918, neither of the two old parties won a majority of the seats in the Storting. In the following years, new parties were formed as a result of the factional struggles in the Labor party. In 1923, the left wing of the Labor party broke away and formed the Communist party. For some years, there were actually three socialist parties after the moderate Laborites also broke away and formed the Social Democratic party in 1919. This party was, however, united with the Labor party in 1927.

The Liberal party was split in 1920, when the Agrarian party was formed. This party was originated on the initiative of the Farm organizations. The Liberals experienced another split in 1933, when the Christian People's party was organized as an expression of the lay religious movement.

In the thirties, several new parties appeared, one of which was the National Socialist party. But none of them won any significant support, and with one exception they never succeeded in being represented in the Storting.

The establishment of a multi-party system resulted in unstable governments which changed rather frequent'y. In the period 1918-45, no single party ever obtained a majority in the Storting. The cabinets were always formed by only one party, but the parliamentary base of the governments depended on political support from one or more other parties in the Storting. From 1918 to 1935, the Liberals, the Conservatives, and the Agrarians succeeded each other in power. In 1927, the Labor party obtained 37 per cent of the votes and became the largest party. The following year it made its first, but unsuccessful attempt to form the cabinet. In the beginning of the thirties, the party increased its vote strongly, and in 1935, it formed a government with the parliamentary support of the Agrarians. The Labor party remained in power until 1940.

During World War II, and in the first months after the war, all parties participated in coalition cabinets led by the Labor party. In the period since

1945, the Labor party has run the government as a result of a plurality or a majority position in the Storting.

Political life in Norway is not complicated by conflicts between different races or nationality groups. There are no problems of contesting religious faiths since about 95 per cent of the population belong to the Lutheran state church. There is, however, some disagreement concerning the position of the Church in relation to the State, and about the role of religion in society. With the exception of the Communists, all parties agree in general on the government's foreign policy, the keystone of which is participation in the Western military alliance, and economic co-operation with Western Europe. Since World War II, there has been almost no disagreement concerning matters of social welfare; all parties accept the principle of the "welfare state."

Economic policy is the main area for dispute between the parties. There are different opinions about the rate of development of national industries, and the means to be preferred for this development. But disagreement on the distribution of goods between various social groups and classes seems to be even more important.

Attitudes on these problems are to a high degree reflected in the parties' stands on the role of the state in economic life. The Labor party and the Conservative party which are the strongest opponents with respect to economic policy represent the two extremes on this dimension. The Labor party must be considered a moderate socialist party similar to the British Labour party. It was originally Marxian in ideology, and some of its symbols still reflect this early orientation. It has not, however, moved far in the direction of nationalization, though it does want a rather comprehensive control of business. The Conservative party, the party that has its strongest support from business groups, wants to reduce state control and encourage private initiative. The Liberals are situated in between these two parties in that they want some state control, although they do not want to move as far as Labor. The Liberals are different from other parties in that they have looser attachment to special groups and classes and tend to identify more with common national values. The Liberal party still reflects its heritage of espousing Norwegian nationalism. It is committed to restoring the pure Norwegian language which existed before the so-called "corruption" by Danish elements. The Agrarians are mainly concerned with farm issues, and, in this respect, they advocate a policy of equalization between farming and industry. On other problems they take stands which are rather similar to those of the Conservatives. The Christian People's party does not fit into this scheme. It is mainly concerned with religious and moral problems, such as religious teaching in the schools, construction of churches and prayer-houses and restrictions on the sale of alcohol. In economic matters, it seems to come close to the stand of the Liberals.

Although there is substantial agreement among the parties on many domestic issues such as social welfare, local party leaders in the Stavanger area in the 1957 election differed in what they saw as the controversial issues dividing the parties (Table 1). Matters of social policy such as housing and labor relations were seen by more leaders in the Labor party as controversial issues than by leaders in any other party. Socialization and individual enterprise were most salient in the thinking of Conservative leaders. Agrarian

Table 1

CONTROVERSIAL ISSUES IN 1957 ELECTION AS REPORTED BY LEADERS*

Party of leaders	Composition of gov't.	Defense and Foreign policy	Socialization, state control, individual enterprise	Inflation, prices, standard of living	Tax policy	Economic policy, interest rates, investments	Agricultural policy	Social policy, housing labor-relations	Educational and cultural problems	Moral issues and Christianity	Other issues	Total
Labor	11.6%	11.6%	9.3%	32.6%	46.5%	37.2%	2.3%	44.2%	20.9%	0.0%	20.9%	43
Liberal	11.5	34.6	23.1	34.6	50.0	23.1	7.7	30.8	15.4	3.8	34.6	26
Christian	3.8	11.5	11.5	26.9	15.4	30.8	7.7	15.4	0.0	65.4	3.8	26
Agrarian	10.5	15.8	21.1	78.9	5.3	21.1	31.6	10.5	0.0	5.3	10.5	19
Conservative	2.9	14.3	57.1	34.3	68.6	25.7	5.7	25.7	8.6	0.0	20.0	35

* Percentages add to more than 100% because question called for multiple answers.

leaders were the group most concerned with problems of inflation and standard of living. Few party leaders thought of defense and foreign policy as controversial with the exception of Liberal leaders.

B. *Regional Differences and the Stavanger Area.* Political development in Norway is characterized by rather large regional differences. The Southern and Western provinces deviate from the rest of the country. The Liberals, the Christian People's party, and the Agrarian party are much stronger in the southwestern region than in the east and north, while the Communists, Labor party, and, to some extent, the Conservatives gain less support in this region than in other parts of the country.

The explanation most commonly given for these regional differences depends on considerations of religion and temperance. The lay religious and temperance movements have their strongholds in the southwestern region, and these movements have close ties to the middle parties, in particular to the Christian People's party. This party originated in the province of Rogaland, and, until 1945, the party had only run candidates in Storting elections in a couple of constituencies on the Western coast. Another hypothesis[2] about the regional differences is that the Labor party and the Conservative party have relatively weak appeal in the South and West because in this region class differences are smaller than in other parts of the country, particularly in agriculture. Thus in other areas where there are noticeable differences in holdings between small and large farmers, the small farmers are more likely to vote Labor than are their counterparts in southwestern Norway.

The province of Rogaland follows closely the pattern of the Southwestern region. But there are rather large variations between the different communes of Rogaland which have been included in the study. How these variations are related to industrialization will be analyzed later. A few observations may, however, be made:

1. Within the communes included in our study the Conservative party gets relatively strongest support in the city of Stavanger and in the town of Sandnes. The Liberals are equal in strength in urbanized and rural areas. The Christian People's party gets some support in urbanized areas, but it is relatively stronger in rural areas.

2. Although voting in Norway is relatively stable from one election to another, considerable changes have occurred in the period 1921–57. Most important is the change in the vote for the Labor party which increased from 22 per cent (together with the Social Democrats) in 1921, to 37 per cent in 1957, and for the Liberals who lost more than half of their vote during this period. In particular the Liberals have suffered heavy losses since World War II. However, in Rogaland the Christian People's party did not take part in the elections until after the war, and the proportion of votes won by this party comes rather close to the proportion lost by the Liberals. The same observation may be made on a nation-wide basis. This suggests that the Christian People's Party has gained most of its votes from groups which traditionally had voted Liberal. This hypothesis will be tested in the analysis of the survey data. But before going into a more detailed

analysis of the party structure in the Stavanger area, some general remarks should be made on Norwegian party structure.

C. Functions of Parties. A primary function of political parties is to organize for the electoral struggle. In running candidates and articulating differences in opinion the parties make it possible for voters to choose between more or less clear alternatives. Although practically all party activities may be referred to the competition for the vote, parties also perform a role in the political decision-making process between the elections.

Compared with the party systems of many other countries, e.g., the United States, the Norwegian parties seem to play a dominating role in the political process. At election it is the parties rather than individual candidates which are made responsible for the policies conducted in the preceding period. This may be partly due to the election system which allows the voters to choose between party tickets and not between individual candidates.' But even more important, it seems that each party tries to develop independent policies, distinct from those of other parties. At elections the parties present a detailed platform to the voters, and the representatives in public office are expected to follow this program. In the Storting and in local assemblies the representatives of each party form a caucus, where matters coming up for decision are discussed. In particular, on issues of principle, the representatives try to arrive at a joint stand which will demonstrate the party's attitude.

In creating a unified policy the role of the party organization is crucial. The platform is decided by the national congress. This assembly, which consists of delegates from all provincial branches of the party, is summoned regularly every second or third year. Ordinarily, committees appointed by the central leadership make proposals to the congress concerning the new policies of the party. But before the congress is held, the proposals are taken up for discussion in local party organizations. Further, the locals have the right to make their own proposals to the congress. In this way the platform is formulated on the basis of thorough discussion at various levels in the party organization, at least this is the protocol of party statutes.

One other task of the national congress is to elect a national committee which supervises the party's policies and organizational activities in the period until the next congress. The national leaders are concerned with the planning and interpretation of long-term policies. They also play an important role in cooperating with the party caucus in the Storting in transforming the platform into practical politics. Although the platform is ordinarily fairly detailed, it does not define the party's stand on every issue coming up for discussion in the Storting. In addition, new problems may arise which were not foreseen when the platform was written, or the situation may have changed so that some problems will have to be considered from a different angle.

The party organization also plays a role in local politics. It should be noted that, in Norway, local self-government is of relatively great importance in the political system. The communal authorities perform functions, which in many other countries are handled by the national administration, e.g., in matters concerning education, economic planning, etc.

The local party organization formulates a more or less detailed platform at local elections, which are held every fourth year, and usually the organization discusses problems with the party's representatives in local office. The participation of parties in local politics obviously contributes greatly in keeping the party organization intact in the period between elections. The local community is the place where the voter gets into most direct contact with the party structure. Therefore, the voter's perception of the differences between the parties and of the relationship between parties and candidates must be influenced by his awareness of party activity in local politics.

The Norwegian parties vary a great deal, however, with regard to organizational structure and practices. Although this problem has never been investigated, some areas may be suggested in which variations between the parties seem to be particularly great:

1. The degree of party unity in propaganda and action. It should be noted that unified policies are only required on issues which are considered by the party to be matters of principle, i.e., matters which are related to the party's ideology or goals. The Communists and the Labor party have the most unified policies, while the Liberals and the Christian People's party seem to be lowest in political unity.

2. The control of the party organization over the party's representatives in public office, on the national as well as on the local level. The Communists, and then the Labor party, obviously have the most disciplined organizations. Again, the Liberals and the Christian People's party probably represent the other extreme with the least organizational control of their representatives. The design of the present study does not provide any measure of the actual control by the party organizations. The problem of how voters and leaders perceive the role of the parties in the local politics will, however, be taken up later in this article.

3. Degree of centralization of decision-making in the party, i.e., the extent to which the party's policies are in fact decided by the central leadership. Nothing is known of a systematic character of this problem.

As has already been suggested, some of these factors are interrelated. For example, it is likely that a strong party discipline will result in a high degree of political unity, and that unity is achieved more easily by centralization of decision-making.

There may be several reasons for the differences in the organizational structure and activities of the parties. Historical traditions may be mentioned as one possible factor. Another is the ideology and goals of the respective parties. But the one thing which seems to be of most importance in this respect is the way in which the parties are tied in with the social structure: which groups and classes do they have to rely upon for support, how close is their relationship with various organizations, to what degree do they have to make compromises in their policies between mutually contesting interests?

Without entering into any detailed analysis of the structural differences between the parties, we may offer certain observations regarding the integration of parties in the society. An important function of parties in any political system is to advance the interests of various social groups and classes. But since groups can also further their interests directly through governmental institutions they are only to a certain degree dependent upon the parties. In the Norwegian system the tie-in between political parties and groups seems to be of relatively great importance. Since the members of the Storting are more or less obliged to follow the party line on major issues, their opportunities to advocate separate group interests when decisions are made in the assembly or in Storting committees are limited. Therefore, social groups and organizations must obtain direct representation of their interests through the parties.

The concern of parties for various interests may be observed in several ways. First of all, it is reflected in the party structure. All parties have sub-organizations for women and youth. In addition, the Labor party has sub-organizations not only of trade unions but also for active Christians and teetotalers, and the Conservatives have an organization for workers. Besides these formal organizations there are several more or less well-structured informal groups in the parties working for various interests. Such "interest factions," formal as well as informal, perform an important function in con-stituting a link between the party and various social organizations and the corresponding categories of voters.[5]

Second, membership in social organizations seems to be an important qualification for the selection of party leaders. Parties tend to nominate organizational leaders from unions and other organizations for public office. Such leaders have the opportunity to advocate their respective group inter-ests when the party platform is written and when the party determines its stand on various issues. In addition, in all matters which have no ideological character from the party's point of view the representative may work more directly for the interests of his organization.

The problems of the relationship between political parties and social or-ganizations which are indeed crucial for understanding the power structure of a Norwegian community, will be dealt with in the next section. At this point, however, we should like to distinguish theoretically among three di-mensions of the relationship between social and political structure.

The first dimension is that of the degree to which an interest group, or a group with common values, has formal representation in the party structure itself. Labor unions in Norway are formally represented in the Labor Party; in the United States they exercise influence within parties more indirectly. The second dimension is the extent to which the group interest and values, reflected within the party, represent latent social structure as against articu-lated, organized groupings. Parties can align certain socioeconomic groupings which may lack organizational structure and formal leaders. Political leaders themselves may serve as the representatives of these unorganized groupings. A third dimension has to do with the multiplicity of groups which the party represents. It may represent a single interest group or only a few closely related groupings. Such a party has, to a certain degree, the character of an interest organization and is little more than the political face of an eco-nomic or social group. Or the party may be an institution which contains many organized and unorganized factions and one of its major functions becomes the reconciling and compromising of competing interests and values.

In this sense, the political party partakes of the character of a sub-state in resolving group conflicts before they reach the top level decision centers of the state.

In the Norwegian political system, two of the parties are "single-interest" parties, the others are "multiple interest" parties. The Agrarian party and the Christian People's party are mostly concerned with narrow interests in their politics, the Agrarians with farm interests, and the Christian People's party with religious and temperance problems. The Labor party, the Conservative party, and the Liberal party, however, include several interests in their platforms; they take stands on all major problems in national politics; and they represent more than one segment of voters. Thus the Labor party has backing not only from organized labor but from independent fishermen, small farmers, functionaries, and professional people, though the last three groups are not dominantly Labor in political preference.

D. Party Organizations in the Stavanger Area.[6] The hierarchical organization of the parties starts with local groups in the communes as the basic unit, moves through an intermediate structure of organization, at the province level, to the highest level, the national organization. This three-level hierarchy is an oversimplification in that large communes are often further subdivided into election districts for purposes of party activity. Thus, in Stavanger a number of parties have assigned responsibility for the eight election districts to specific leaders or committees. The political youth and women's organizations are more or less independent and are moulded after the party organizations. But in addition, these sub-organizations are affiliated with the party organizations on all levels in the hierarchy. Party and sub-organizations are mutually represented on the commune, provincial, and national committees. Further, members of the sub-organizations are automatically regarded as members of the party, and frequently they participate in joint meetings with the party organization.[7]

The number of local party organizations in each commune varies with the size of the commune and with the parties. The Liberals, the Christian People's party and the Agrarians ordinarily have only one organization in each commune. The Labor party and the Conservatives, however, may have several groups in large communes, in particular in the cities. When there are several organizations the party activities in the communes are co-ordinated through a representative assembly or council in which local party organizations, women and youth organizations participate.

On the local level, the Labor party has collectively associated trade unions in addition to ordinary party groups, women and youth groups. Local unions may decide with a majority vote that they will join the party.[8] The local union then gets an additional function as a party organization, which is represented in the party equally with other local groups. It should be observed, however, that the collectively associated trade unions do not form a separate nation-wide organization within the party similar to women and youth organizations, and in Norway, national unions never join the party as national unions join the Labor party in Britain. This structural difference has important implications in that the Labor party political leadership is more than another set of roles for the leaders of the national unions.

In the province of Rogaland, the Labor party, the Liberal party, and the Conservatives have both youth and women's organizations. The Agrarian party has a youth organization, but no women's organization. In the Christion People's party the women are organized, but not the youth.

All parties, except the Liberals, have local organizations in about three-fourths of Rogaland's fifty-four communes. The Liberals are organized in only half of the communes. In the four communes included in our study, all parties have local organizations with the exception of the Agrarians who have no organizations in Stavanger and Sandnes, and the Christian People's party which has no organization in Sandnes. Altogether there are twenty-one political women's and youth organizations in the area, thirteen of which are located in Stavanger and Sandnes.

E. Party Membership. The heavier involvement of Norwegians, compared to Americans, in the political process is indicated by the fact that some 21 per cent of all Norwegian citizens are dues-paying members of some political party. Though this figure would be reduced to some 17 per cent if union collective association were omitted, it would still be higher than the proportion of people who make even an occasional financial contribution during a political campaign in the United States. In Detroit, for example, some 11 per cent of the people reported that they or some member of their families had contributed money to a candidate or a party during the 1956 campaign.[9]

The Stavanger area shows a lower percentage of party members than the country as a whole, partly because fewer union members are collectively associated with the Labor party in this area. In fact, the Labor party is the only party which is appreciably weaker in members in the Stavanger area than in the nation as a whole. The Liberals have the same strength in this area as in the rest of the country but this is not a good showing since Rogaland is supposedly one of the main Liberal strongholds. By way of contrast, the Christian People's party has 8 per cent of the voters in the Stavanger area enrolled as members whereas their showing in the nation as a whole is only a little over one per cent. The Liberal vote in the 1957 elections, however, showed a slight gain over the 1953 record in this part of Norway, though the long-time trend has been running against the Liberal party in almost all sections of Norway.

The Liberal tradition in the Stavanger area is maintained in part through the effort of the party press. In Norway most of the newspapers are more or less committed to some political party. The papers advocate their respective parties' viewpoints, not only during the campaigns but also between the elections. In this way the party press contributes strongly in articulating the differences between the parties. The Liberal paper in Stavanger (*Stavanger Aftenblad*) is one of the leading Liberal papers in the country, and it is by far the biggest paper in the province of Rogaland. Altogether this paper sells some 35,300 copies, of which 19,000 are distributed in the Stavanger area. Next comes the Labor paper (*Rogalands Avis*) with 12,700 copies in all, and 7,900 in the Stavanger area. Then the Conservative paper (*Stavangeren*) with 8,300 copies in all, and 4,600 in the Stavanger area.[10] For the Agrarian paper (*Rogaland*) which is the smallest one, there is no available information.

Table 2

VOTING BEHAVIOR IN THE STAVANGER AREA IN RELATION TO PARTY MEMBERSHIP AND PARTY IDENTIFICATION*

Party Supported	Com.	Lab.	Lib.	Chr.	Agr.	Cons.	Non-Voter Uncertain	Refuses	NA
COM.									
Member									
Identifier	38%							2%	
LABOR									
Member	6	10						2	
Identifier	25	67	2	1		1	14		16
LIBERAL									
Member		5							
Identifier	0	53	6				7	2	14
CHRISTIAN PEOPLE'S PARTY									
Member		1	12						
Identifier	0	3	49				2	2	
AGRARIAN									
Member		1	1	42					
Identifier	0	1	2	42	2		1	4	3
CONSERVATIVE									
Member						15		2	
Identifier			1			45	5	4	3
INDEPENDENTS	25	16	29	17	10	27	62	38	50
REFUSES DK, NA	6	7	4	12	6	10	9	44	14
Total	100%	100%	100%	100%	100%	100%	100%	100%	100%
N	16	365	171	90	95	113	84	46	36

* Party identification was measured by the following question (to those who were not party members): "Apart from formal party-membership would you say that you wholeheartedly support one special party; in other words, do you consider yourself a **Liberal**, a **Conservative**, a **Laborite**, or what?"

F. Party Identification. People who were not party members were asked whether they identified with some special party. As Table 2 shows, there are more identifiers than members. The bulk of the vote for every party, save the Communist party, comes from party members and identifiers but there are interesting differences among the parties in their ability to attract votes from people who do not otherwise support the party. If we group together party members and identifiers into the one category of party supporters, we find that the Agrarian vote is the most heavily drawn from party supporters (84 per cent). And conversely very few Agrarian supporters defect to the other parties on election day. The Labor party vote is next in dependence upon party supporters (77 per cent) though it loses more supporters to the non-voting category than any other party. The other parties are grouped with respect to dependence upon party supporters at approximately a sixty per cent level with the exception of the Communist party which falls to 38 per cent. There are too few cases (sixteen to be exact) of Communist voters to warrant generalization, but it would appear that it is easier to admit Communist voting than more consistent support of the Communist party — not a single Communist voter would admit to party membership.

Perhaps the most surprising finding in these data on party support and party voting is the apparent lack of clarity about the Conservative party as a political party. It was expected that the Agrarian and Labor parties, with clear goals and programs, would have the highest overlap between voters and supporters. And it was expected that the Liberal Party, with a more diffuse program and with less concern for strong centralized party organization, would have fewer party supporters among its voters. To put it another way, the independents may be more attracted to a middle party like the Liberal party which takes a position between Labor and the Conservatives concerning the problem of the state control of the economy. The Christian People's party also would not have high identity of party supporters and party voters since this party gives little emphasis to formal political organization. But the Conservative party, the political function of which seems to parallel that of the Labor Party at the other end of the continuum, draws as heavily upon the independents for its vote as do the Liberals and the Christian People's party. It may be in part that many of the independents are not in sympathy with present governmental policy and in voting Conservative are voting against Labor though they are not willing to call themselves supporters of any political party. It may also be that the Conservative party's acceptance of Labor party reforms has made its position and program more ambiguous than that of the Labor party. But it could be that the Conservatives have a certain flavor of being a party of prestige and respectability, and this may appeal to independents with weak identification with specific social groups and classes. Finally, there is reason to believe that some people with high status and education are reluctant to reveal their party attachments. Some regular Conservative voters probably prefer to call themselves independents.

Another measure of party support comes from the feeling which people express about the importance of their own party putting up a ticket in the Storting election. Party members and identifiers were asked: "Suppose that your party for one reason or another was prevented from presenting a ticket of candidates at the Storting election in the province of Rogaland; would that mean a great deal to you, a little, or would you not care?" Respondents were classified as strong in party commitment if they said, "a great deal" and weak in party commitment if they said, "a little," or did not care. More of the supporters of the Christian People's party show stronger commitment than of any other party (Table 3). The Liberal party is at the bottom of the list in percentage of its followers showing strong commitment with less than a fourth of their supporters in this category. Again the unusual character of the Liberal party as a political organization is in evidence. Many people apparently vote for the Liberal candidates as an expression of their allegiance to certain symbols and values rather than for a political instrumentality for achieving specific programs.

In general a high proportion of party supporters vote for their respective parties and strongly committed supporters are more consistent in their party vote than are weak supporters. This finding corresponds to what has been observed in studies of the American electorate. In Norway, party supporters

Table 3

VOTING BEHAVIOR IN RELATION TO STRENTGH OF PARTY COMMITMENT

VOTING BEHAVIOR 1957

Party supported	Strength of commitment	Com.	Lab.	Lib.	Chr.	Agr.	Cons.	Did not vote and uncertain	Re-fuses	NA	Total N=100%
Com.*											7
Lab.	Strong	1%	95%	1%				2%		1%	123
	Weak	2	85	1	1		1	7		3	144
	NA		97							3	40
Lib.	Strong		92	4				4			27
	Weak	2	83	5				5		5	75
	NA*										17
Chr.	Strong			8	89						36
	Weak			18	74			4	4		23
	NA*										7
Agr.	Strong			3	3	94					34
	Weak		2		4	82	4	2	4	2	50
	NA*										8
Cons.	Strong						96			4	28
	Weak		2				85	6	7		47
	NA*										3
Independents		1	21	18	5	3	11	18	16	7	284
DK, Ref. NA		1	25	8	12	6	12	9	22	5	92

* Too few cases for computation.

are, however, much more consistent in voting for their own party than are identifiers of American parties at presidential as well as at congressional elections.

Relationships between various Norwegian parties could hardly be read from the way in which deviant party supporters vote, because they are scattered around among almost all parties. The Christian People's party is an exception in this respect; a significant proportion of its supporters vote Liberal. About 40 per cent of the independents belong to the categories of non-voters, refusers, and not ascertained (Table 3). This finding also corresponds to observations in America: people who say they are independent in relation to the parties tend to be less politically active than party identifiers.

G. *Political Stability.* In Table 4, voting behavior in the 1957 election is compared with first-time voting. Although in Norway only small changes occur in vote distribution from one election to the other, the number of voters who switch between the parties is not significant.

The Labor party, the Agrarians, and the Conservatives had the highest degree of stability in the 1957 election. They were supported by the about two-thirds of their first-time voters. As might be expected, the Liberals haxe the least stable electorate; only about 40 per cent of their first-time voters were consistent in their preference in 1957. On the other hand, the Liberals

Table 4

VOTING BEHAVIOR IN THE 1957 ELECTION COMPARED WITH FIRST-TIME VOTING

VOTING BEHAVIOR 1957

First Time Voting	Com.	Lab.	Lib.	Chr.	Agr.	Cons.	Non-voter, Refuses Uncertain	NA	Total	N
Stavanger:										
Communist*									100%	7
Labor	3%	72%	9%	3%	0%	3%	9%	1%	100%	242
Liberal	1	14	40	12	1	19	11	2	100%	112
Christian Peoples*										3
Agrarian*										2
Conservative		6	8	4	2	69	9	2	100....	53
Others*										6
Don't remember, Refuses		16	13	3		10	45	13	100%	31
NA	3	31	9	6	3	14	17	17	100%	35
										491
Southern Community:										
Communist*										2
Labor	1	69	6	6	3	1	11	3	100%	169
Liberal	1	8	43	20	12	6	8	2	100%	133
Christian People's*										12
Agrarian		6	8	12	63	4	7		100%	98
Conservative		4	12	8		65	11		100%	26
Others*										1
Don't remember, Refuses		3	10	7	14	7	59		100%	29
NA		25	11	7	5	11	20	21	100%	56
										526

* Too few cases for computation.

are the party that has received most first-time voters from other parties. The relatively high circulation in the electorate of the Liberals must be explained as another effect of the party's position as a middle party. When the people change party preference they are not likely to move between the extremes in the party system; they seem to prefer the moderate party in the center. Only two percent of those originally voting Labor now vote Conservative and some five per cent originally voting Conservative have moved over into the Labor camp.

The Christian People's party is the party which has received the highest proportion of Liberal first-time voters. This finding supports the hypothesis that the Christian People's party has drawn most of its vote from traditional Liberal voters.

H. The Demographic and Socioeconomic Composition of the Electorate. We have already touched upon the fact that the Labor party and the Conservatives are relatively stronger in the city of Stavanger than in the semi-rural southern community, while the three other parties, in particular the Christian People's party and the Agrarians, have more the character of rural parties. As Table 5 shows, this is partly due to the farm vote which goes

Table 5

VOTING BEHAVIOR IN RELATION TO OCCUPATION, SEX AND AGE. (OWN OCCUPATION OR OCCUPATION OF HEAD OF HOUSEHOLD.)

Occupation	Sex:	Com.	Lab.	Lib.	Chr.	Agr.	Cons.	Did not vote or un-certain	Re-fuses	NA	Total N= 100%
					VOTE PREFERENCE						
STAVANGER											
Workers Less than 35 years	M	7%	67%	3%	7%	3%	3%	7%	3%		30
	F	5	48	16	11	2	9	7		2	44
36 - 50 years	M	6	76	6			2	6	4		49
	F		53	16	3		5	11	5	7	62
More than 50 years	M	7	58	9	2		7	5	5	7	43
	F	3	63	9	5		3	9	7	2	59
White Collar and Less than 35 years	M		36	14	7		25	14		11	28
	F		27	27			27	7	3	3	30
Business People 36 - 50 years	M	3	22	19		3	40	8	5		37
	F		11	33	14	3	22	8	3	6	36
More than 50 years	M		21	26	7		26	5	14	2	43
	F		7	33	10		37	3	10		30
SOUTHERN COMMUNITY											
Workers Less than 35 years	M	2	43	14	4	16	4	6	4	8	51
	F		46	9	5	5	7	23		5	43

Table 5 (Continued)

VOTING BEHAVIOR IN RELATION TO OCCUPATION, SEX AND AGE. (OWN OCCUPATION OR OCCUPATION OF HEAD OF HOUSEHOLD.)

Occupation:		Sex:	Com.	Lab.	Lib.	Chr.	Agr.	Cons.	Did not vote or uncertain	Refuses	NA	Total N= 100%
	36 - 50 years	M	2	53	6	4	2	6	13	6	6	47
		F		37	9	20	4	4	13	9	4	54
	More than 50 years	M	3	63	9	13		3	3	3	3	32
		F		40	13	24	3		7	3	10	30
Farmers	Less than 35 years	M*										11
		F*										11
	36 - 50 years	M		10	14		66		3			29
		F*										17
	More than 50 years	M			13	18	48	8	5	5		38
		F		5	10	20	50	5	10			20
White Collar and	Less than 35 years	M		8	25	4	8	25	21	8		24
		F		21	37	13	4	13	8		4	24
Business People	36 - 50 years	M		29	33	19	5	9	5			21
		F		18	41	26	3	6	3	3		34
	More than 50 years	M*										13
		F		7	41	7	4	22	7	7	4	27

* Too few cases for computation.

heavily to the middle parties . It may also be observed, however, that there are differences between the two types of communities with regard to workers and the white-collar professions. In Stavanger the Labor party mobilizes much more of the vote of both the blue-collar workers and the white-collar groups than it does in the semi-rural southern community. The defection of the workers in the more rural area is largely to the Christian People's party and the Farmers party, with the Liberals profiting little from the break in the labor ranks. The Liberal party, however, gets stronger support than the Christian People's party among the white-collar groups outside Stavanger as in the city. Some of these gains in the middle class vote are at the expense of the Conservative party as well as the Labor party.

The differences in vote distribution may be explained by the differences in degree of industrialization. The southern community is characterized by more occupational mobility than Stavanger. While Stavanger has a labor force with long traditions in industrial production, a high proportion of the workers in the southern community have a background in agriculture. A similar tendency is likely to be observed among the white-collar workers in the two communities. It is not surprising that people who have moved from agriculture into the labor force or into white-collar jobs tend to be influenced politically by their background milieu which is dominated by the Liberals, the Christian People's party, and in particular by the Agrarians.

To the extent that there is a female vote in the larger Stavanger area it would favor the Liberal party and the Christian People's party (Table 5). The Labor party gets less support at the polls from women than from men both within Stavanger and in the three southern communes. The Farmers party and the Conservative party are less affected by vote division between the sexes. The greater appeal of the Liberal party and the Christian People's party to the women may be due to the emphasis of both these parties on moral issues. In the rural area the Christian People's party is relatively more attractive to the older women. The Labor party may mobilize less voting support among women because the norms of the shop and the union may exert less pressure upon housewives than upon working husbands.

Table 6

VOTING BEHAVIOR IN RELATION TO CLASS IDENTIFICATION

Q.: "If you had to place yourself in one of these groups, would you say that you are in the upper class, the middle class or the working class?"

PARTY PREFERENCE

Class Identification	Com.	Lab.	Lib.	Chr.	Agr.	Cons.	Didn't vote or un-certain	DK and re-fuses	NA	Total (N= 100%)
Upper or middle class*	..	15%	25%	12%	14%	20%	7%	4%	3%	439
Working class	3	56	11	6	4	4	9	4	3	516
Other classes or would not take a stand		15	17	6	19	8	12	15	8	48

* Only 10 respondents classified themselves as "upper" class.

Table 6 shows voting behavior in relation to class identification. Laborites are heavily working-class identifiers, while the Conservatives are mostly middle-class. The Liberals, the Christian People's party, and the Agrarians lie in between the two extremes although they attract predominantly middle-class identifiers. When class identification is broken by occupation the data indicate that white-collar people who vote Labor tend to call themselves working-class, while workers who vote bourgeois are inclined to consider themselves as middle-class people.

Class identification of political leaders goes in the same direction as for the voters (Table 7). For the Labor party this result is interesting in that almost half of its leaders belong to white-collar occupations. The notion of class differences seems to be an important factor in political conflict even in

Table 7

PERCEPTION OF OWN CLASS OF PARTY LEADERS

Party	Upper or middle class*	Working class	Other classes wouldn't take a stand	NA	Total N=100%
Christian People's	73	12	11	4	26
Labor	7%	74%	19%		43
Liberal	58		38	4	26
Agrarian	68		32		19
Conservative	63	3	26	8	35

* Only 5 respondents have classified themselves as "upper" class.

the Stavanger area where differences between classes are usually thought to be small compared with the eastern and northern part of the country.

The leaders are more reluctant than the voters to identify with either the working-class or the middle-class. Some political leaders may prefer not to be labelled as representing a single class. Then, too, the leaders are more sophisticated and they may have found our class distinctions too crude. In particular, it may be difficult for the farmers to identify with either of the two classes. Some of the leaders, particularly the Liberals, may be reluctant to accept any class identity for ideological reasons. As has previously been noted, the Liberals identify strongly with national values and are opposed to the struggle between social groups and classes.

I. The Role of Parties in Local Politics. One aspect of the role of political parties in community affairs concerns the involvement of citizens in local-governmental decisions. For example, the decisions of the municipal council can be made by the elected officials themselves or they can be made by these officials after discussion by the official with the rank-and-file of his party or some group representative of the party. If there is opportunity for participation at local party meetings in decisions on community matters, there is likely to be clearer perception of the role and program of the different parties. Parties rather than individuals will be held responsible for political decisions. Party activity of this sort may help the party organization maintain its vitality in the period between elections.

Except for the Communists, all parties had tickets or slates of candidates at the last elections (in 1955) in the four communes included in the study. In Stavanger, Sandnes, and Hoyland, separate partisan slates have been maintained in all local elections since the war. But in the commune of Time there had previously been a tradition for the bourgeois parties to present a joint slate.

In our interviews both leaders and party supporters were asked about their perception of the role of parties in local politics. Most of the political leaders in our sample were people with present or previous positions in public office. Presumably they were well-informed on the practices of their respective parties. Table 8 shows how they reacted to the question. The Labor

Table 8

LEADERS' REPORT OF DISCUSSION OF ISSUES WITHIN THE PARTY

Q.: How is it in this commune? Do the representatives in the chairman's council and the municipal council usually make decisions on important issues independently of the party, or are the issues first discussed within the party?

	Lab.	Lib.	PARTY Chr.	Agr.	Con.
Issues first discussed within party	65%	46%	27%	11%	37%
Issues discussed on important matters only	5%	11%	16%	16%	9%
Decisions made independently of party discussion or only taken to party after representatives decide		8%	15%	26%	11%
Don't know	2%	4%	15%	5%	9%
Not ascertained	28%	31%	27%	42%	34%
Total 100%	N=43	N=26	N=26	N=19	N=35

leaders who replied agreed that the party discusses local issues. Agrarian leaders and leaders of the Christian People's party were more inclined to believe that representatives take an independent stand, with the other parties taking a position somewhere between the extremes of Labor and Agrarians.

Party supporters (Table 9) showed smaller differences in perception of the parties' role. Nearly half of the Labor supporters believe that representatives discuss issues with their party, but in general the practices as reported by the leaders were not paralleled by similar perceptions of the party supporters. There was a considerable number of respondents who could not answer the question and there were relatively more such "don't know" responses among the Christian People's party leaders and supporters alike. This finding accords with the notion of the Christian People's party as the least politicized of the parties. Politics is seen more or less as a necessary

Table 9

REPORT OF DISCUSSION OF ISSUES WITHIN PARTY
BY PARTY SUPPORTERS

Q.: What happens when your party's representatives in the muncipality in this city (commune) take their stand on important matters, do the individual representatives take their stand independently of the party, or do they discuss the matters with people in the party beforehand?

PERCEPTION OF ROLE OF PARTY

	Party supported Representatives take independent stand	Representatives discuss with party	Other answers, refuses	Don't know	Not ascertained	Total (N=100%)
Communists*						7
Labor	11%	49%	0	21%	19%	291
Liberal	7	42	3	27	21	113
Christian People's	15	36	5	36	8	63
Agrarian	22	45	4	19	10	90
Conservative	20	45	0	24	11	75

* Too few cases for computation.

evil in the struggle for the Christian values. Therefore, the party's leaders and supporters tend to have a vague perception of the role of the party in local politics.

Relations between Political Parties and Social Groups

The relationship between political parties and social groupings is facilitated in Norway by the direct representation of social organizations in the party structure. In addition to this institutional linkage between political and social structure there are, of course, other bonds created by overlapping membership in parties and other groupings apart from formal representation. In this section we shall attempt an empirical description of the integration of political and social groupings through an examination of the organizational memberships of party leaders and party followers. The perceptions and attitudes of the voting population about the relationship of political and non-political organizations will also be presented, e.g., to what extent do people perceive norms relevant to political action in their social groupings.

A. Organizational Memberships of Voters and Political Leaders. Table 10 presents the basic data on number of organizational memberships held by the voters and the leaders outside their parties. Four essential facts are apparent here: (1) Labor party voters and leaders belong to fewer organizations than do the adherents or leaders of any of the other parties. (2) No matter what the party allegiance, leaders have more ties to other organizations

Table 10

NUMBER OF MEMBERSHIPS OF VOTERS AND POLITICAL LEADERS IN ORGANIZATIONS OUTSIDE THE PARTIES

NUMBER OF MEMBERSHIPS

Party:		One org.	Two org.	Three or more org.	No memberships or not ascertained*	Total N=100%
Communist Voters**						16
Labor	Voters	42%	13%	7%	38%	365
	Leaders	33	13	28	7	43
Liberal	Voters	34	18	14	34	171
	Leaders		27	69	4	26
Christians	Voters	38	21	22	19	90
	Leaders	11	27	62		26
Agrarians	Voters	35	23	26	16	95
	Leaders	32	16	47	5	19
Conservatives	Voters	30	21	13	36	113
	Leaders	17	17	52	14	35
Did not vote or uncertain		43	7	12	38	85
Voting not ascertained		30	15	5	50	82
	Voters	38	16	13	33	1017
	Leaders	19	25	49	7	149

* Only 20 NA's altogether.
** Too few cases for computation.

than do voters. These two facts are consistent with the general sociological finding that membership in groups is a function of socioeconomic status with relatively fewer joiners among the low income groups. But other factors are at work here as the following results indicate. (3) The Conservative party voters coming in large part from upper income groups, are more like the Labor party than the center parties in having a small number of organizational membership. (4) And finally, the Liberal party shows the greatest discrepancy between the amount of outside group activity of leaders and followers.

In regard to the types of organizations to which the voters and leaders of the five parties belong, in general there is a correspondence between the outside membership pattern of leaders and followers with the notable exception of the Liberal party. Even allowing for the generally higher level of leadership participation in outside groups, the Liberal leaders are much more involved in religious, charitable, humanitarian, and community-centered organizations than the leaders of other parties. And although the Liberals get over ten per cent of their vote from trade union members, not a single one of their leaders has membership in a trade union. The many ties which the Liberal leaders have with their community do not seem to be effective in integrating their party into the social structure. Instead of the group efforts of the Liberal leaders having a political function, it is more a case of their political leadership expressing their social function as community leaders. Liberal leaders seem to be in politics as one more of their many community activities. This finding indicates that overlapping membership of political leaders in social organizations is not sufficient in itself to mobilize support for a party.

Something of the character of the various parties can be grasped from a study of the organizational ties of their supporters. The Agrarian and the Christian People's party are more representative of single interest, or value ' groups than the other parties. Both leaders and followers in the Agrarian party are drawn heavily from members of the Farmers' organization and the Christian People's party has strong ties to the lay religious and temperance organizations. The Labor party shows less concentration in the trade unions than might have been expected. The data suggest that the Norwegian party system is made up of parties which differ significantly on the dimensions previously indicated. Some are more practical institutions, which reconcile competing claims; others are the embodiment of single interest or value groupings and are the political reflection of a religious movement or an economic organization.

The basis of the Labor party in the trade unions deserves further comment. Only 41 per cent of Labor party voters in Rogaland are members of trade unions whereas the Agrarian party draws 73 per cent of its vote from farm organizations. If we examine the data from the point of view of how the members of the organizations vote, we still find that the farmers' organizations show more solidarity than trade unions: 76 per cent of their members vote Agrarian and 67 per cent of trade union members vote Labor. The Labor party shows less concentration in the trade unions than might have been expected. In spite of the close contact between the unions and the party, the trade unions are only one of several interest groups which contribute to its strength.

b. *Organizational Image of Party Ticket.* Politicians often hold the belief that they can strengthen their party and their ticket by a slate of candidates representative of the important interests in the constituency. Our samples of political leaders was of this conviction. When these leaders were asked to state why the five top candidates on their slate had been chosen, 65 per cent mentioned group representation. On the direct question of whether the composition of the ticket would affect the distribution of the vote, some 45 per cent of the leaders answered in the affirmative. Geographical and occupational groups were the most frequently mentioned as important in securing a representtaive slate.[11] Party leaders are sensitive to the party image created in the minds of the electorate by the specific composition of the party slate. They are also alert to the potential value of representing various groups not only because of the direct appeal to the voters but also because of the enlistment and energizing of workers from the groups which the candidates represent.

How correct the political leaders are in their emphasis upon this specific form of linkage with other social groups is a difficult question. The voters do not show quite as much support for this position as do the leaders when their opinion is sought directly. Nevertheless, some 40 per cent say they would hesitate to vote for a ticket which did not contain a representative of

Table 11

INTEREST GROUPS WHICH VOTERS THINK SHOULD BE REPRESENTED ON THE PARTY SLATE*

Q.: Of course the candidates who are nominated on the slates belong to different groups and strata in the population. Here is a list of some groups and strata. Would you please tell me if some of these groups are so important to you that you would hesitate to vote for a ballot which did not contain a single spokesman for this group in an important place?

Vote Preference	Own occupa-tional group	Own commune or the neighboring commune	The Women	The Youth	Actively religious people	Temperance people	No importance; No group mentioned	NA	Total
Communist**	—	—	—	—	—	—	—	—	13
Labor	24%	5%	10%	9%	4%	7%	55%	6%	341
Liberal	15	8	14	10	17	16	54	6	156
Christian	5	3	10	6	48	27	40	7	88
Agrarian	43	1	8	9	7	17	37	7	91
Conservative	17	14	7	6	6	3	57	8	105
Non-Voters and Uncertain	12	6	11	13	14	19	53	7	85
NA	8	4	4	14	14	12	53	23	77
									956

* Percentages add to more than 100 percent because question called for multiple answers.

** Too few cases for computation.

some group important to them. The supporters of the Agrarian party and the Christian People's party show the highest percentages who demand such representation (Table 11). Less than 20 per cent of the Conservative adherents agree on any one group which needs representation on the party ticket before they would support it; whereas 48 per cent of the Christian People's party want the actively religious represented and 43 per cent of the Farmers party want the farmers represented. This is consistent with the previous interpretation that the Agrarian and Christian People's parties are not institutions which integrate or compromise the views of various factions. Rather, they are political expressions of a single set of interests or values. Again there is more apparent apathy among Labor party supporters with the overwhelming majority not concerned about the representation of workers on their ticket. This may well be because representation is no longer a problem for them. They have had a Labor government in power for so long with trade union officials in the government that this question about representation was an academic one for them.

Though many voters want representation of their groups on the party ticket, they do not implement this desire with specific knowledge about the actual composition of the various party slates. Norwegian voters have little knowledge about the candidates running for seats in the Storting. Forty-five per cent of the voters could not name a single candidate for the Storting from the Stavanger area. Of the ninety-six candidates nominated by the six parties for the province of Rogaland, fifty-four lived in the Stavanger area. Thirty per cent knew from one to three candidates and only twenty per cent knew four or more. When asked about the organizations the candidates belonged to, only nineteen per cent of the voters could mention any organizational ties of candidates. Eight per cent knew about one candidate and 11 per cent were knowledgeable about the organizational memberships of two or three candidates. There is a clear contrast here between the politician's emphasis upon the composition of the ticket and the awareness by the voters of who the candidates are and what groups they represent. Nonetheless there may be a cumulative effect over the years so that though voters cannot specify how their groups get represented they may have a global impression that one party rather than another does provide representation. It may be very much like the problem of issues. The voters are not very knowledgeable about specific issues but they still have a good idea of the direction in which the parties are moving in terms of their own interests.

Finally we should mention that the nomination of group candidates also helps in linking the parties with various social organizations. The candidates are drawn from the active elite in the community. Most of them hold a leading position in one or more organizations. The overlap in leadership between parties and organizations makes it necessary for the parties to take a stand on problems with which the organizations are concerned. The leaders may work for the interests of their organizations through their respective parties. The nomination of organizational leaders on party slates may, therefore, have an important function in integrating the political parties in the social structure.

C. *Voters' Perceptions of Political Norms of Organization.* The tie between social organizations and political behavior may exist at two levels.
Membership in an organization may result in many influences which pre-
dispose people to accept certain political views and political preferences.
Or the relationship may be very direct, in that there are clearly preceived
political norms in the social organization, namely a belief that the great
majority of the group vote in a certain way and that it is eminently appropriate for them as group members to vote in such a fashion. Among our
Norwegian respondents the relationship seems to be much more of the indirect type. Members of trade unions were asked whether they thought a
trade union should take a stand on political matters or whether it should
be politically neutral. It was surprising to find that 62 per cent said that
the union should be politically neutral. It could be that the pure and simple
trade unionism of Samuel Gompers would find support among the rank-
and-file of Norwegian labor. It is also possible that Norwegian workers felt
that since the union is integrated into the party structure there is no point
in the union itself taking a stand. Against such a sophisticated interpretation is the fact that some members of the Labor party, who belong by virtue
of the trade union being collectively associated with the Party, are not aware
of their party membership.

At any rate those who feel the trade union should take a stand on political
matters are more likely to vote Labor than are union members who favor
political neutrality (Table 12). And those who are neutralists contribute

Table 12

MEMBERS' ATTITUDES TOWARD POLITICAL ACTIVITY
OF TRADE UNIONS RELATED TO VOTING

Q.: Do you think that a trade union should take a stand on political matters,
or should it be politically neutral?

Vote Preference	Union should take a stand	Union should be neutral	DK or NA
Communist	6%	4%	5%
Bourgeois	8	16	18
Labor	77	65	50
Uncertain or Not ascertained	9	15	27
Total	**64**	**138**	**22**

double the vote to bourgeois parties of those who favor the union taking
a stand on political matters. Length of membership in the union also contributes to the political orientation of the member in the direction of the
Labor party. Those who have joined trade unions since the war are close
to the 60 per cent mark in their Labor vote whereas 75 per cent of the
older trade unionists vote Labor. There is an interesting progression of
support for the bourgeois parties from the old unionists to the newcomers.
Only 7 per cent of the members who go back thirteen years or more vote
bourgeois, 15 per cent of members of eight to twelve years' standing vote

similarly, while 23 per cent of the newcomers support the bourgeois parties. Moreover, this stronger Labor position of old members may not be so much a matter of length of years in the union as a matter of types of experience in the labor movement. Old members may have been through a period of struggle before Labor victories were common. It must be added that all the evidence presented so far shows much less militancy and involvement of the rank-and-file of trade union members than would be expected in a country where Labor has steadily increased its political strength over the past twenty years.

Members of farm, religious, and temperance organizations show the same reluctance as labor union members to say that their organizations take a stand on political matters. Those who are or have been officers in religious or farm organizations are more likely to say that the organization does not take a stand on political matters than are the rank-and-file members (Table 13). The reverse is true in the temperance organizations. Only six per cent of the members of religious organizations and 13 per cent of members of

Table 13

POSITION IN ORGANIZATION IN RELATION TO PERCEPTION OF WHETHER ORGANIZATION TAKES A STAND ON POLITICAL MATTER

PERCEPTION OF POLITICAL STAND

Type of Organization	Position in Organization	Organization takes a stand	Organization does not take a stand	DK	NA	Total
Farm Organization	Never held Office	29%	46%	17%	8%	72
	In office now or previously	27	55		18	11
	NA	13	50	12	25	8
Religious Organization	Never held Office	7	63	11	19	94
	In office now or previously	5	79	4	12	58
	NA		48		52	21
Temperance Organization	Never held Office	8	63	11	18	38
	In office now or previously	30	45	5	20	20
	NA		75	13	12	8

temperance societies would admit that their groups occasionally took a stand on anything political. This is interesting in view of the way in which these same people have formed their own political party to give them adequate political representation — the Christian People's party. But in their own eyes they have still not entered politics. Farmers in similar fashion do not believe that farm organizations take political stands (only 27 per cent would make this admission). For a group to take a political stand in Norway apparently has some connotation of undesirable activity — perhaps functioning as a pressure group.

Among members of farm organizations there is a clear and well nigh unanimous perception of how the group votes. Only 4 per cent saw members as voting anything else but for the Agrarian party (Table 14). Some 48 per cent of the members of religious organizations did not answer this

Table 14

PERCEPTION OF VOTING BEHAVIOR OF MEMBERS IN FARM, RELIGIOUS, AND TEMPERANCE ORGANZATIONS

Q.: For which party do you think that most members in the group are voting?

Organization	Com.	Lab.	Lib.	Chr.	Agr.	Cons.	Combinations several parties	DK	NA	Total
Farm Organization			2%	1%	83%		1%		13%	91
Religious Organization	1	2	5	37	4	1	12	15	23	173
Temperance Organization	1	6	12	14	11		9	27	20	66

question but of those who did the great majority named the Christian People's party. When the question was put negatively, namely whether there were parties for which group members should not vote, about 40 per cent of the people in religious and temperance groups would not answer or stated explicity that membership in the group had no relevance to voting behavior.

SUMMARY

This paper presents some of the findings from a study of party leaders and the electorate in the city of Stavanger and the surrounding semi-rural community in southwestern Norway. This area differs from the rest of Norway in giving greater support to the center parties, namely the Liberal party, the Christian People's party and the Agrarian party and less support to the parties of the left and of the right, the Labor party and the Conservative party. The following conclusions are suggested by the data:

1. The Agrarian party and the Christian People's party differ in basic structure from the other parties in being the political expression of a single interest or value group. The Conservative, Liberal, and Labor parties are more like American parties in representing and reconciling the interests of a number of groups. Only forty per cent of the vote of the Labor party comes from the trade union members or their families in the Stavanger region. The objective facts are reflected in the perception of party followers. Supporters of the Agrarian party are much more insistent than supporters of the Labor party that the party ticket have candidates representing the related organizations.

2. The level of political participation in Norway is higher than in the

United States both with respect to turn-out and party membership. The Stavanger area is lower in party membership than the rest of Norway partly because of the loose nature of the Liberal party organization (this is a section where the Liberals are more numerous than in other parts of Norway) and partly because there are fewer collective trade union memberships in the Labor party in southwestern Norway.

3. The independent vote in the Stavanger area goes more heavily to the Liberal party and the Conservative party than to the other parties. Apparently part of the support of these two parties comes from people in groups where there is no clearly perceived political norm. In general, however, the frame of reference for political choice in Norway is strongly influenced by identification with some social or economic grouping.

4. Psychological identification with social class is a factor in voting preference in Norway. The majority of factory and manual workers support the Labor party but those who do not tend to regard themselves as belonging to the middle rather than the working class. And the members of the white collar occupations who vote Labor tend to see themselves as belonging to the working class. Leaders of the Labor party who objectively would be classified as belonging to the middle class still see themselves as members of the working class.

5. Though there is great stability in voting preferences in Norway the changes that do occur have affected the Liberal party more than the extreme parties. On the one hand the Liberals have lost to the Agrarian and Christian People's parties. On the other hand, they have also gained votes from people moving out of the more extreme parties. It is easier for the Conservative shifting allegiance to vote for a party of the center than for the Labor party.

6. The parties are integrated into the social structure partly through the organizational membership of party supporters and leaders. In general the organizational ties of the leaders are similar to those of their followers save that they are more active than their followers in number of such memberships. The one exception is the Liberal party in which the pattern of leadership linkage to other types of organizations would not be predicted on the basis of an analysis of the composition of the Liberal party vote. The Liberal party does not gear into interest groups very effectively and seems to be the expression of people who cherish certain traditional values and symbols.

7. The workers give greater support to the Labor party in the city of Stavanger than in the three semi-rural communes outside of Stavanger. This is partly due to the late industrialization of these communes and also to the group atmosphere of an area where the prevailing norms have not favored the Labor party.

8. The belief that one's group takes stands on political matters is related to voting for the party associated with the group's interest. For example, workers who feel that the union takes a stand on political matters are more likely to vote Labor than those who do not think the union takes a stand.

9. Though the evidence indicates a considerable degree of integration between political parties and social groupings there is a reluctance on the part of voters to perceive these organizations as possessing political norms. This may merely reflect the adequate institutionalization through which the interests of groups are already channeled.

NOTES TO CHAPTER VI

1. The findings from this detailed investigation in the province of Rogaland will also have a broader context for interpretation in terms of the results of two waves of a national cross-sectional study of all Norway conducted by Stein Rokkan.

2. A complete report on the study for monograph publication is in process which will deal with the primary design of the study, namely, the relating of party functioning to voter perception and behavior.

3. Gabriel Öydne, *Litt om motsetninga mellom Östandet og Vestlandet* (On the differences between East and West), Sym og Segn, 1957.

4. At local elections however, the voters are permitted to split their ticket. It should be noted that the election system at both general and local elections is a proportional one. Each party runs a slate which contains several candidates.

5. The function of factional activities in political parties is discussed in an article by Henry Valen, "Factional Activities and Nominations," forthcoming in *Acta Sociologica*.

6. Information on party organization in the Stavanger area was obtained from the Rogaland province secretaries and the secretaries of the local party organizations in the communes included in the study.

7. Sub-organizations, such as the Labor party's Christian Workers' Association, and the Conservative party's Workers' Association, are independent and have weaker ties with their respective parties than youth and women's organizations. In the Stavanger Area the first mentioned organizations play a role of minor importance in the party structure. Therefore, they will not be further commented upon.

8. Members of collective associated trade unions have the right to ask not to be regarded as members of the Labor party. Such a reservation has, however, no effect on the membership dues which are paid to the party by the unions and not by the individual union members.

9. From the Detroit Area Project conducted by Samuel Eldersveld and Daniel Katz on political participation in 1956–57.

10. Information on the distribution of the newspapers is obtained from the Norwegian Newspapers National Association. The Stavanger Area, as used here, consists of a few more communes than those included in the study.

11. It should be noted that the election system is a proportional one and that each constituency, which covers a province, elects from four to thirteen deputies. Each party names six more candidates on its slate or ticket than the total of candidates elected from a province. For example, the province of Rogaland elects ten candidates to the Storting and each party nominates sixteen candidates.

Review: The Judicial Process in Two African Tribes

BY *VICTOR AYOUB*

I

ANTHROPOLOGISTS HAVE long provided source materials for other disciplines both in the social sciences and the humanities. The use to which the works of Sir James Frazer and Lewis Morgan, to name perhaps the most notable providers, have been put by some psychoanalytical theorists, literary critics, and social and economic theorists is so well known as to require only mention. Margaret Mead and Ruth Benedict are also names which abound in the literature of other fields. The list of names is clearly increasing. Anthropological sources have, however, been most frequently used either to reconstruct a hypothetical society in an unrecorded past for the purpose of elucidating some theory of social and cultural evolution, or they have been used simply to provide illustrative materials, examples of contrast, in order to highlight the social institution, mechanism, or custom with which a writer is primarily concerned. The use of such materials, however, for systematic comparative study has not been significantly evident.

Of course, some may judge that there is no basis for the systematic comparison of the kind of societies and cultures anthropologists most often study and the kind that members of the other social sciences predominantly study. For example, the political scientist, in his concern with the general problem of the allocation of power and responsibility and the processes of social control attendant upon such allocation, finds his locus of study in a special set of institutions developed within the society to resolve this problem. The anthropologist, concerned with exactly the same issue but in the context of so-called "simple" or non-literate societies, is not often likely to find a similar set of institutions. The problem for these societies is more than likely to be resolved within institutions which serve other functions as well, e.g. kinship, marriage or blood brotherhood. What value can the study of the political processes of such fundamentally different societies have for the political scientist? Is the apparent difference as fundamental as it appears? These questions are always, implicity or explicitly, of concern to the anthropologist, if only for the reason that while his primary attention is usually drawn to societies and cultures other than his own he finds it incumbent upon himself to show the relevance of his studies in terms of his culture.

II

This review of two books, one by Max Gluckman[1] and the other by Paul Bohannan,[2] may serve particularly well as examples of anthropological studies which may be relevant to the problems of political science. In both books, the case method is used to describe and analyze the processes of jural control characteristic of African society.

The Tiv, of whom Bohannan writes, are an African Negro tribe of about 800,000 living in Northern Nigeria under British rule. They are subsistence farmers.

In order to understand social relations among the Tiv, and consequently judicial processes, one fundamental concept must be known and understood. The concept is known as *Tar*. It is part of the Tiv's own cultural idiom, that is, a concept they explicitly use in order to organize an aspect of their experience.

A *Tar* is identified by the association of a lineage segment with a particular territory. The Tiv organize themselves in terms of genealogies which are traced through the paternal line of descent, back seventeen or eighteen generations to an original ancestor, named "Tiv," from whom the people take their name. A social group whose members can identify themselves as being descended from a common ancestor going back four or five generations represents a "lineage segment." It is this social group which is identified with the smallest politically relevant territory. Two such segments, occupying discrete *tars,* whose members are descended from a more remote common ancestor form a larger *tar*. This social group and territorial association is further extended into similar but more inclusive groupings until the largest tar is *Tar Tiv*. At each level, the *tar* bears the name of the common ancestor who serves as the locus of unity for all the members of the social group associated with the territory. Anthropologists have come to call this a segmentary lineage system. In such a system the political organization is intimately bound up with the kinship structure of the community.[3]

The *tar* as country and the *tar* as smaller associations of group and territory within the "country" represent the frame of reference in terms of which the Tiv perceive some important relationships with one another. The unity of the *tar* is, at any level, a condition which ought to be maintained. In this regard, a recurrent expression which prevails among the Tiv is "to spoil the Tar." Whenever the recognized order of social life is disturbed by such acts as war, theft, witchcraft, or quarrels, it is a case of "spoiling the tar." To bring social life back to its expected and recognized order — to normalcy — is "to repair the tar." Although there is more than one way to "repair the tar" in the event of disputes, the proper means to achieve this end is arbitration. As the author puts it, "repairing *tar* is government."

In his analysis of jural processes among the Tiv, Bohannan is primarily concerned with courts which are officially designated by the British colonial administration as Grade "D" courts. These are courts which are authorized to maintain jurisdiction over civil claims not exceeding £25 and criminal cases involving a maximum penality of 3 months' imprisonment or £10 fine. They are "native courts" viewed from the perspective of European residents; they are "government courts" viewed from the perspective of the Tiv themselves. The significance of this distinction will be clear later. It reflects the author's preoccupation, theoretical as well as methodological, with keeping distinct the points of view of the indigenous members of the society, of the non-indigenous members of the society (i.e., Europeans) and of the author as investigator.

In the operation of jural processes involved in the adjudication of a case, there are no stated rules of procedure or rules of codified substantive law which guide the participants in the case. That is, from the point of view of the Tiv, social acts take place and issues are resolved, but there is no explicit reference to rules or norms or law. (The investigator may, as Bohannan does, formulate statements which express rules inferred from the observation of social acts, but this is the investigator's view, not the Tiv view.)

The function of a court action is "to repair the tar," to resolve the breach in relations which has led to court action so that the community may again begin to function smoothly. It is a *modus vivendi* which judges seek, a mode of action which shall, at worst, lead to a resolution of the dispute, and prove least unsatisfactory to contending parties. Moreover, Bohannan points out, if no agreement can be reached and the judges have to settle the matter arbitrarily (probably reflecting the role they must play from the point of view of the Colonial Administration) they lose their reputations. It is not a Tiv conception that the court has authority to carry out its decisions. They believe that every dispute has a right answer and they take court action as a means of discovering that answer. When the answer is "discovered" and the disputants concur in it, a resolution has been effected. There is, from this point of view, no "corpus of law" to provide a ready-made standard for determining right answers.

This conception of the "government courts" fits in with the Tiv conception of their indigenous system of jural control, referred to by the author as "moots," which now have a more restricted jurisdiction than in the past, but which serve the same function, i.e., "to make the community run smoothly and peacefully." On the other hand, Europeans conceive of these "native courts" as they do of their own systems of jural control and believe that court action is intent upon applying, within a restricted jurisdiction, "native law and custom," something which, as indicated before, the Tiv do not "have." That is, they do not conceive of their actions in this regard as a system of rules representing part of a special institution dealing with jural control and derived from the rules and actions which make up the institutions of marriage, family, property, etc. Judges settle disputes, in Bohannan's words, "in terms of their knowledge of Tiv institutions; they do not do so in terms of rules of those institutions which have been resystemized specifically for the purpose of jural action."[4]

If these two kinds of systems of rules are not kept terminologically distinct, semantic difficulties in the definition of law immediately arise which are bound to have unfortunate consequences in the analysis of jural processes and jural control in different societies.

Bohannan, writing from the point of view of the analyst, provides a third organization of thought by which Tiv court action can be understood. He states, diagrammatically and discursively, the processes which characterize the events which lead to, are present in, and are the consequences of, court action.

These processes are identified as (1) breach of norm, (2) counteraction, and (3) correction. They are social acts. For example, a "breach of norm" is not the opposite of a norm. The opposite of a norm such as "No smoking" would be a similar type of statement, "Smoking allowed," which is itself a norm. The relevance of this distinction will be immediately evident. A "breach of norm" spoils the tar. It is a deviant act which precipitates the need for some kind of "counteraction." Jural action is but one kind of "counteraction" resorted to by the Tiv. Other kinds fall into the category of "self-help." If a "breach of norm" leads to jural action, "It is possible — and is often done — for Tiv to defend themselves by attempting to maintain that their action was not a breach of norm — that it was an act in accordance with some norm or another."[5] If a jural type of counteraction is successful, i.e., a resolution satisfactory to all is found (the means are found to "repair the tar"), the third social action will be precipitated, namely "correction." There are several social actions which constitute "correction" for the Tiv, i.e., will "repair the tar." There is restitution of the norm. An act will be committed in line with the original standard, thus reaffirming it. There is punishment in the shape of fines and penal action. There is compensation as a substitution for the norm.

Here, again, Bohannan points to confusions that may arise if we use concepts derived from a system of jural control peculiar to one society in the interpretation of a system indigenous to another society. The concept of "correction," he explains, may be considered the equivalent of "sanction," if the latter is understood in its technical sense "which refers to that portion of a law which sets forth the penalty to be expected for infringing the rest of it." However, "sanction" is not only part of our law as a legal institution but it is also part of a set of concepts by which Western lawyers and jurists analyze systems of Western law. The danger of using this concept in place of that of "correction" is that it may easily lead to the confusion of misconstruing what jural action actually does involve for the Tiv.

III

Thus by describing and analyzing cases adjudicated in the native courts, the author elucidates the characteristic processes the Tiv go through in order to resolve litigations. The processes are described as they are understood by the Tiv themselves. This point reflects the main thesis of the book over and above the purpose of documenting the jural processes of the group as such.

Bohannan contends that to describe and analyze the system of jural control of another culture in terms of our own system and from a frame of reference derived from the observation and interpretation of it is to commit an act of distortion. In order to clarify his point, the author makes a distinction between a "folk system of interpretation" and an "analytical system." The folk system is that one represented by the inevitable efforts of human beings to interpret their experiences in order to provide themselves with a rationale for action as they interact within both a physical and social environment. This is a direct cognition of experience, providing the individual with a system of thought organizing and ordering his relation to the physical and social world in such a way as to make action effective. The analytical system, on the other hand, is the organization of the outside investigator's observations of human beings, their actions, and their interpretive systems, into a system of thought based upon techniques and methods of observing and recording these experiences and canons of reasoning identified, to a greater or lesser extent, as the "scientific method."

For example, the interpretation of one set of Tiv social relationships as determined by genealogical links through the male line of descent is part of the Tiv folk system. Another way of stating this is that the Tiv cognize these relationships in terms of their own cultural "idiom" which stresses those social bonds established through the male line of descent. The same set of relationships cognized by the investigator as part of a "segmentary lineage system" illustrates an interpretation at the level of an analytical system.

According to Bohannan, the "folk system" is an ordering of experience by the human beings within the society. The investigator attempts to reconstruct it. The analytical system, however, is a direct ordering of his observations, involving both the behavior and the cognitions of his subjects. This system he *constructs*. Herein lies an inconsistency in Bohannan's dichotomy, I believe. Bohannan contrasts the point of view of the participant *in* the culture with the point of view of the investigator *of* it. However, the set of statements which the latter uses to describe the "folk system" are *his*, just as are the set of statements which he uses to interpret that first set of statements and which he designates as his "analytical system." True, the investigator quotes participants of the culture and uses key words, such as *tar*, in providing his description of the "folk system." In fact, Bohannan writes that "the key to the folk system — almost the only key — is the language in which it is stated." However, such terms as are taken from that language to give the effect of providing the reader with *the* folk system of the group are meaningless until the investigator has explained their meaning in his own language. It is only too well known that this often involves extraordinary circumlocution in order to reach the closest approximation to the meanings which the terms have in their indigenous contexts. And then, after this is done, the investigator can use a term taken from his informants' language, but he could as well, coin a new term[e] and point to his explication of the informants' term to indicate the meaning which should be given the new term thereafter.

This is, in effect, what happens when the investigator merely utilizes the terms taken from his informants' language. After explaining the meaning of the term in *his own language*, he incorporates the term into *his own idiolect*[f] which could in time become part of the language. The word "taboo" is probably a good example of this kind of occurrence. The point is that whatever means the investigator uses to describe his observations, he is not providing us with a description of *the* "folk system" of the society. This may seem a trivial point on which to dwell so long, but it can be made immediately apparent with reference to Bohannan's own statements that confusions can easily arise if this distinction is not observed. He writes that "folk systems are *never* right or wrong. They 'exist.' They are." This is certainly true about *the* folk system, but I doubt that any investigator would ever say this of his description of that system. Again, Bohannan explains that "Tiv ideas and actions concerning family and marriage form the folk system of their family institutions." Actions can hardly be part of a folk system unless "cognitions" are to be interpreted as "actions." This is not the definition of *the* folk system of a society, but "the concrete structure" which the investigator first describes in a set of statements and then interprets with another set of statements which are related to one another in a logically coherent and consistent order and identified as an "analytical structure."[8]

The relevance of this discussion is the issue it raises regarding the comparative study of institutions, political or otherwise. At what level of analysis is a comparison relevant of "primitive" societies and the complex societies of industrial capitalistic development? While "concrete structures" do not really permit discrimination between what is political, economic, or social, analytical structures are different ways of looking at the same things. Keeping these "structures" sharply apart helps to clarify the relationship of the several social sciences (or several analytical structures) to one another, and of each to the single society which might be under scrutiny. In addition, the distinction seems to me to clarify the relations of a discipline (or an analytical structure) to the job of investigating on a comparative basis two or more concrete structures (i.e., societies or parts thereof). It is not ultimately a matter of what anthropology can contribute to political science, ouside of the detailed descriptions of the political aspects of many concrete structures, or what political science can contribute to anthropology, outside of the detailed descriptions of the political aspects of one or more concrete structures identifiable with so-called modern, complex societies. The issue is finally — what kind of analytical structure can be formulated so as to be the interpretative frame of reference for the analysis and explanation of the political *aspects* of several concrete structures which are of different degrees of complexity in regards to size, elaboration of special institutions, subsistence level, etc. It may be that such a "structure" will not be developed or cannot be developed. There will be no unified theory, as it were. This is an answer, however, which can be given only on the basis of conceptualization, not on the basis of evidence.

While there is a danger of transforming an analytical structure or elements thereof into a concrete structure, Bohannan points to the danger of transforming a concrete structure (i.e., *folk system*) into an analytical structure (i.e. *analytical system*). He is intent on keeping the distinction as sharp as possible in order to prevent the investigator from elevating a "folk system" of his own society to an analytical system with which to interpret and analyze the social relationships characterizing another society. For example, law, as it is represented by a special set of institutions in our own society, is a "folk system" by which we, or at least lawyers, judges, and other representatives of these special institutions, organize social facts for social action. To use this "folk system" to explain that of another society which systematizes institutions and processes of social control on a different basis is akin to the once prevailing habit of grammarians to fit the structure of various languages to the paradigms of Latin grammar. The comparison of folk systems may be made, but, I might add, and lead again to a point made previously, that comparisons which will result in "explanations" of differences and similarities must be made in terms of an analytic system characterized by concepts and statements of relations between concepts which will "fit" all the "folk systems" being compared. Comparisons, of course, may be valuable in terms other than the one just suggested. It may be heuristically valuable. The political scientist may find a treasure house of suggestive leads in the analysis and explanation of one "folk system" of social control if he explores the anthropological literature dealing with other such systems and makes *ad hoc* comparisons. However, analogy serves neither to explain nor confirm. It serves only to suggest. This will be made clearer by example below in the discussion of Gluckman's book.

IV

The Judicial Process Among the Barotse is but one part of a projected trilogy[9] intended to analyze the legal system of an African tribal society under British authority.

"Barotse" is a general term used to refer to several tribes which live in an area of Northern Rhodesia known as Barotseland. The term includes the Lozi, who established themselves as sovereigns over the tribes in the area well before the middle of the Eighteenth Century, and are the rulers of Barotseland. It is their law of which Gluckman writes. Although British overlordship of the territory dates back to 1900, indirect rule has been the means by and large through which it has exercised authority. Thus, in regard to jural actions the Barotse courts have jurisdiction over the people of Barotseland, but with some explicitly prescribed "limitations of power and relations with British courts."

The natural environment in which the Lozi live provides opportunities for agriculture, animal husbandry, and fishing. Living in a flood plain adjacent to woodlands, they have been able to establish trading relations with surrounding tribes, and thus, have developed a complex economy.

The village is the basic unit within which their social organization is set. It is the locus for kinship groups; it is a basic political unit. Economic exchange and co-operation is effected primarily between individuals who are related by both kinship bonds and political bonds. In addition, each village population is linked to a wider political organization which has its ultimate locus of identity in the office and authority of a king. This link is most notably established through the headman of the village, who is related to his villagers both as a kin and as a political representative of the higher authority (i.e., the king). In this setting, the same kind of relationships between individuals can serve many interests. This is identified by Gluckman as a "multiplex tie." He has established relations in more than one village and therefore in more than one kinship group. He has established relations with many others as neighbor, as blood-brother, as friend, and he has several sets of political relationships. This network of ties by which each Lozi is linked with others represents a "multiple membership of diverse groups and in diverse relationships." These conditions precipitate many quarrels; but they are also the conditions promoting cohesion within the society.

Both of these consequences affect the character of jural action in the society. The Lozi disapprove of dissolving relationships in any permanent manner. Villages should remain united; kinfolk and kin groups should remain united; lord and underling not separate. Thus, the function of the judges throughout a hearing is to prevent an irremedial break in the relations of the contending parties. "Therefore," writes Gluckman, "the court tends to be conciliating; it strives to effect a compromise acceptable to, and accepted by, all the parties." However, the judges do not reconcile the disputants without casting blame on the wrongdoers. Since a grievance brought before the court is examined in terms of those norms of behavior which are expected of people, those who have broken these norms will be chastized. Such judgments have the ring of sermons, "for they all lecture on the theme: your station and its duties." The norms of the social position and the relation, e.g., filial, parental and, brotherly love, of the wrongdoers determine the standards according to which they are admonished. The aggregate of norms expressed under these conditions form a hypothetical figure to which Gluckman gives the name "the reasonable man," a figure present in all legal systems. (Bohannan acknowledges this conception among the Tiv.) The "reasonable man" is, in the Lozi legal system, a legal concept used as a basis for cross-examination (e.g., "Would a reasonable man behave that way?") by judges as they try to ferret out the truth.

The procedures of the court in examining grievances reflect the chief aim it sets itself. To seek a resolution, conciliate and reestablish harmonious relationships between the contending parties, the judges extend their inquiry to elicit information about the totality of past relations beween the litigants. The proceedings are not conducted in a manner intended to elicit and consider only those facts which are relevant to legal claims involved in the suit and defined in the narrowest way possible. In the proceedings, therefore, moral and legal rules are hardly discriminated, although in enforcement the discrimination is more evident. The court has the authority to enforce legal rules; it does not have the authority to enforce moral rules, although it seeks ways, e.g., administrative action, to do so.

Gluckman treats of this judicial process in relation to the Lozi legal system. It is the interplay of "legal concepts," "law as *corpus juris*," and "law as adjudication," or judgments ("legal rulings") as interpreted and applied by judges that characterizes the process. "Legal concepts" are a set of concepts of great generality and flexibility (both multiple and elastic in meaning), carrying important ethical implications. For example, "law," "justice," "certainty of law," "guilt," "innocence," "right," "duty" are such concepts. "Law as corpus juris" is "the body of rules . . . on which judges draw to give a decision." The "process by which cases are tried and judgments or legal rulings are given on them" identifies "law as adjudication." Lozi judges derive "legal rules" (i.e., judgments) from the whole body of law, which includes among other things, "rules accepted by all normal members of the society as defining right and reasonable ways in which persons ought to behave in relation to each other and to things." In doing this, they follow principles of reasoning which are fundamentally the same as those followed by Western jurists, and also give themselves considerable latitude because of the flexibility of standards implied in such "legal concepts" as customary and reasonable.

V

Gluckman has described in considerable detail the manner in which a Lozi court trial is conducted. As he does so, he exposes the logical processes operating in the behavior of the judges, litigants, and witnesses as they progress toward a resolution of the dispute. These processes represent the ethnographer's articulation of what apparently lies implicit in the conduct of a trial. It is not likely that any Lozi judge or "student" of jurisprudence could have laid bare the mechanisms operating the trial system as Gluckman has done.

However, there is a difficulty in Gluckman's analysis. There is, it seems to me, a lack of conceptual discrimination between the description of the judicial system and the interpretation of that system, that is, between the "concrete structure" and the "analytical structure." Gluckman is either describing the judicial system in the same or similar terms as he uses to interpret that description, or he is not clearly distinguishing between the terms when he is describing and when he is interpreting. For example he writes that he will restrict the use of the term "law" to one referent — "the body of rules, the *corpus juris,* on which judges draw to give a decision." Other references of "law," he will designate by other terms, including "statute." Elsewhere, he identifies the Lozi *corpus juris* "with statutes and other rules." The reader cannot know whether this is merely a minor error, or whether *corpus juris* is being used differently in different contexts. The example would be trivial if it stood alone. It does not.

Gluckman engages in a brilliant analysis of "The Paradox of the 'Uncertainty' of Legal Concepts and the 'Certainty' of Law," in order to demonstrate the socially valuable function that is served by the multiple and elastic nature of "legal concepts" which makes their meaning uncertain and ambiguous (although not necessarily vague). The flexibility of "legal concepts" allows their manipulation by judges in the interest of seeking justice. In this manner, the *corpus juris* can remain certain, while legal rulings can adapt to changed social conditions. If I have understood this argument correctly, it is, I believe, more the result of the author's repetition of the argument than the result of conceptual clarity in stating it at any one time. This point can be demonstrated directly from the text. The author indicates that law as *corpus juris* is one of the "legal concepts," and therefore, by definition it must be considered uncertain. Later, explaining the reasons why certainty characterizes the law, he writes, "My conclusion is that the law as a *corpus juris* remains certain," It is not difficult to understand Gluckman's argument as to why flexibility in "legal concepts" has social value, but it is very difficult to understand what relation "law," which is uncertain has to "law" which is certain. Are they on two conceptually distinct levels? Are they on the same conceptual level, but refer to two different kinds of "law"? This is not really clear, and it is primarily the repetition which provides any ease in following the argument, not logical and coherent conceptualizing. Gluckman himself senses that there might be some conceptual fuzziness in his argument, since he adds at the end of the chapter, "I hope my flexible use of 'certainty' here does not negate entirely the value, or the resolution, of this paradox."

The ambiguity increases. Gluckman invokes a concept, "alegal," which is clearly an analytical concept, that is, one created to interpret those things which are part of a concrete structure. It is applied in order to identify 'law' in a society where "legal action" is not present, where there are no legal rules and institutions. "We might then adopt," Gluckman writes, "the . . . distinction between societies which have legal rules, and those which are *alegal,* without legal institutions, but which certainly are not *lawless.*" Therefore, Gluckman suggests, "law" be specialized "to cover a body of accepted rules," that is, *corpus juris.*[20] "Legal and alegal," he adds, . . . "define rules which are enforced in a different way in the same society, and in societies at different stages of political development." Thus, a society without courts would have "rules of law" but no "legal rules." Here, the confusion of conceptual levels seem self-evident. "Alegal," on the one hand, refers *to a society without "legal rules"* and institutions but with law; on the other hand, it *defines rules within a society* which are enforced in ways other than by "legal action." Thus, "legal," since it is set in apposition to "alegal" partakes of the same confusion, only more so. For, (1) it refers to a society characterized by the presence of legal rules and institutions within it, as opposed to a society without them;[21] (2) it refers, within a society, to those institutions, e.g. "procedures, processes, and sanctions of the courts," in which legal action is implemented; and (3) it refers to the legal rules, themselves, as they are applied in legal action. The confusion may be compounded. It was noted before that Gluckman considered "law" (*corpus juris*) as a "legal concept." This point raises a question. In a society which is "alegal," i.e. has "law" but no "legal rules," etc., are there any "legal concepts," e.g. ideas of right, duty, reasonable man, etc.? Without doubt, there are. But what relation does the term "legal" in "legal concepts" have to the term "legal" in "alegal," in "legal" (in apposition to "alegal") and in "legal rules." If "legal concepts" is used to identify certain elements in a "legal" society (as a "concrete structure"), then it is, for example, associated with "legal rules" and one meaning of "alegal." If it is a concept used to codify the concept of "legal concepts" as applied in a "legal" society and the corresponding concepts in an "alegal" society for which there is no name given, then it is part of an analytic system of interpretation, but apt to be confused with the same phrase used at the concrete level. This possibility of confusion is, it seems to me, prevalent in Western jurisprudence, because the concepts used in "the law" (i.e., American, British, French, etc.) are often used in the 'study of the law,' as well. Undoubtedly, Gluckman and others know what they are referring to and can keep their ideas distinct in their own minds when they are discussing concepts of 'the law' or concepts of the 'study of law.' However, the contribution to systematic comparative analysis is limited when the language of jurisprudence permits such ambiguity.

I could be tempted to say, perhaps unfairly, that Gluckman, having found virtue in ambiguity in one context, was promoting it in other contexts. He, rightly and brilliantly, points out that the undoubted ambiguities in legal concepts serve socially valuable functions in providing for scope and development of the legal system. That the body of rules that men live by must have, at least, the illusion of certainty, while at the same time, being adaptable in the face of social and cultural change hardly seems possible to refute, and this is especially the case with a body of rules which are embodied in a separate institution of the society, being derived from, but no longer reducible to, the norms, values, rules of other institutions within the society. That the flexibility in meaning of some of the concepts associated with this body of rules should permit the neat balance between the illusion of permanence and the inevitableness of change is a matter of strength, not weakness. However, this is the legal system as an "action system." To use Bohannan's concept, it is one "folk system" of interpretation "devised" for the purpose of social action. It must be flexible in order to cope effectively with experience. If ambiguity serves this function, therein lies its strength. Legal concepts developed to interpret the legal system of a society form an analytic system. This is a system organized for analysis — a kind of action, certainly, but not social action. In this context, ambiguity is no virtue. It exists. It will always exist, either because of the intellectual limitations of particular men, of the culture, or because "analytic systems" "respond" to experience as much as "folk systems," both being the organization of men's thought, though for different reasons. Since this system is meant for analysis, the reduction of ambiguity and the increase of conceptual clarity and consistency are always goals for which to aim. I believe that in these books Bohannan has attained this to a far greater degree than Gluckman has.

VI

If my remarks could appear to deny the value of Gluckman's work, let me correct the impression immediately. This is an extraordinary book. It is penetrating and subtle in its suggestiveness. Ideas abound in it. Certainly, more than one reading is necessary to absorb its richness. Moreover, the author frequently puts his insights, drawn from his analysis of the Lozi judicial processes, to work on our Western procedures. That he can do this is undoubtedly related to the fact that it is from the point of view of Western jurisprudence that he directs his attention to the Lozi. This procedure has dangers for analysis, but it has led, in this case, to some heuristically valuable suggestions. I have remarked already on the author's discussion of ambiguities in the language of the law and their functional value. A fuller example will show, I believe, a stimulating mind at work.

Rejecting one view as to why Europeans mistakenly believe that African courts consider a man guilty until he is proven innocent, Gluckman explains the process of cross-examination in order to suggest another explanation. It is the judge who cross-examines, as each contending party does not have separate lawyers to cross-examine the other side. In this situation, only by assuming that the one being questioned is lying can the evidence be tested and therefore, the judges proceed in this way. If the examinee is the defendant, the judge *acts* as if he assumes he was guilty. Thus, from the judge's point of view, guilt must be discharged before innocence is established. Gluckman turns from the Lozi to Western systems. Among the British and Americans, lawyers do the cross-examining and it is they who act as if the examinee is lying. The judge is impartial. He remains aloof from the cross-examination. In a French court, the judge does not remain aloof while the lawyers battle. He has responsibility for seeing the truth established, and, thus, he may join in the cross-examination. His relation to a defendant, then, would be rather like that between the African judge and a defendant. Thus, Gluckman suggests, this action of the judge in the French courts may be what gives English jurists and others, I might add, the impression that in the French court system a man is considered guilty until proven innocent. I found this suggestion fruitful. It should not however be forgotten that such excursions of thought suggest avenues of analysis and interpretation, but are not themselves appropriately so. Thus, they are referred to as heuristically valuable.

In contrast, Bohannan seldom bridges the gap between the Tiv system and ours in this manner. This is not fortuitous. He is intent upon not confusing the Tiv "folk system" with any other, and he shuns the jurisprudence of the West as a system by which to analyze Tiv jural action. Therefore, his attention is not likely to be attuned to seeking cross-references between the Tiv jural process and our own.

Thus, if I say that the conceptual clarity of Bohannan's book is greater than Gluckman's I must also say that the heuristic value of Gluckman's book exceeds that of Bohannan's. Furthermore, I believe that this order of difference owes much to the differences in their theoretical approaches.

VII

In the preface to his book, Gluckman writes that, "in analyzing legal problems in an African society one has to use terms and concepts which have been employed by jurists through two millenia . . ." For an anthropologist, he adds, this is an unattainable ideal. Nonetheless, the ideal directs the mind to the extent that it can, and this is Gluckman's frame of reference. He sees Lozi law from the point of view of Western jurisprudence by and large. Bohannan, on the contrary, explicitly avoids this approach. To view the judicial processes, and other processes of social behavior, through the "folk system" of a social group other than the one being studied is, to him, to misrepresent. Bohannan seeks first to describe the "folk system" which represents Tiv ordering of jural action; and, second, to interpret Tiv jural action in terms of an "analytical system" which is his own.

The comparative results are interesting. Gluckman stresses repeatedly that the Lozi judicial processes do not differ fundamentally from ours. Bohannan sees the Tiv conceptions and our concepts as quite distinct. This is no more forcefully shown than in the description of how Europeans and Tiv in Tivland cognize the Grade D courts. First, the former refer to them as "native courts"; the latter refer to them as "government courts." The former, secondly, assume that the "native courts" apply 'native law and custom,' that is, assume the existence of a *corpus juris,* while the other sees the "government courts" as a place to arbitrate disputes, without authority to carry out decisions. Of course, it may well be that our judicial processes actually show greater similarity to those of the Lozi than to those of the Tiv. The difference in analytical systems may not have made the difference in interpretation.

However, when Lozi and Tiv are considered together, the results, too, are interesting. In both groups, the main function of the court is to conciliate and to reintroduce harmony in the social relations of the contending parties, so that in effect the community itself will return to a state of smooth functioning. Both have the conception of the reasonable man, a figure present in all legal systems according to Gluckman. In the court's examination of a case, in both groups, the information sought reaches far beyond the kind or amount needed for and relevant to the pursuance of the specific claim which brought the contending parties before the court. There are other similarities but these seem the most significant ones.

There is one striking difference, however, striking because there are some notable similarities between the two societies, and because both authors have taken great care to document and analyze the respective characteristics which make this difference. Gluckman writes that "In at least one sense of *'law'* — the sense of corpus juris — all societies have 'law' whether or not they have courts to enforce rights and punish wrongs under the law." Almost as though he was responding directly to Gluckman's assertion, Bohannan writes, "The organization of the rules is the institution itself. There is no second organization for specifically jural purposes, no discipline of law and no *corpus juris* in the Tiv folk system." At the least, these statements may express no more than a difference in the definition of one concept in isolation, *corpus juris;* at the most, this may be a difference in the level of analysis. In one, the concept is part of a description of a folk system, whereas, in the other, the concept is part of a set of analytical statements. In either circumstance or whatever the circumstance, the statements are so dramaically juxtaposed that they make emphatic the need to consider what kind of comparative analysis will prove more than heuristically valuable. The problem, then, really is to find the kind of analytical system which will do the service. Therefore, again, the issue is not what can anthropologists contribute to political science or what can political scientists contribute to anthropologists. The issue is what kind of analytical system is empirically most viable. Both of these books, in one way or another, contribute to an understanding of this problem, particularly if read together. Both books, I believe, are important reading for anyone interested in the comparative study of social institutions.

NOTES TO REVIEW

1. Max Gluckman, *The Judicial Process Among the Barotse of Northern Rhodesia,* Glencoe, Ill.: The Free Press, 1955.

2. Paul Bohannan, *Justice and Judgment Among the Tiv,* London: Oxford University Press, 1957.

3. See John Middleton and David Tait (eds.), *Tribes Without Rulers,* London: Routledge and Kegan Paul, 1958, for descriptions of the political organizations of several societies with segmentary lineage systems.

4. There is a point here about which I am not clear. (1) Do the Tiv codify in explicitly formulated normative and moral statements the rules of these institutions, e.g. marriage, family, property, etc., which the judges use in settling disputes in place of substantive law (which represents a reorganization of at least some of these rules "for the specific purpose of action in courts;" or, (2) On the occasion of specific disputes involving jural action, do they infer from their knowledge of social actions and social relationships associated with marriage, family, etc., a "rule" befitting that occasion, which again is not "applied" as a rule, but can (by another observer) be inferred from the action taken by the judges in suggesting settlements and resolutions to the disputes? In a chapter on court actions involving marriage cases, Bohannan provides a series of statements regarding rules and norms constituting the institution of marriage among the Tiv, but these statements represent *his own* codificaton of rules, not those of the Tiv. I was never certain whether the Tiv had a similar set of explicitly formulated rules and norms.

5. Bohannan does not note this following point but it might well be a good reason for keeping clear the difference between norms embodied as an institution identified as that of the law — or "legal," and norms which identify other institutions which constitute the society. It seems reasonable to assume that the set of rules codified in legal institutions is more likely to be internally consistent and coherent (though never abso-

lutely so) than the set of norms which identify the other institutions in the society and from which the legal norms are derived. This makes it less of a possibility in the "legal" system (though not absolutely so) to defend oneself by the assertion that the ostensible breach of norm was really an act in accordance with another norm. At the same time this line of defense seems admirably suited to a situation wherein the ideal resolution to a dispute is to find an answer with which everyone involved will concur because it increases the range of possible resolutions.

6. See Stanislaw Andrzejewski, *Military Organization and Society,* London: Routledge & Kegan Paul, Ltd., 1954, for an extensive use of this alternative.

7. That is, "Generally speaking, the totality of speech habits of a single person at a given time . . ." Charles F. Hockett, *A Course in Modern Linguistics,* New York: Macmillan, 1958, 321.

8. This does not mean a chronological sequence of mental acts. Obviously, description is often interspersed with interpretation in the discursive analysis of a subject. For the concepts of "concrete structure" and 'analytical structure," see Marion Levy "Some Aspects of 'Structural-Functional' Analysis and Political Science," in Roland Young, ed., *Approaches to the Study of Politics,* Evanston: Northwestern University Press, 1957, 52-66.

9. The other titles are *The Role of Courts in Barotse Social Life* and *The Idea of Barotse Jurisprudence.*

10. He defines law as *corpus juris* as "the body of rules . . . on which judges draw to give a decision." It seems reasonable to assume that "a body of accepted rules" refers to the same thing, but here, in a context where they do not provide the basis for "legal rules," i.e. what the judges decide.

11. However, no society identified as "Legal" would be without "Alegal" attributes.

Bibliography

BY *MELVIN REICHLER*

THE STRUCTURE OF POWER

Agger, Robert, "Power Attributions in the Local Community: Theoretical and Research Considerations," 34, *Social Forces* (May, 1956), 322-331.

Agger, Robert and Ostrom, V., "The Political Structure of a Small Community," 20, *Public Opinion Quarterly* (Spring, 1956), 81-89.

Belknap, George and Smuckler, R., "Political Power Relations in a Mid-West City," 20, *Public Opinion Quarterly* (Spring, 1956), 73-81.

Blumer, Herbert, "Social Structure and Power Conflict," in *Industrial Conflict,* A. Kornhauser, ed., New York: McGraw Hill, 1954, 232-239.

Coleman, James, *Community Conflict,* Glencoe, Illinois: The Free Press, 1957.

Fanelli, A. A., "A Typology of Community Leadership Based on Influence and Interaction within the Leader Sub-system," 34, *Social Forces* (May, 1956), 332-338.

Griswold, L., "The Community as a Social System: A Study in Comparative Analysis." Unpublished Ph.D. thesis, University of Kentucky, 1956.

Hunter, Floyd, *Community Power Structure,* Chapel Hill: University of North Carolina Press, 1953.

Kaufman, Herbert and Jones, Victor, "The Mystery of Power," 14, *Public Administration Review* (Summer, 1954), 205-12.

Lynd, Robert S. and Lynd, Helen, *Middletown in Transition,* New York: Harcourt, Brace and Co., 1937.

McKee, James B., "Status and Power in the Industrial Community: A Comment on Ducker's Thesis,' 58, *American Journal of Sociology* (January, 1953), 364-70.

Miller, Delbert C., "Industry and Community Power Structure," 23, *American Sociological Review* (February, 1958), 9-15.

Pelligrin, R. J. and Coates, C. H., "Absentee Owned Corporations and Community Power Structure," 61, *American Journal of Sociology* (March, 1956), 413-419.

Rossi, Peter H., "Community Decision Making," 1, *Administrative Science Quarterly* (March, 1957), 415-443.

Schulze, R. O., "Economic Dominants in Community Power Structure," 23, *American Sociological Review* (February, 1958), 3-8.

Underwood, K. W., *Protestant and Catholic,* Beacon Hill, Boston, The Beacon Press, 1957.

Vidich, A. and Bensman, J., *Small Town in Mass Society,* Princeton, New Jersey; Princeton University Press, 1958.

Warner, W. L., *Democracy in Jonesville,* New York: Harper Brothers, 1949.

Wilson, E. K., "Determinants of Participation in Policy Formation in a College Community," 7, *Human Relations,* 1954, 287-312.

SOCIO-ECONOMIC BASES

Andrews, W. H., "Some Correlates of Rural Leadership and Social Power among Intercommunity Leaders." Unpublished Ph.D. thesis, Michigan State University, 1956.

Baltzell, E. D., Jr., *Philadelphia Gentlemen,* Glencoe, Illinois: The Free Press, 1958.

Blough, M., "A Study of the Current Role of Organized Labor as a Pressure Group in the Political System of an Urban Community." Dissertation in progress, University of Chicago.

Blumberg, Leonard, "Community Leaders: The Social Bases and Social Psychological Concomitants of Community Power." Unpublished Ph.D. thesis, University of Michigan, 1955.

Bouma, D., "An Analysis of the Power Position of the Real Estate Board in Grand Rapids, Michigan." Unpublished Ph.D. thesis, Michigan State University, 1952.

Davis, Allison and Gardner, B. B., *Deep South,* Chicago: University of Chicago Press, 1944.

DeLora, J., "Patterns of Locality Involvement of Urban Small Businessmen." Unpublished Ph.D. thesis, Michigan State University, 1957.

Dollard, John, *Caste and Class in a Southern Town,* New Haven: Yale University Press, 1937.

Dreer, H., "Negro Leadership in St. Louis: A Study in Race Relations." Ph.D. thesis, University of Chicago, 1955.

Fuchs, Lawrence H., *The Political Behavior of American Jews,* Glencoe, Illinois: The Free Press, 1956.

Gilson, T. Q., "Social and Civic Activities of Executives: A Case Study." Unpublished Ph.D. thesis, Massachusetts Institute of Technology, 1954.

Gosnell, H. F. *Negro Politicians: The Rise of Negro Politics in Chicago,* Chicago: University of Chicago Press, 1935.

Haer, John L., "Social Stratification in Relation to Attitude toward Sources of Power in a Community," 35, *Social Forces* (December, 1956), 137-142.

Jones, Alfred W., *Life, Liberty, and Property,* Philadelphia: Lippincott, 1941.

Karsh, B., "The Labor Strike in a Small Community." Unpublished Ph.D. thesis, University of Chicago, 1955-1956.

Kimbrough, Jr., "The Role of the Banker in a Small City," 36, *Social Forces* (May, 1958), 316-322.

Mayntz, R., *Soziale Schichtung und sozialer Wandel in einer Industriegemeinde,* Stuttgart, 1958.

Miller, Delbert C., "The Seattle Business Leader," 15, *Pacific Northwest Business* (February, 1956), 5-12.

Palmer, S. H., "The Role of the Real Estate Agent in the Structuring of Residential Areas." Unpublished Ph.D. thesis, Yale University, 1955.

Spence, R. B., "Some Needed Research on Industry within the Community," 27, *The Journal of Educational Sociology* (December, 1953), 146-151.

Walter, G., "Human Relationships and Brickmaking: A Sociological Analysis of a One Industry Town." Unpublished Ph. D. thesis, University of Pittsburgh, 1953.

West, James, *Plainville, U.S.A.,* New York: Columbia University Press, 1945.

Whyte, William F., *Street Corner Society,* Chicago: University of Chicago Press, 1955.

Wurzbacher, G., ed., unter Mitarbeit von R. Pfaum (Mayntz), *Das Dorf in Spannungsfeld industrieller Entwicklung,* Stuttgart, 1958.

MECHANISMS OF POWER ALLOCATION

Agger, R. and Goldrich, D. "Community Power Structures and Partisanship," 23, *American Sociological Review* (August, 1958), 383-392.

Berelson, B., Lazarsfeld, P., and McPhee, W., *Voting,* Chicago: University of Chicago Press, 1954.

Campbell, Angus, "The Political Implications of Community Identification," in *Approaches to the Study of Politics,* Evanston: Northwestern University Press, 1958.

Counts, George S., *The Social Composition of Boards of Education,* Department of Education, 1927.

Election Study Group, ed., "Local Election and the Organized Labor-Research Report of the Mayor and City Assembly of Nagoya," Nagoya Daigaku Hosei Ronshu, 1, *The Journal of Law and Politics,* 1951.

Fauvet, J., *Les Paysons et la politique dans la France contemporaine,* Cahier de la Fondation Nationale des Sciences Politiques, No. 94. Paris: Librairie Armand Colin, 1958.

Forthal, S., *Cogwheel of Democracy,* New York: William Frederick Press, 1946.

Freeman, J. Leiper, "Local Party Systems: Theoretical Considerations and a Case Analysis," 64, *American Journal of Sociology* (November, 1958), 282-289.

Gosnell, H. F., *Machine Politics: Chicago Model,* Chicago: University of Chicago Press, 1937.

Graf, Hans, *Die Entwicklung der Wahlen und politischen Parteien in Gross-Dortmund, Hannover und Frankfurt,* 1958.

Hoshino, Mitsuo, "Votes and Political Consciousness in the Last Local Election," 42, *Toshi Mondai* (Municipal Problems), 1951.

Janowitz, Morris, *Community Press in an Urban Setting,* Glencoe, Illinois: The Free Press, 1952.

Jones, Joseph H., Jr., "A Comparative Analysis of Community Leaders and Non-Leaders in a North Central Kentucky Community." Unpublished Ph. D. thesis, University of Kentucky, 1956.

Katz, Elihu and Lazarsfeld, Paul, *Personal Influence,* Glencoe, Illinois: The Free Press, 1955.

Lawrence, R. D., "Kansas Publishers: A Professional Analysis," 15, *Journalism Quarterly* (December, 1938), 337-348.

Long, Norton E., "The Local Community as an Ecology of Games," 64, *American Journal of Sociology* (November, 1958), 251-261.

Mailey, H. V., *The Italian Vote in Philadelphia between 1928 and 1946,* Philadelphia: University of Pennsylvania Press, 1950.

Matthews, Thomas, "The Lawyer as Community Leader: One Dimension of the Professional Role." Unpublished Ph.D. thesis, Cornell University, 1953.

Mayntz, R., "Lokale Parteigruppen in der kleinen Gemeinde." *Zeitschrift fur Politik,* 2 Jg., 1955, Heft 1.

Mendras, H., *Etudes de sociologie rurale: Movis (Aveyron) Virgin (Utah),* Cahier de la Fondation Nationale des Sciences Politiques, No. 40. Paris: Libraire Armand Colin, 1953.

Miller, Delbert C., "Decision Making Cliques in Community Power Structures," 64, *American Journal of Sociology* (November, 1958), 299-309.

Miller, Paul A., "The Process of Decision-Making within the Context of Community Organization," 17, *Rural Sociology,* 1952, 153-161.

Munke, Stephanie, "Wahlkampf und Machtverschiebung," *Geschichte und Analyse der Berliner Wahl vom 3 December 1950.* Mitarbeit, Redaktion und Einleitung von A. R. L. Gurland, Berlin, 1952.

Nakamura, Kikuo and Nakamura, Katsunori, "Political Consciousness of Local Elections — Research in Mie Prefecture," 29, *Hokagu Kenkyu (Journal of Law)* Politics and Sociology, 1956.

Ogata, Norio and others, "Various Types of Voting Behavior in Hokkaido," *Hogakukai Ronshu (Law and Political Science Review of Hokkaida University),* No. 4, 1956.

Olmstead, D. W., "Organizational Leadership and Social Structure in a Small City," 19, *American Sociological Review* (June, 1954), 273-281.

Parenton, V. J., and Pellegrin, R. J., "Social Structure and the Leadership Factor in a Negro Community in South Louisiana," 17, *Phylon* (March, 1956), 74-78.

Peel, R. V., *The Political Clubs of New York City,* New York: G. Putnam & Sons, 1935.

Research Group of Election Actuality, ed., *Actuality of General Election,* Tokyo: Iwanami Book Company, 1955.

Rhyne, E. H., "Party Politics and the Decision Making Process: A Study at the County Level." Unpublished thesis, University of North Carolina, 1957.

Rose, Arnold M., "Power Distribution in the Community Through Voluntary Association," in Hulett, J. E., Jr., and Stayner, Ross, eds., *Problems in Social Psychology,* Urbana, Illinois: University of Illinois, 1952, 74-83.

Salter, J. T., *Boss Rule,* New York: McGraw-Hill, 1935.

Smith, L., "Political Leadership in a New England Community," 17, *Review of Politics,* (July, 1955), 292-309.

Smuckler, R. H., and Belknap, G. M., *Leadership and Participation in Urban Political Affairs,* Governmental Research Bureau, Political Research Studies No. 2, Michigan State University, East Lansing, 1956.

Stewart, F., "A Sociometric Study of Influence in Southtown," 10, *Sociometry* (February, and August, 1957), 11-31, 273-286.

Storer, N. W., "Patterns of Change in the Leadership of a Small Community." Unpublished Master's thesis, University of Kansas, 1956.

Takahashi, Akira, and others, "Political Consciousness of Urban Working People and Mass Communication Activities," *Shinbun Kenyujo Kiyo (Bulletin or Journalism)*, Tokyo: Institute of Tokyo University, No. 7 (March, 1958).

Warren, Roland L., "Toward a Typology of Extra-Community Controls Limiting Local Community Autonomy," 34, *Social Forces* (May, 1956), 338-341.

GOALS AND POLICY ISSUES

Banfield, Edward, *Government Project*, Glencoe, Illinois: The Free Press, 1951.

Carpenter, D. B., "Some Factors Associated with Influence Position in the Associational Structure of a Rural Community." Unpublished Ph. D. thesis, University of Washington, 1951.

Charters, W .W., Jr., "Social Class Analysis and the Control of Education," 23, *Harvard Educational Review* (Fall, 1953).

Freeman, Charles, and Mayo, Selz C., "Decision Makers in Rural Community Action," 35, *Social Forces*, 1957, 319-322.

Goldhammer, K., "The Roles of School District Officials in Policy Determination in an Oregon Community." Unpublished Ph.D. thesis, University of Oregon, 1954.

Hunter, Floyd, Chaffer, R. C. and Sheps, C. G., *Community Organization*, Chapel Hill: University of North Carolina Press, 1956.

Larson, J. A., Jr., "Community Participation in Locating Industries in non-Metropolitan Tennessee." Unpublished Ph.D. thesis, Northwestern University, 1956.

Meyerson, Martin and Banfield, Edward C., *Politics, Planning and the Public Interest*, Glencoe, Illinois: The Free Press, 1955.

Miller, Delbert C., "The Prediction of Issue Outcome in Community Decision Making," *Proceedings of the Pacific Sociological Society*, Research Studies of the State College of Washington, 25 (June, 1957), 137-147.

Miller, Paul A., "A Comparative Analysis of the decision process; community organization toward major health goals." Unpublished Ph.D. thesis, Michigan State University, 1954.

Royama, Masamichi, ed., *Anatomy of Political Consciousness*, Tokyo: The Asahi Press, 1949.

RESEARCH TECHNIQUES

Agger, Robert E., "Power Attributions in the Local Community," 34, *Social Forces* (May, 1956), 322-331.

Arensberg, Conrad C., "The Community Study Method," 60, *American Journal of Sociology* (September, 1954), 109-124.

Baltzell, E. D., "Who's Who in America," and "The Social Register," and "Elite and Upper Class Indexes in Metropolitan America," in *Class, Status and Power*, Bendix, R. and Lipsett, S., eds., Glencoe, Illinois: The Free Press, 1953.

Blackwell, Gordon W., "A Theoretical Framework for Sociological Research in Community Organization," 33, *Social Forces* (October, 1954), 57-64.

Foskett, J. and Hohle, R., "The Measurement of Influence in Community Affairs," *Research Studies of the State College of Washington*, 25 (June, 1957), 148-154.

Green, James W., and Mayo, Selz C., "A Framework for Research in the Actions of Community Groups," 31, *Social Forces*, 1953, 320-327.

Hill, M. C. and Whiting, Ann, "Some Theoretical and Methodological Problems in Community Studies," 29, *Social Forces* (December, 1950), 117-124.

Kaufman, H., Sutton, W., Jr., and Edwards, A., "Toward a Delineation of Community Research," The Social Science Research Center, Social Science Studies Community Series, No. 4 (May, 1954), Mississippi State College.

Kimball, S. T. and Piersall, M., "Event Analysis as an Approach to Community Study," 34, *Social Forces* (October, 1955), 58-63.

Long, N. and Belknap, G., "A Research Program on Leadership and Decision Making in Metropolitan Areas," (Mimeographed), New York, 1956.

Lowe, Francis E., "The Measurement of the Influence of Formal and Informal Leaders of Public Opinion during the 1950 Senatorial Election Campaign in Madison, Wisconsin," Unpublished Ph.D. thesis, University of Wisconsin.

Schulze, R. O. and Blumberg, L. O., "The Determination of Local Power Elites," 63, *American Journal of Sociology* (November, 1957), 290-296.

White, James E., "Theory and Method for Research in Community Leadership," 15, *American Sociological Review,* 1950, 50-60.

Index